Fighter pilot Manfred von Richthofen (the Red Baron) lacked innate aerobatic ability. As a tyro, he attempted to solve this problem through denial, going so far as to sneer at stunting as pointless. Great War air combat experience proved quite the reverse, and so we would anticipate a short and sad fighting life for the fellow. Yet the Red Baron became the Great War's single greatest scorer, as measured by total victories. How did he do it?

This book is concerned with tactics, especially those tactics used by the Red Baron and his opponents. It offers the how and why of Great War aerial combat. The author leans heavily on his expertise in engineering and aerodynamic techniques to explain this, with his reasoning presented in a readable, non-mathematical style. Absent are both the usual propaganda-laced Air Service reports and psychobabble. Offered instead is the logic behind Great War aerial combat; i.e., those elements determining success or failure in the Red Baron's air war.

Gunnery experience led to the machine gun as the weapon best suited for aerial combat. Joined with a suitable aircraft, the extremely successful Fokker diving attack resulted. In reaction, effective defensive techniques arose, using forms of shrewd tactical cooperation by two-seater crews: pilot and gunner. These are detailed. Numbers mattered, establishing the level of assault firepower. Tactics of machines flying together in formation are given, as well as those of 'formation busters', intent upon reversing the odds and turning large numbers into a disadvantage. A pilot's nature and emotions had much to do with choosing between the options defining tactics. What were the aces like? How were tactics tailored to suit personality? What traits made for the ability to grapple with a jammed machine gun? A dozen high achievers are examined in terms of tactics and background. In a fascinating study Leon Bennett covers all of these aspects of WWI aerial combat, and more.

Similarly, the author turns his attention to examining the cause of von Richthofen's death, employing the tools of logic, rather than merely acccept one of the many conflicting eyewitness reports as truth. In doing so, much testimony is exposed as unlikely. The bullet scatter to be expected from ground anti-aircraft fire matters greatly, and is developed, along with the odds against lone riflemen hoping to hit a fast-moving low altitude target. The most dangerous altitude for front-line crossing is established. The author concludes by rating the possibility of a rifleman downing the Red Baron as quite realistic - certainly as likely as any of the more celebrated possibilities.

This is an important book, offering a ground-breaking account of WWI aerial tactics, and a thorough examination of the final combat and death of the Red Baron.

Leon Bennett is a graduate of the New York University College of Engineering, with both Bachelor's and Master's degrees in Aeronautical Engineering. He continued as a research worker at the University, attaining the rank of Senior Research Scientist, and also lectured on prosthetic devices at the NYU Medical School. Upon the closing of the Engineering College, he transferred to the Veterans Administration, where his research efforts won the 1984 award for vascular research by the American Congress of Rehabilitation Medicine. His military service was spent as a researcher at the Ballistics Research Lab, at Aberdeen, MD. His research output consists of 36 articles on subjects such as insect flight, blood flow, and load dissipation by human tissue. Following retirement, he has written two highly-regarded books about World War I aerial combat, *Three Wings for the Red Baron*, and *Gunning for the Red Baron*. He has also prepared numerous how-to articles for hobby magazines featuring model aeroplanes, including *Flying Models*, *Model Aviation* and the *Flying Aces Newsletter*.

FALL OF THE RED BARON

WORLD WAR I AERIAL TACTICS AND THE DEATH OF VON RICHTHOFEN

Leon Bennett

Helion & Company Ltd

Helion & Company Limited
26 Willow Road
Solihull
West Midlands
B91 1UE
England
Tel. 0121 705 3393
Fax 0121 711 4075
Email: info@helion.co.uk
Website: www.helion.co.uk

Published by Helion & Company 2012. Reprinted in paperback 2016

Designed and typeset by Farr out Publications, Wokingham, Berkshire
Cover designed by Farr out Publications, Wokingham, Berkshire
Printed by Lightning Source, Milton Keynes, Buckinghamshire

Front cover: *Rittmeister* Manfred von Richthofen standing in front of an iconic Fokker Dr.I Triplane (Ullstein Bilderdienst).
Rear cover: Boelcke's Swarm – a loose group of roughly half a dozen Albatros fighters was typical of *Hauptmann* Oswald Boelcke's 1916 approach (*Flugsport*, June 1917, p.373).

ISBN 978-1-911096-11-5

British Library Cataloguing-in-Publication Data.
A catalogue record for this book is available from the British Library.

For details of other military history titles published by Helion & Company Limited contact the above address, or visit our website: http://www.helion.co.uk.

We always welcome receiving book proposals from prospective authors. We are particularly keen to hear from authors interested in publishing First World War aviation titles with us – please contact us with your book proposal or for details of titles we are actively seeking to commission.

Contents

List of Illustrations

The publishers and author are aware that not all of the images in this book are of perfect quality. Nevertheless, we have chosen to include them as many are very rare, having seldom – if ever – appeared in print for nearly a century.

List of Illustrations

List of Illustrations

List of Illustrations

Acknowledgments

The path of creation is never clear. In this instance, youthful enthusiasm plus the wonders of model airplanes played a part. Adult immersion in aero engineering and ballistics research came next, a process leading to familiarity with key British sources at the IWM (Imperial War Museum) and TNA (The National Archives). It is their vaults that currently hold the world of Red Baron raw data. Given the files, an understanding of the contradictory literature surrounding Richthofen and his achievements became possible. It was only necessary to nail it down.

Through all, my ever-patient wife R. made the book possible by assuming far more than her share of the ancillary chores. Her ability to translate both French and German made for comprehension of otherwise hopeless memos. In her hands, even loony software instructions were turned into clear English, resulting in the text you now hold.

Prologue

Shooting down enemy aircraft was an important achievement in WWI. Success was vital to the infantry, serving to stop frontline strafing, and prevent observation by the enemy. Convinced of the need, every Air Service struggled for maximum combat success. Much effort went into locating the source of a pilot's air fighting ability. To some it seemed a personal knack–rather like hitting a curve ball–a skill beyond training or even logical description. One either had it or one did not. How were those gifted few to be identified? Was it all a matter of the right genes? An early display of brilliance?

Turning to the most successful of all, Manfred von Richthofen, (the Red Baron) we anticipate quick learning, and the natural combat skills of a born hunter. Instead, we find a mediocre student pilot and a poor shot, unable to hit the target with an airborne machine gun. Lacking any feeling for aerobatics, he opted for sullen denial, disparaging loops as useless stunts.

We sense the man as lacking in important skills, despite the right sort of ancestors, properly military. Given so hapless a start, we uneasily anticipate his end, and a quick end at that. Yet, it was not so.

Richthofen had another side, one that was all-important: the ability to reason and change his mind as circumstances altered. For example, early in the war, speed seemed critical to Richthofen and the Albatros series of fighters supplied that speed. Later in the war, he traded speed away for the extra maneuverability granted him in the form of the Fokker Triplane. His tactics changed accordingly.

He was that rare pilot with a grasp of the relationship between design and tactics. If he could dive away from trouble, diving had virtue as a tactic. However, if his machine had little to offer as a diver, with enemy aircraft easily out-speeding his airplane in descent, then no tactic was more stupid than evasion by diving. In short, tactics did not stand alone. Much had to do with the nature of his machine, as compared to the enemy's.

Granted the importance of tactics in winning or losing, other factors were also important. How did tactics rank? After much combat experience, Canadian ace Billy Bishop[1] supplied a priority rating for tactics, granting it second place, one immediately after shooting skill. As for telling good from bad, he used a prudent rule: "take a minimum of risk and whenever things look at all doubtful or bad, immediately make my escape."[2] The important thing was "to use one's head." Guile and stealth were vital; bravado was so much nonsense. In his estimation, flying skill itself deserved third, or last place.

Even as we sense the self-preserving wisdom underlying Bishop's conclusions, there came a severe criticism of Richthofen for employing that same level of caution; this given by Captain A. Roy Brown, an ace credited by many with the downing of the Red Baron himself. In Brown's view, Richthofen sought mainly easy victims: "He picked off lame ducks pulling [away] from a fight. He specialized in swooping on slow-motion artillery planes."[3]

Whether the accusation was true or not, the tone of condemnation was clear. We sense a demand that acceptable tactics embrace more than the limitations of one's aircraft and skill–they must pass muster as properly heroic.

To some extent, this burden of selflessness derived from the demands of strategy. The British were convinced that an offensive outlook was crucial to the production of ultimate victory. In practice this meant that every British airplane in good repair was to fight nearby enemy machines, no matter what the circumstances, and without concern for immediate victory. This approach was precisely the opposite of Bishop's. As a tactic 'always fight' amounted to an anti-tactic; one ignoring immediate prospects in the hope of achieving a long-term goal: the exhaustion of the enemy under the blows of an overwhelming number of British, French , Italian and American flyers. Ignored was a bitter truth: to join combat in the wrong circumstances meant only a suicidal sacrifice.

To Richthofen a certain nobility of tactics was important. One must not pretend to be wounded in order to lure an unsuspecting enemy to his doom. At the same time 'always fight' was judged to be stupid, for only a fool could ignore the plain lessons and odds of combat. As Richthofen well understood, there are times when it is best to flee rather than fight.

This book is concerned with tactics; especially those tactics used by the Red Baron and his opponents. We open by freshly considering the means of Richthofen's death. Competing claimants are examined in terms in terms of logic, rather than the usual contradictory eyewitness reports. Ground anti-aircraft fire is examined in terms of hit probability. Richthofen's crossing of the frontlines on the fatal day, and the most dangerous altitude for doing so are developed. His attacker's chances are viewed by means of machine gun scatter studies. We conclude by rating the possibility of Richthofen's death by rifleman as quite possible; certainly as likely as any of the more celebrated possibilities.

The history of aerial tactics is lightly sketched. Guns and gunnery influences leading to machine gun usage as the tool best suited for air combat are given, followed with the highly successful Fokker diving attack procedures. Treated next are the corresponding defensive techniques, leading to cooperation by shrewd two-seater crews – pilot and gunner – in fighting off attack.

Numbers were important in determining the level of assault firepower. Tactics of formations are given, as well as those of formation busters, intent upon reversing the odds and turning large numbers into a disadvantage.

A pilot's nature and emotions had much to do with making a choice between options. What were the aces like? What traits and backgrounds made for the ability to grapple with a jammed machine gun when in combat? How were tactics tailored to suit personality? A dozen high achievers are examined in terms of tactics and background.

Our goal is to satisfy those who care about the 'how and why' of Great War air combat. Our method throughout leans heavily on engineering and aerodynamic techniques, treated in a popular style. Absent are serial numbers, squadron personnel listings and propaganda-laced reports. Offered instead is the logic of those men behind "big fuss" air combat – the elements defining the Red Baron's air war.

Those readers with a long memory will sense altered thinking about certain issues treated in earlier volumes by this author. For example, the Red Baron's killer, though still uncertain, is now regarded as unlikely to be Captain Brown, portrayed as the principal suspect in the initial volume *Three Wings for the Red Baron*. Why the change? Months of study have had their effect and perhaps we know a bit more. Chapter 1 will introduce you to the chancy evidence and conclusions, much of it dependent upon possibilities and probabilities. Hopefully, we have moved closer to the truth, but that is for you to decide. Best wishes for a fascinating, if rocky journey.

1

Richthofen versus the Rifleman

We are certain that Richthofen's life was ended by a single bullet on April 21, 1918. Though the basic facts are clear, the precise method remains unknown. In brief summary: while pursuing one aircraft, Richthofen was attacked by another. The fight moved to a low altitude, attracting bullets from small arms anti-aircraft units and infantry riflemen. At some point in this struggle, the fatal bullet was fired; a bullet that many claimed was their own. To date, detailed examination has not resolved the issue.

Sifting through the many possibilities – some reasonable, some strange indeed – and applying a careful skepticism to all, we are left with three likely, completely different possibilities: (1) he was brought down by a bullet fired by Canadian fighter pilot Captain Roy Brown; (2) he was killed by one of several teams of Australian anti-aircraft gunners armed with Vickers and Lewis machine guns; (3) he was hit and killed by a single shot fired by an unknown, ground-based rifleman.

Each of these possibilities has received support from knowledgeable veterans and historians. Though the destructive bullet itself was lost, Richthofen's fatal wound was consistent with that resulting from a single standard .303 bullet used in British rifles and machine guns, or the equivalent German 7.92 mm. bullet.

Much has been said concerning the likelihood of methods (1) and (2) above. However, little has been offered concerning (3). This chapter's purpose is to examine (3) in depth, using standard, accepted ballistic and engineering concepts.

For air defense, we instinctively turn to fighter planes, with anti-aircraft guns sensed as a less effective, secondary line of defense. In the 1914-1918 war, small arms fire, though recognized officially as a significant portion of anti-aircraft defense, was regarded as an inferior, limited weapon. Doubts were partly those based on range, for aircraft at altitudes greater than 2500 feet were beyond the reach of both machine gun and rifle fire.

Riflemen had additional limitations, even when firing against low flying aircraft. To work a hand operated, bolt-action gun meant aiming freshly before each round was fired. For serious marksmen, the result was a painfully slow firing rate, amounting to approximately 10 rounds per minute against a fixed, but distant target. Add on the difficulties inherent in targeting a fast moving aircraft – likely covering a distance of 7000 feet in that same minute – and grave doubts resulted concerning rifleman effectiveness.

These doubts were expressed by American ace Captain Eddie Rickenbacker, a man whose firsthand knowledge was indisputable, for some of it was gained by serving as the target of rifle fire. In his words:

> How many riflemen can compute the exact point ahead of their gun muzzle where the bullet and the pilot's head must meet? Not one! Occasional hits are made at random, but the percentage is ridiculously low ... [it is] a hundred to one that no hits will be received.[1]

His case is clear and simple, and to a considerable extent correct. Certainly the prospects of an individual sharpshooter were not good. Yet, there were other, very different, and equally valid views. Consider those of British Captain Ira Jones, credited with 40 victories, many over the Western Front in 1918, at the time when Richthofen was brought down. Achieving such feats as the destruction of two Fokker D.VIIs in a single encounter,[2] his expertise was beyond question. Concerning Richthofen's death, Jones said: "It's my belief that the fatal shot was from a rifle."[3]

The conflict of views is obvious. Yet, each view contains much that smacks of the truth, in the way of possibility and probability. A closer examination is warranted.

The major difficulty with Rickenbacker's argument was not the estimated rifleman's odds – worse than 'one in a hundred' – for such a ratio may well have been realistic – but in a failure to pursue his own line of reasoning. Perhaps accuracy was not possible for any one rifleman. However, why limit consideration to only a single shooter? Imagine hundreds of riflemen firing at a low flying aircraft, with each man able to get off only two carefully aimed rounds in the course of a single overhead pass. The resulting spray of bullets made it possible that at least several would hit the aircraft, and that one bullet might hit a vital spot through pure chance. In other words, even if the possibility of any one rifleman's bullet doing harm approached the negligible, as Rickenbacker indicated, the firing of many hundreds of bullets could well change the outcome.

At heart, this revised plan drops the traditional prospect of defense through the skills of experts in favor of defense produced by masses of men, each possessing little skill, and perhaps not even that. As everyone learns, given enough falling raindrops, we are likely to be hit, no matter how poor the aim of the rain gods.

How large were the number of shooters? Were hundreds really positioned to respond quickly enough to be effective? The mere existence of many hundreds of potential shooters, say a battalion of troops, didn't mean that every man fired effectively. Some would fail to get the order, some were busy with other concerns and would sullenly ignore the order, some had inoperative rifles, or lacked ammunition, or froze in fear, or were away on leave, or were hopelessly inept. Given an unprepared battalion, perhaps the equivalent of one company's rifles might be fired effectively. Were these enough?

For a real life example, consider a typical 1918 strafing run[4] involving three American SPAD 13 aircraft against an estimated full company of German infantry soldiers, caught by surprise. In a single pass, one aircraft went unharmed and the other two were hit by a total of three bullets. None of the bullet strikes were fatal, though one machine required major repairs.

In another 1918 instance, American Captain Ray Bridgeman, crossing the lines in his SPAD 13 at about 500 feet, was brought down by a single bullet to his engine.[5] Survivor Bridgeman believed the bullet came from the American side of the lines; the action of a misguided or embittered rifleman. Bridgeman wasn't the only such victim. Rumors of false aircraft insignia employed to deceive the enemy were widespread,[6] leading to ground-based shots from both sides, sometimes directed against the same machine.

Typical Machine Gun Sections

(top) British, Antwerp, 1914. (bottom) Russian, 1916. Heavy machine gun sections employed dozens of riflemen as helpers and defenders. They proved useful in the role of anti-aircraft marksmen. Source: (top) Baer C.H., Ed. *Der Völkerkrieg* (Stuttgart: Hoffmann, 1914) p.149; (bottom) Anon., *The Times History of the War* Volume 9 (London: *The Times*, 1916) p. 204

Triplane Similarity

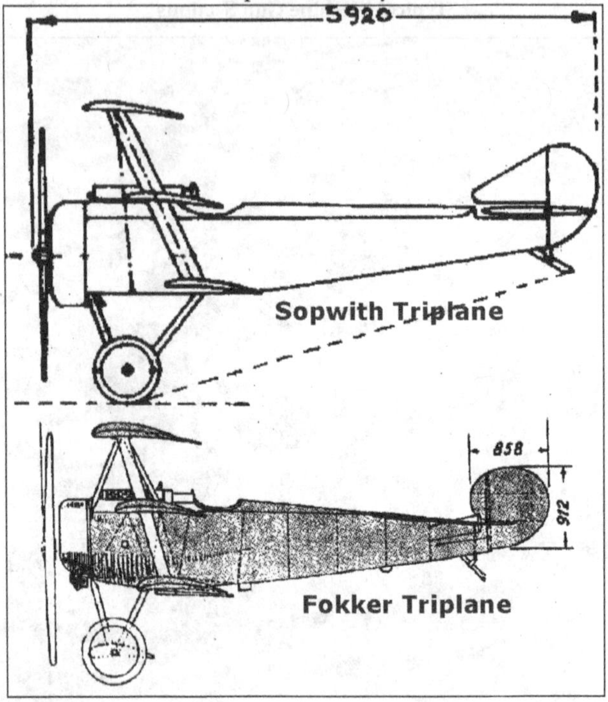

Wartime German illustrations pointed to the striking similarity between British and German three-winged aircraft; a factor leading to mistaken bullets from a confused infantry. Source: (top) *Flugsport*, February 1918, p.104; (bottom) *Flugsport*, July 1918, p.n/a

Each side shared in this curious belief. For example, German General von Hoeppner[7] noted that his troops were convinced that "foes were marking their planes with German insignias." As a result, many Germans fired at anything that flew. The similarity of many designs, for example British and German triplanes, fostered the notion. See sketch.

Americans were also caught up in this paranoid world, consisting of flight under false colors. Innocent victims included anti-balloon ace pilots Frank Luke and Joe Wehner. One day commander Harold. E. Hartney found them[8] "heatedly discussing the thousands of bullets fired at them, from our side of the lines as they made their way home … it happened many times." The mere flying of clearly and correctly marked aircraft wasn't enough. To certain minds, all aircraft were potentially those of the enemy. For such men, flight at a low altitude itself was sensed as proof of evil intent.

Luke and Wehner, concerned with shooting down observation balloons floating at a negligible altitude, required the lowest possible route for approach and return. As given by Hartney, "you have to come down within 100 feet of the ground … [and face] 10 to 20 machine guns and countless rifles." [9] Unfortunately, this was exactly the path assigned by the paranoids to their enemies. Hence the "thousands of rounds" – much of it rifle fire – offered up by American troops to their own aces.

At times a low altitude did indeed indicate harmful intent. British pilot Lieutenant Sholto Douglas,[10] intent on destroying a vital railroad bridge near Cambrai, France and fearful of missing with his too light bombs (20 lbs. each) flew over at a height of only 130 feet, receiving "much rifle fire" and "12 to 15 hits on my machine." He survived, for his aircraft surface area (BE2c) was large and the truly sensitive area small, but the lesson was clear. The light damage his bombs inflicted upon the train line reinforced the moral – avoid low altitudes – because the penalties were large and the payoff small.

Ground strafing didn't permit evasive tactics, for successful attack required flight approaching ground level. The inevitable results were frequent hits from return fire and a certain cool judgement about receiving aircraft hits. To American Elliot Springs,[11] conducting strafing runs "at a couple of hundred feet," the finding of a "few holes scattered about the plane, but nothing serious" reflected a typical day's effort. Again, the aircraft's critical area was small, and not easily struck.

Other strafers were not as lucky. American Lieutenant Bill Lambert, ground strafing in SE5's with members of his 48th Squadron in April 1918, saw six of their machines crash as a result of return fire.[12] Yet, oddly enough, "none of our pilots was badly hurt … " Chance and luck could be very picky. Or perhaps it was a matter of that truly tiny sensitive area – that of a man plus engine plus fuel and oil tanks, along with a few vital control points.

To British intellectuals reaching for some sense of certainty in the uncertain world of return fire, the figure for truly sensitive target area was usually taken to be 20 square feet. A hit anywhere in this sector was interpreted as a total loss – be it of man or aircraft. This number arose from the pre-war work of British engineer M. O'Gorman.[13] To determine the likelihood of return fire hits, he arranged for a locomotive to tow a large box kite containing a marked 20 square feet of sensitive area, serving as a target. Test shooters included regular Army riflemen numbering as many as 48, or a single Vickers machine gun. In the course of many runs 1587 rifle bullets were fired, and there were eight sensitive area hits, or roughly one in 200. Next, an expert machine gunner fired some hundreds of rounds and achieved the same level of accuracy: roughly one critical area hit per 200 rounds fired. In sum, the tests showed that whether fired by a rifle or machine gun, bullets had about one chance in 200 of hitting a sensitive spot on a remote, moving kite serving as a mock aircraft.

Modern criticism of the O'Gorman test would feature two serious departures from reality – those of kite speed and range. Certainly the kite speed of roughly 25 mph was too low to simulate an aircraft, and served to ease the shooting task. On the other hand, the range employed was too great, by some hundreds of yards, greatly increasing the difficulty of the shooters. These failures to duplicate actual wartime shooting conditions prevent serious consideration of the O'Gorman 'one in 200' result. We suspect that his result reflects only the proper order of magnitude, i.e. 'one downed per hundreds fired.' However, whatever the exact ratio might have been, it was apparent that given enough rounds fired, there would be successful hits in sensitive areas and aircraft would be brought down. Furthermore, there was reason to believe that every rifle round fired was about as effective, per bullet, as one fired from a machine gun in terms of hitting a distant, moving target. What mattered in mass firing was the number of bullets fired, and not the weapon. At a time when machine guns were in short supply, the prospect of employing readily available rifleman as anti-aircraft defenders was most appealing.

Not only were riflemen present by the many thousands, but each had an easy flexibility of aim denied to many machine gunners. Early anti-aircraft machine gun mounts were notoriously poor, offering a limited capability for shifting one's aim, or in other cases, inadequate stiffness of support, such that recoil force altered the aim of all rounds following upon the first. By comparison, the rifleman was more nearly in full control of his direction of fire at all times.

Anti-Aircraft Defense, German 1914.

These early German machine gun mounts permitted changes in elevation, but not those of azimuth (left-right) – a serious defect. Any rifleman offered greater flexibility.
Source: Baer, C.H. *Der Völkerkrieg*,(Stuttgart: Hoffmann, 1914) p.164.

Even so, the sources of his aiming errors were many. For one, it was necessary to know the aircraft speed and range in order to plan for the simultaneous arrival of plane and bullet. Should the aircraft pass over at a range of, let us say 600 feet, the usual rifle or machine gun bullet's speed was such that roughly 1/3 of a second was required for the bullet to arrive. Moving at typical fighter combat speeds of 120 feet/second, the aircraft would move forward by some 40 feet in the course of this time delay. As a result, aiming directly at the aircraft was useless, for the bullet would pass 40 feet behind the aiming point. Instead, it was necessary to aim and shoot at empty space some 40 feet ahead of the aircraft; a distance larger than the length of most fuselages. While gun sights could be set to automatically supply this amount of deflection or "lead", the correct value of offset depended on the range and the aircraft velocity, both of which had much to do with happenstance and were usually beyond the shooter's ability to judge both quickly and accurately. As a result, the actual lead employed was generally a matter of split-second guess work, set into place as the aircraft passed over. Unhappily for riflemen, the loss of accuracy owing to mistaken lead allowance was serious.

There were yet other forms of major aiming error. Just as long range led to serious aircraft targeting errors, too short a range produced another form of aiming difficulty – that resulting from the need for pivoting the rifleman's upper body to follow his fast moving target. A very

Why Shooting at Long Range is Difficult

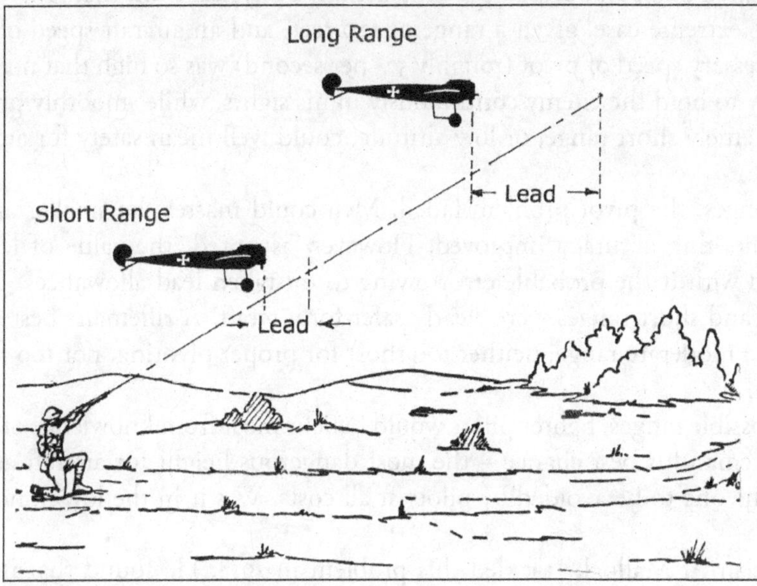

Lead, a certain distance aimed ahead of the aircraft, was required to permit the bullet to meet its target. As range increased, lead became huge, resulting in large errors in setting the right amount. In turn, accuracy vanished. Source: Original sketch by author.

Why Shooting at Short Range is Difficult

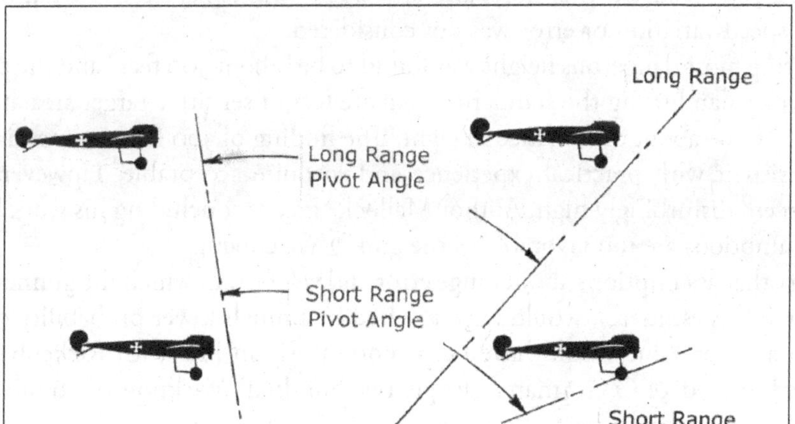

To keep the aircraft within his sights, it was necessary for the rifleman to pivot; the shorter the range, the faster the pivot. Few had fast pivoting ability. As a result, hits were unlikely at extremely short ranges. Source: Original sketch by author.

short range required a fast and precise pivoting action; a physical stunt that few could perform properly. In the extreme case, given a range of 120 feet, and an aircraft speed of 120 feet per second, the necessary speed of pivot (roughly 52° per second) was so high that no man had the ability necessary to hold the enemy continuously in his sights, while smoothly pivoting. Thus, flight at an extremely short range, or low altitude, could well mean safety for aircraft passing over the front.

At longer ranges, the pivot problem faded. Men could master the smaller angle of pivot required and shooting accuracy improved. However, as noted, the value of lead increased with range, and with it the probable error owing to mistaken lead allowances. In sum, both extremely long and short ranges were clearly safer for aircraft. A rifleman's best chance came with aircraft at a moderate range; neither too short for proper pivoting, nor too far for proper lead assessment.

Of all the possible ranges, fighter pilots would benefit most from knowledge of that altitude offering the rifleman his best chance – the most dangerous height for aircraft attacked from the ground – the one to be avoided by pilots at all costs. Was it in the low hundreds or high hundreds?

Mathematician A. Mallock[14] tackled this problem in 1918. He found that its complexity forced the use of simplifications. For example, the range was taken as purely vertical; i.e., the aircraft was to pass directly over the shooter. The issue of range and range error was handled by assuming a standard plus or minus 3% error for all range estimates. At say, 200 feet of altitude, this amounts to an allowable error of plus or minus 6 feet. We believe that few men can judge altitude so precisely. The effect of the 3% assumption was to minimize that shooting error owing to range and lead. Furthermore, aircraft velocity was considered fixed at 100 mph, and the effect of speed variation or error was not considered.

The resulting most dangerous height was found to be "about 300 feet" and the probability of an ordinary rifleman hitting the standard 20 square feet of sensitive target area at this altitude was estimated to be about one chance in eight. The finding of 300 feet as most dangerous was roughly consistent with practical experience and so quite acceptable. However, the 'one in eight' odds seem disturbingly high. Author Mallock agreed, concluding his work by admitting that his "assumptions are too favorable to the gun."[15] We concur.

Inserting other assumptions about range error and velocity, in which the gunner was granted less accuracy in his estimates, would have resulted in a much lower probability of hitting the target. Such a lower value would have been more nearly in line with Rickenbacker's 'worse than one per hundred' or O'Gorman's 'one per two hundred'. We know of no subsequent work exploring Mallock's assumptions.

Also wanted was that number of riflemen necessary to assure destruction of an overflying aircraft. From the theoretical point of view, calculating this number required more than knowing the odds of getting a hit in a sensitive spot. An extra computing step was necessary.[16] For example, let's assume the odds of destruction are 'one per hundred.' It would be wrong to conclude that employing 100 shooters would assure destruction. This case falls into that branch of probability theory dealing with 'independent events'. If given a hundred shooters, each with a 1% chance of bringing down their target, the proper expression for the probability of destruction is: $\{1 - (.99)^{100}\}$. The resulting 63% probability value strongly suggests destruction, but doesn't guarantee it; there is still a better than 1/3 chance that the enemy would survive. To be fairly certain about destruction, let's say 95% certain, many more than 100 shooters were required. Infantry officers, seeking practical answers to the number of riflemen necessary to shoot down aircraft, pooled their experience in the form of how-to-manuals. A set of official German instructions, issued in September 1917, offered this solid advice:[17]

> Fire from single rifles is useless. Only the concentrated fire of 80 to 100 rifles can lead to success. Fire control, quick decision on the part of the commander, good fire discipline and rapid delivery are necessary.

These views were a good fit to probability theory predictions, and also met the test of combat reality. Masses of riflemen, properly handled, could indeed bring down overflying aircraft. As for single shooters, no matter how skilled, experience showed they were most unlikely to achieve significant destruction.

Army manuals offered practical aiming advice as well. In some cases, this advice was useful for pilots as a guide to that which was best avoided. For example, aircraft crossing the

Front Line Crossing Angle

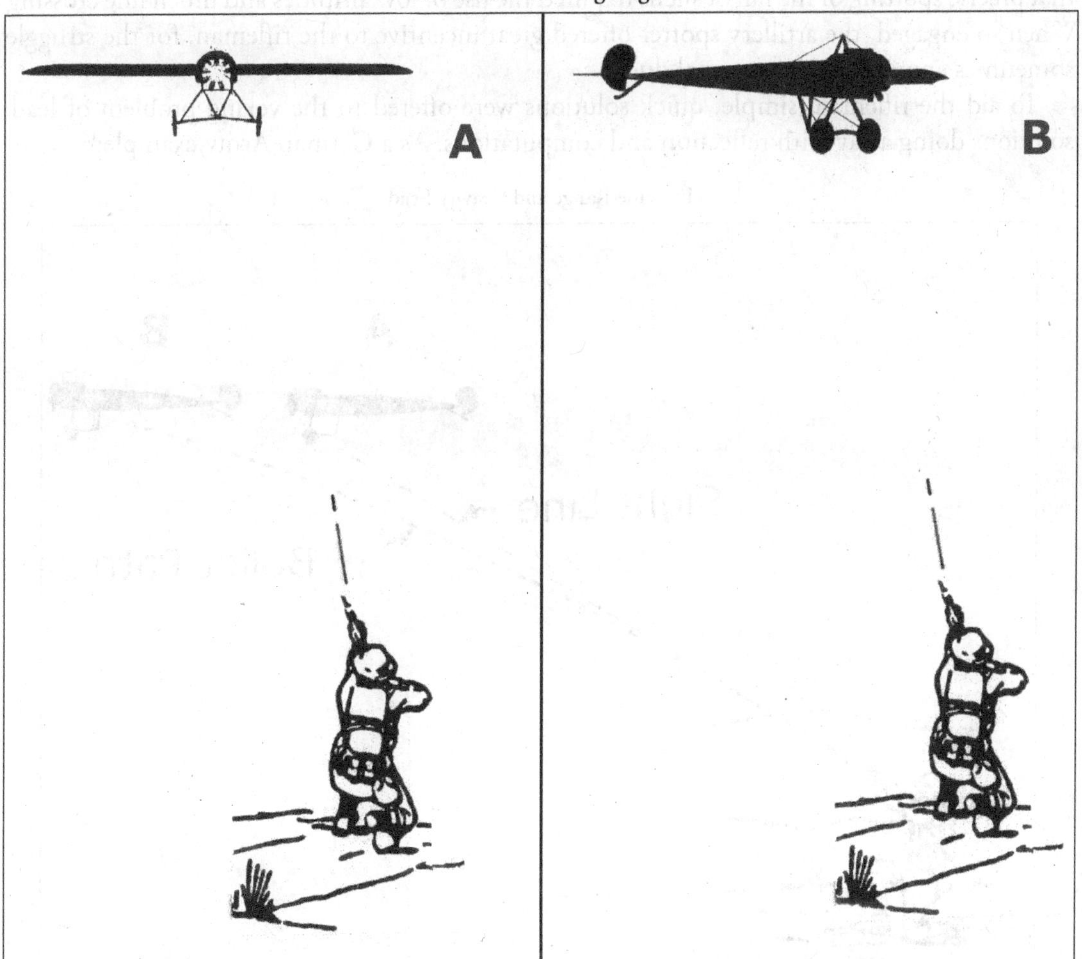

Crossing at an angle (B) other than a right angle (A) made for trajectory and lead uncertainty, lowering the rifleman's chances. See text. Source: Original sketch by author.

frontlines at a right angle were noted[18] as more likely to be shot down than those moving along a trajectory inclined to the frontlines. This had to with the rifleman's difficulty in predicting the future flight path of his target. Given only an oblique view of a distant aircraft, to spell out the resulting angular trajectory was not easy. Consider this problem in detail.

When crossing at right angles, as shown in (A), the future path was obvious. When moving at a slant to the front as in (B), determination of the angle and future path was far from obvious. Furthermore, a devious pilot could hold his machine at say, 10° of yaw with respect to his flight path. As a result, even a perfect knowledge of the machine's angle with respect to the shooter could prove of little value in determining future trajectory. Yet future trajectory, to be judged within seconds, was a key step in the aiming process. As a result, (B) proved to be the wiser path for pilots when crossing frontlines.

To many pilots it seemed that crossing at a high altitude, out of small arms reach, was the best move. However, fresh problems arose as altitude increased. For one, anti-aircraft cannons tended to become effective at higher altitudes – 1000 meters or more – and secondly, flying at great values of range hampered vision and prevented good reconnaissance. Experience showed that precise spotting of the fall of shells required the use of low altitudes and much line crossing. When so engaged, the artillery spotter offered great incentive to the rifleman, for the struggle sometimes amounted to a personal duel.

To aid the rifleman, simple, quick solutions were offered to the vexing problem of lead; solutions doing away with reflection and computations. As a German Army example:[19]

Extreme Range and Gravity Lead

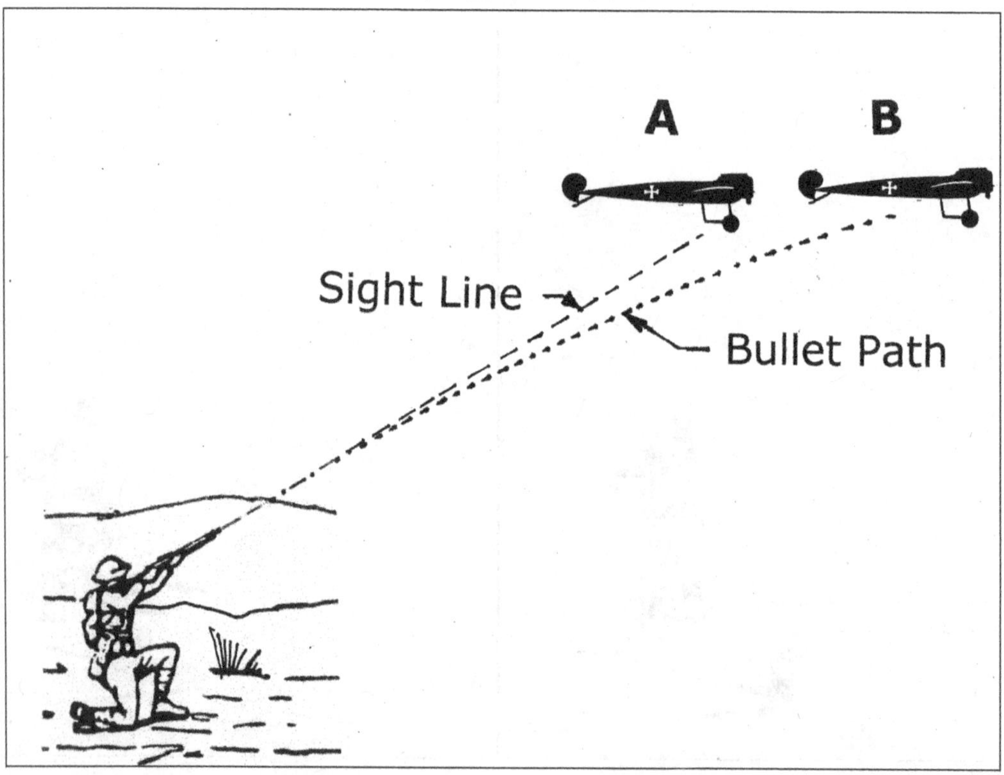

At extreme range, aiming directly at the aircraft (A) could supply adequate lead, by means of bullet drop caused by gravity, yielding a hit, as at (B). Source: Original sketch by author.

When the aeroplane is flying away, aim will be taken *below* the aeroplane, up to a range of 1000 meters, and *directly at it* above that range. (italics sic.)

The wisdom of the 'aim below' suggestion is evident upon checking those prior illustrations concerned with lead. To aim below a departing aircraft was to aim ahead of the machine. Properly done, and given a reasonably short range, the bullet caught up to the aircraft.

The second suggestion – aiming directly at the aircraft – makes use of the bullet's drop in height, that resulting from gravity. At extreme ranges, requiring several seconds of bullet travel, the drop was a matter of many feet. The effect was to bend the bullet path downward, as it moved forward.

Despite their basic merit, both these suggestions suffered from a lack of detail. For example, aiming below departing aircraft at short ranges, though correct in principle: yes, but how much below? Not only was the precise amount all-important, but the answer varied with range and speed. To incorporate these factors, the rifleman needed much more advice. In sum, what was offered fell far short of practical application. Similarly, aiming directly at a departing aircraft, positioned at a great range, was a sound notion. However when at great range, half a mile or more, many other factors influenced the outcome: such as the rifleman's stability, visibility, and ability to predict the aircraft's future path. As a result, for most shooters the likelihood of a hit at extreme range was very low – even when shooting against a fixed target. Finally, there remained the unresolved issue of how one located the transition point for aim – given as 1000 meters distant. Ordinary gunsights were of little use and there was no easy answer. Once again, the advice offered was seriously inadequate.

Why give soldiers advice of dubious value? Perhaps the object was to encourage riflemen to shoot, even if their individual chances were negligible. Bullets were cheap and there was much logic behind mass fire as a means of achieving the desired destruction through sheer numbers.

Competing anti-aircraft service cannons, working at their best altitudes, offered a sense of the extreme difficulty found in achieving proper aim. Over the entire war,[20] the French fired an average of 3225 shells to destroy each of those aircraft downed. The corresponding British figure was one downed per 1800 fired, and that of the Americans, 1055. The inferior French figure represented years of learning how, while the superior American values reflected both late entry and use of the latest French arms. Taking as the average, an Allied order of magnitude figure of 'one downed per thousands fired', offers us a means of comparing the success of cannons, as against rifles. Summing up all considerations, the order of magnitude of the rifle success ratio was probably 'one downed per many hundreds fired'. Therefore the rifleman's expenditure of bullets in downing aircraft was no less effective, per aircraft downed, than the firing of shells, and quite possibly more effective. Certainly rifle fire was much cheaper.

However, the rifle's reach was extremely limited as compared to that of the cannon – at times, an overwhelming disadvantage. Still, there was considerable logic to deploying riflemen as an anti-aircraft auxiliary. Accomplishing more than the bringing down of enemy aircraft, the threat of the rifleman itself served to alter tactics over the front.

For example, Flt. Lieutenant R. M. Foster's wartime experience[21] detailed the acceptance of mass fire effectiveness, along with its tactical implications. He first noted the changes wrought by infantry units with "their rifles and guns at the ready – sufficiently concentrated to produce that volume of fire which, by the law of averages, brings about the lucky hit."

As a result, he would restrain the employment of low flying aircraft over the enemy's established defenses, using such flights "as little as possible." Instead, he would employ strafing in periods of "moving [i.e., mobile] warfare … [when] … the employment of low-flying aircraft in large numbers will amply justify the losses sustained." In other words, aircraft losses arising when flying low over established infantry units were large indeed, so large as to be acceptable only when crucial to the success of a big push.

Given this desirable condition – a mobile frontline – how should one go about strafing? As given by Foster, safest was never to climb above 50 feet of altitude. However, this altitude led to great difficulty in selecting targets, for when flying extremely low, targets flashed by before action could be taken. One effective compromise was to initially fly over at an altitude beyond small arms range, selecting targets at about 2500 feet, and then to dive down to less than 50 feet for the actual strafing run. Regaining height was sensed as a mistake: it offered one's profile for every shooter below and took too long. Simply returning home was much better, when done at that most desirable altitude of 50 feet or less.

Foster's views were prevalent, for they offered much in the way of universally shared experience and common sense. In sum, the rifleman, when in massive numbers, was a menace to all low flying aircraft. Fifty feet up was the only safe height for crossing over the lines. At more than one hundred feet of altitude, major troubles were anticipated from riflemen; troubles not to cease until a few thousand feet were gained.

What of Richthofen, and his end? Did death by rifleman fit the facts of his case? Despite the confusion and contradictions surrounding his death, certain useful data and claims do exist. Examination with the tools of engineering permits us to separate fact from fantasy, thus spotting mistaken or lying claims and allowing for the entrance of logic. We end, still unsure of Richthofen's killer, but relieved of much burdensome nonsense and with an improved sense of the odds favoring each claimant.

Consider Richthofen's flight path on the fatal day.[22] As leader of *Jasta* 5, he flew as part of a loose formation, that of fighter groups *Jasta* 5 joined to *Jasta* 11, guarding a number of observation machines, totaling roughly 20 aircraft in all. While still on the German side of the lines, and moving towards Australian-held territory, they met approximately a dozen British machines somewhere between Cerisy and le Hamel. These included the Camels of ace fighter pilot Captain Roy Brown (12 victories) and beginner Lieutenant Wilfred May. The latter had been given sound advice: he was to observe, rather than participate. If somehow caught up in fighting, he was to drop to the 50 feet of altitude recommended by Foster and streak for home.

As the melée developed, May was singled out by Richthofen as his next victim. Realizing that he had become a target, May followed instructions and speeded towards the Australian lines, though not at 50 feet of altitude. Instead, he flew at a height in the low hundreds – an exactly wrong, but understandable error – for the terrain was hilly and overgrown with trees. Richthofen followed, determined to blast May's Camel.

In the midst of combat, Brown looked down and saw May under close pursuit, and clearly in trouble. Concerned with saving May, he attacked the pursuing all red triplane, employing a single shooting pass at roughly right angles to the triplane's path. Brown's review of the encounter[23] placed the combatants "at not more than 200 feet above the ground and directly over the Australian first line trenches." He saw infantrymen staring at the intruding aircraft,

Richthofen's Last Flight

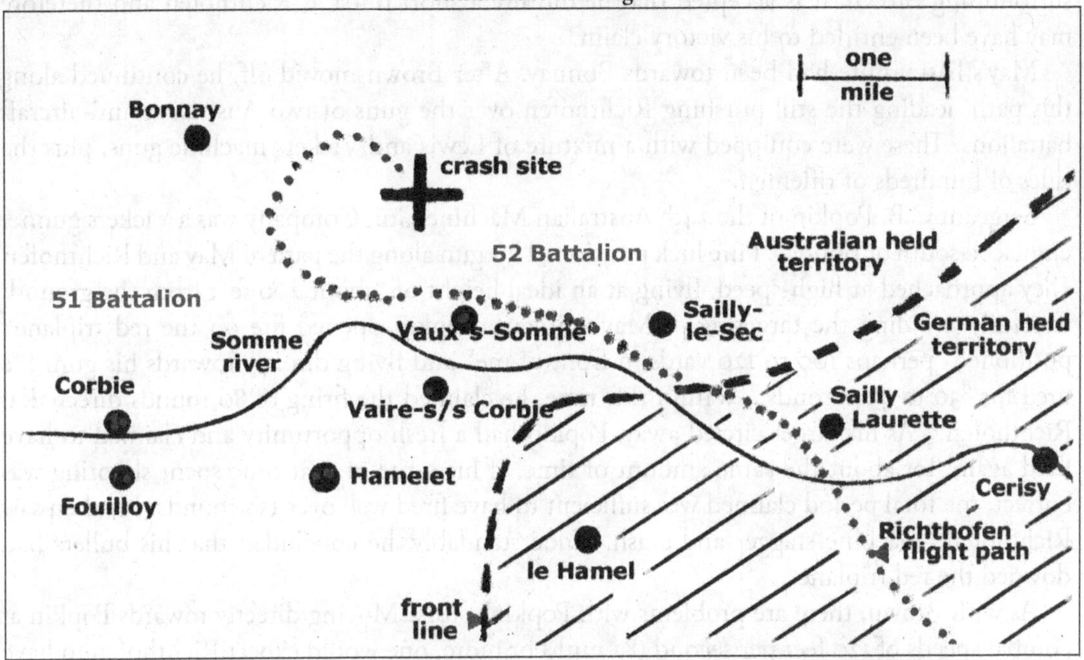

Crossing over German held area into unfriendly territory, he encountered British fighters and Australian ground fire. Somewhere along the path shown, he was hit and killed by a single bullet.Source: Original sketch by author, guided by old auto maps.

with machine gunners shooting at the "red plane." He next saw Richthofen's machine "waver and fall to the ground between the first line and the support trenches of the Australian infantry." Brown turned away, convinced that though many below had fired, he personally had ended Richthofen's threat. However, a number of observers disagreed.

For one thing, the location of the downed red triplane as given by Brown, was roughly two miles distant from its actual resting place (see map). Perhaps the error reflected only a post-combat lapse in judgement concerning a detail, but it was an important detail, for if Richthofen had flown on for some appreciable distance after Brown's attack, it was possible that someone else had brought him down. Secondly, Brown himself made a poor witness, for he was clearly disturbed and in the early stages of a nervous breakdown; a man who readily admitted to living exclusively on a diet of milk and brandy.[24] The contrast between the lifestyles of the two men produced doubt that Brown could possibly have won a mortal duel against Richthofen. Finally, despite claims of word-for-word authenticity and official acceptance of his detailed story, obtained through interview, as part of RAF history, certain sentences were prepared in too writerly a fashion to be acceptable as Brown's actual words – for example, the description of his Camel aircraft after that day's fighting as: "a sorry sight with twisted wires and punctuated wings … with only two cylinders working."[25] The voice heard was not that of a combat pilot, but that of a journalist. Inevitably, doubts have arisen concerning the authenticity of Brown's story.

Within a few more days he succumbed to the nervous disorder that had been plaguing him for many weeks, and was invalided out of frontline service. Still, whatever the doubts surrounding Brown, it is accepted that he did fire a short burst at Richthofen and therefore may have been entitled to his victory claim.

May's basic route had been towards Bonnay. After Brown moved off, he continued along this path, leading the still pursuing Richthofen over the guns of two Australian anti-aircraft battalions. These were equipped with a mixture of Lewis and Vickers machine guns, plus the rifles of hundreds of riflemen.

Sergeant C.B. Popkin of the 24th Australian Machine Gun Company was a Vickers gunner emplaced south of Bonnay. Pure luck positioned his gun along the path of May and Richthofen. They approached at high-speed, flying at an ideal height of "about 200 feet from the ground." Carefully avoiding the targeting of May's aircraft, Popkin opened fire on the red triplane[26] positioned "perhaps 100 to 120 yards in front of me" and flying directly towards his gun. He fired for "30 to 40 seconds." Within this time, he claimed the firing of 80 rounds directed at Richthofen.[27] As his target circled away, Popkin had a fresh opportunity and claimed to have fired again, for about the same amount of time. If his sense of that time spent shooting was correct, the total period claimed was sufficient to have fired well over 150 rounds. He then saw Richthofen's machine stagger and crash. Understandably, he concluded that his bullets had downed the red triplane.

As with Brown, there are problems with Popkin's story. Moving directly towards Popkin at combat speeds of 120 feet per second (82 mph) or more, one would expect Richthofen to have overflown the claimed intervening distance of 120 yards in roughly 3 seconds. How Popkin managed to fire effectively for a claimed "30 to 40 seconds" in the course of a 3 second straight line approach period is far from clear. We suspect that Popkin was seriously mistaken in his time and bullet estimates. In sum, we believe that he overstated his period of fire by a factor of 10 fold, and that the true number of bullets fired effectively were relatively few. For a corrected figure, we shall use the official Vickers figure for rapid fire: some 250 rounds[28] per minute. The resulting number for 3 seconds of firing: 12 rounds.

Regarding Richthofen's subsequent circling maneuver and Popkin's second firing opportunity, the path and distance numbers necessary to check the results have never been available. As a result, the prospects of Popkin's second chance remain unexamined. It is likely that as before, a dozen bullets were fired. However, it is accepted that Popkin did indeed fire at Richthofen, who then crashed, mortally wounded, some time after Popkin's second firing run.

One more claimant for the role of Richthoften's killer was Sergeant Robert Buie of the 14th Australian Field Artillery Brigade. Working one of the two post-mounted Lewis machine guns assigned to the 53 Battery, he found himself in position to shoot just as May and his pursuer hurtled by. His alignment with respect to the aircraft was similar to that of Popkin: both aircraft were on a nearly head-on path, one behind the other, and inclined slightly to one side.

Buie claimed that he opened fire at 200 yards and kept shooting until "my last shots finished at a range of 40 yards."[29] Applying a straight line aircraft flight speed value of 120 feet per second (82 mph) to the distance of 160 yards (i.e., 200 minus 40), yields an elapsed time result of 4 seconds. Buie claimed to have carefully aimed and fired off the entire drum (47 rounds) in careful bursts, all within this 4 second time period.

His first 20 rounds were spent in registering the target, with Richthofen moving straight ahead and slightly towards the right of his position. May's aircraft location, a bare 60 feet ahead of the red triplane, was a major problem. To shoot at the rear aircraft, without hitting the one out in front was far from easy. Yet Buie claimed to have done so, and also to have noted changes in Richthofen's posture as he hunched down behind his twin Spandau machine guns[30] to fire at May's aircraft. He also claimed to have noted a "sharp change in engine sound" signifying the stoppage of Richthofen's engine, an event suggesting that Buie's bullets were well-aimed. Richthofen then moved into a low altitude glide, finally hitting the ground in a crash landing.

As with Popkin and Brown, there are difficulties of belief. Firing off a full drum of Lewis gun bullets in careful bursts, so as to avoid hitting May, while noting Richthofen's position within his cockpit, etc., and all done within 4 seconds, seems unlikely. Even the official maximum cyclic firing rate[31] of the Lewis gun, given as 500 to 600 unaimed rounds per minute, does not aid the Buie claim. In reality, his firing rate would have been much lower, forced down by necessary pauses. Some were made necessary by cooling requirements; i.e. a short halt after the firing of each 6 to 10 bullet burst.[32] Additional pauses were necessary to re-aim the gun at Buie's tricky target, trailing behind May's aircraft, and as such, partly hidden. With pauses forcing a much lower time-averaged firing rate, many more than 4 seconds were required to empty a full drum. In sum, constraints upon firing rate suggest strongly that Buie didn't fire a full drum at Richthofen. We do believe that Buie did fire some rounds at Richthofen – likely far fewer than a dozen bullets in all – preceding Richthofen's crash. However, the connection between bullets and crash, if any, remains unclear.

The difficulties with belief noted above in connection with the stories of Richthofen protagonists Brown, Popkin and Buie suggest a search of other eyewitness reports. There were other such reports, by British airmen and Australian ground troops. RFC/RAF pilots routinely submitted a combat report listing claims and, where possible, the names of eyewitnesses. Thus, in concluding his description of the Richthofen encounter,[33] Brown stated: "I got a long burst into him [Richthofen] and he went down vertical and was observed to crash by Lieutenant Mellersh and Lieutenant May."

Eyewitness Lieutenant F.J.W. Mellersh's own report[34] noted: "… a red triplane crashed quite close to me and as I looked up I saw Captain Brown's machine." However, mere presence on the scene wasn't equivalent to shooting down an enemy aircraft. Even if the triplane did in truth crash in the presence of Brown, and there were dozens of ground-based viewers who did not agree, Mellersh's statement failed to confirm a victory for Brown.

Lieutenant May was far more positive.[35] "While he [Richthofen] was on my tail, Captain Brown attacked and shot it down. I observed it crash to the ground." Surely no witness was better placed, or had more at stake in Richthofen's crash than May. Yet, a great many Australians saw no such thing. A shooting pass by Brown, yes; but the only immediate result was Brown's departure, after which Richthofen's pursuit of May continued for several miles. During the pursuit, following much shooting from the ground, May was able to escape and Richthofen was finally brought down at a spot remote from May's path. In sum, May couldn't possibly have seen Richthofen "crash to the ground" immediately after Brown's attack, for the good reason that it didn't happen at that time. This negative view, taken from the reports of many dozens of Australians,[36] is unlikely to be mistaken. In weighing the truth of evidence, numbers count.

It's the evidence of single witnesses that tends to prove troublesome. Not only have the odd views of May and Mellersh produced doubt, but as shown above, those of the individual claimants Brown, Popkins and Buie were also unconvincing. Unfortunately, this has also proved to be the case with reports of presumably disinterested observers. For an example, consider the evidence submitted by Lieut G.M. Travers of the 52nd Battalion.

Equipped with field glasses, and assigned the task of observer, he seemed well suited for the task. Choosing a spot near Popkin's Vickers gun, he was in a perfect position to see Popkin's attack as May and Richthofen swept by. His eyes convinced him of Popkin's success in shooting down the pursuing red aircraft: "the enemy plane [Richthofen] swerved to the right so suddenly … " as to suggest a serious hit. After the crash he "had a look … at the driver who was dead, a machine gun bullet had passed from the left side of his face and near the bottom of his jaw and came out just behind his right eye."[37]

However, there was no such wound. Autopsies conducted by two medical teams pointed to only one serious wound, at heart level.[38] A single bullet had entered his torso at the right arm pit, and exited at the left nipple. There has never been a question about the location of the single, fatal wound. Travers, with his strange, totally mistaken story, proved himself inept in the role of observer. The practical effect of his tale was to greatly reduce the value of his support for Popkin as the killer of Richthofen.

Yet another witness of this type was Sergeant H. Hart, 53 Battery. Hart was in position to see Buie fire, after which "splinters flew from it [the red triplane] and it veered … and crashed about 500 yards from the battery."[39] Rushing over to inspect the corpse, he saw " … the wounds, they were frontal, in the chest, abdomen and legs – all in the front … "

Once again, the medical autopsies did not agree. In addition to the death-dealing single bullet wound, the body did exhibit other wounds including "minor bruises" and a broken jaw caused by the crash, but these were not pertinent to Richthofen's death. What might have been strong evidence by Hart faded under the influence of his mistaken observations.

In sum, the eyewitness evidence offered by Brown, May, Popkins, Buie, Mellersh, Travers, and Hart was all seriously flawed. Certain mistaken trends were evident. One such concerned the number of bullets fired; a number always exaggerated by those who reported on the shooting itself. A second error was in the number of serious, death-dealing wounds reported as sustained by Richthofen; a number always given as higher than the true value: exactly one.

Errors of excessive bullets and wounds served to back the concept of a machine gun as the weapon employed. In popular thinking, machine guns spew out bullets, and so a great many must have been fired. With so many fired, if well-aimed, numerous hits must have occurred. The existence of a single bullet wound was disturbing to this way of thought, for a single bullet strike suggests a rifle and not a machine gun. Was it indeed possible to shoot at a man-sized target with a well placed machine gun at a reasonable range and miss with every bullet – except one? If almost all the machine gun bullets managed to miss, why the exception?

The answer has to do with the scatter and spread of the emerging bullets. Each bullet had slightly different dimensions, and came with a slightly different amount of gunpowder, leading to correspondingly changed natural paths. Then, machine gun barrels whipped, and recoil vibration changed aim a bit. Over long ranges, the difference in path caused by these factors could be considerable. However, given a short range, if firing a full burst right on target, hitting a man with only one bullet was unlikely. Consider the implications of scatter result test data when applied to the death of Richthofen – a death caused by a single bullet.

Tests of new Lewis guns, bolted down securely, yielded a tight group of bullets. Firing results[40] showed "all the shots falling within a [one] foot circle at 300 yards [range]." Noting that the range used in shooting at Richthofen was a good deal less than 300 yards, and that scatter decreases in a straight line fashion with range, we calculate a total scatter diameter of less than 8 inches at 200 yards. At this range, well-aimed test guns, bolted down to a rigid

Machine Gun Scatter (not to scale)

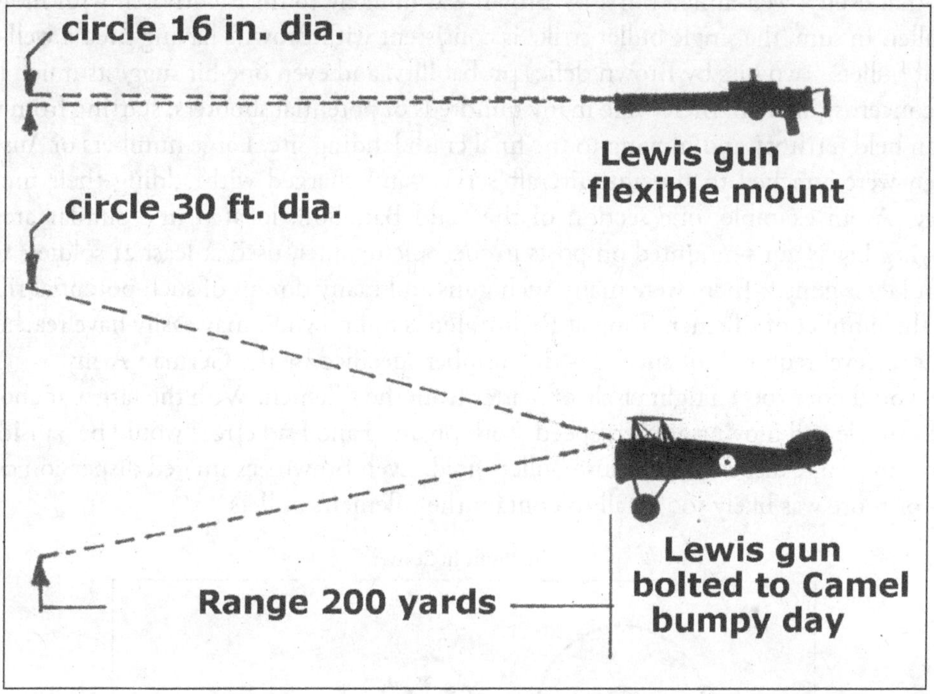

Richthofen's single fatal wound suggests a high scatter source, likely that of multiple rifles or an airborne machine gun, rather than a well-aimed, ground-based machine gun. Source: Original sketches by author.

framework, and firing a full burst, were most unlikely to hit a man with only one bullet. If one bullet struck an armpit, many of the others were likely to strike his body as well.

However, in reality the ground placed guns of Buie and Popkins were not rigidly held. They were flexibly mounted to permit following a target. Orfordness tests with a moving gun as compared to a fixed gun, showed the dispersion diameter to roughly double; i.e., we might expect a scatter diameter of about 16 inches at 200 yards. Into this area would pour some 70 to 80% of the bullets fired. The remaining bullets, considered "wild" rounds, might go far afield.

The effect of the change in mounting was to lower the probability of multiple strikes. Applying these findings to the cases of Buie and Popkin, and as before assuming that each gunner fired a well-aimed full burst, we would still expect several bullets to strike Richthofen. However, in reality there was no second wound, and we must conclude that in all probability, Buie and Popkin fired poorly aimed bursts. If one of their bullets did strike Richthofen, it could only have been a wild round. As for the bulk of their bullets, they went elsewhere.

Brown's bullets were also subject to scatter. Even when fighter plane guns were fixed and bolted down, as were those of Brown, their bullets experienced a greatly increased spread owing to the lack of rigidity of the aircraft structure and the softness of air support. The bumpiness of the day's weather was also a factor, acting to further increase the spread. Tests pointed to spread circles as large as 5 feet in diameter being necessary to contain ¾ of the Lewis gun bullets fired from a light aircraft at 250 yards range, on a calm day.[41] Correcting for range, at 200 yards we would expect a scatter diameter of 48 inches, or three times that experienced by comparable ground gunners. On a bumpy day, and April 21 has been described as "gusty" and "turbulent"[42], the scatter diameter could increase to more than 30 feet. So great a scatter meant that even a well-aimed burst by Brown was unlikely to hit Richthofen with more than one bullet. In sum, the single bullet strike is consistent with Brown's having fired a well-aimed burst of bullets. Two hits by Brown defies probability, and even one hit suggests much luck.

As concerns riflemen, there were many hundreds of potential shooters, starting from within German held territory and moving to the final crash landing site. Large numbers of Australian riflemen were attached to the anti-aircraft service and charged with adding their fire when possible. As an example, one section of the 22nd Battalion, located in a similar area, and employing Lewis guns mounted on posts in the Buie manner, used at least 21 soldiers to man its twin Lewis guns.[43] There were many such guns and many dozens of such potential riflemen. While the number of riflemen firing at Richthofen is unknown, it may easily have reached that "80 to 100" level required for success – the number specified by the German Army.

We would not expect a tight circle of scatter from the riflemen. With the target at about 200 feet of altitude and moving at high-speed, both pivoting and lead errors would be considerable, resulting in a large dispersion of those bullets fired. Even Brown's estimated dispersion circle of 30 feet or more was likely too small to contain the riflemen's bullets.

The Profit in Scatter

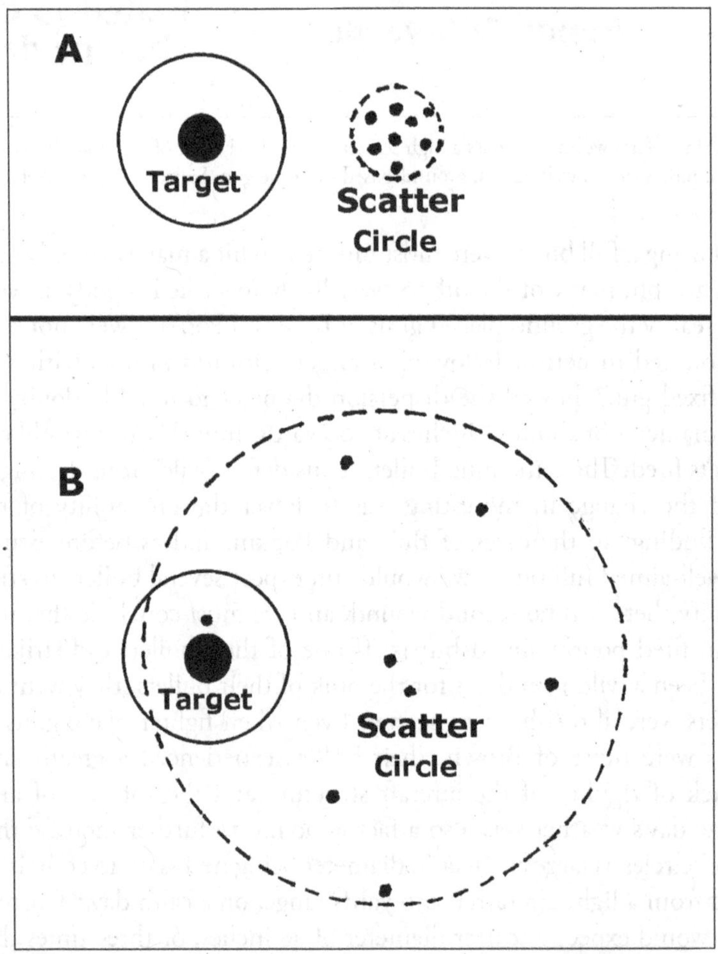

(A) A poorly aimed burst, fired with a small scatter, will miss the target with every bullet. (B) The same poorly aimed burst, fired with large scatter, may place a bullet on target through sheer chance. Source: Original sketch by author.

Still, there was an advantage to wide dispersion. At times, imperfect aim could be offset. Unlike a perfect, zero scatter gun, whose bullets went only where aimed, a mass of riflemen had the advantage of large scatter, possibly hitting the target despite poor aim. As shown above, a large scatter was capable of compensating for even dreadful aim – if enough bullets were fired.

Were there enough? Everything rests on the number of shooters. If a hundred or more men were able to get off two rounds apiece, they had a good chance of hitting Richthofen with a single bullet. In ignorance of the number of shooters, any prediction of the likelihood of success is impossible. It can only be said that the rifleman prospect is real and deserves consideration, not as an afterthought, but as a main contending possibility.

And so we conclude our study of Richthofen's death; one concentrated on gunnery and chance. Though none of the "usual suspects" have been eliminated in our study, something has been achieved by identifying the mistaken eyewitness accounts and false logic that dominate this area. We next deal with an even stranger result of defective official reasoning: proof that air war itself was impossible.

2

Air Combat: Real or Nonsense?

For the most part, Richthofen's war was fought against the British. His 80 air combat victories amounted to an extraordinary success. So one-sided a result creates doubts, for Richthofen was an improbable top ranking winner. He had too many drawbacks. One's natural skepticism rises in protest.

He was no student. More to the point, he was no student pilot, flunking his flight exam twice before an ever-patient flight school accepted his uncertain efforts. In turn, he made for a poor aerobatic pilot at a time when aerobatic skill seemed a requisite for success; for example, that considerable score and fame achieved by Immelmann.

The one characteristic shared by all the great aces was fierce determination, offered at a level far beyond military requirements. Yet Richthofen's record was that of a drifter, rather than an achiever. He served first in the cavalry and then in the Army food and provisions section. There was also service as an aerial observer and even some time spent training as a bomber pilot in an

The Red Baron, 1917

As he truly was, handsome and carefully watchful. Source: *La Guerre Aerienne*, January 1918, p.183.

outfit hoping to become a strategic air force. He compiled a lackluster record in each of these positions, ending by transferring out. Finally, he hit upon service as a fighter pilot, and to our astonishment, accumulated those 80 victories.

Are we to believe that he had found his true calling at last? Perhaps, but it seems a bit much. We cast about for a more likely explanation. Was it possible that his success came from shooting down a series of inept opponents, unequal to the challenge?

In pre-war days it was widely believed that France led the world in the design of aircraft and Germany held the lead in engines. Were opposing British war planes simply second rate? Was that the key to his success? For that matter, did British pilots receive proper training? In short: how well prepared were the British to fight Richthofen?

A look at pre-war British air planning turns up a curious official attitude: there were grave doubts that air war would ever happen. As a result, those few fighting types ordered were designed for air-to-ground attack, rather than aerial combat. When air combat came, British machines proved poorly suited for the task. Given time– more than a year–the British caught up, but in the meantime casualties were heavy, boosting the scores of those like Richthofen, who were truly prepared for air combat.

The British inability to sense the coming air war amounted to a startling lapse of judgement; a failure entitled to a closer look.

By early 1912, flight was an everyday reality, with air show aerobatics a popular attraction. It was also a time of loud European nationalism, of contempt for one's neighbors and diplomatic threats. British Army planners moved to find solutions for the looming next war. What of aircraft, and their role?

Much was uncertain. The airplane was too new. One couldn't be sure. The experts announced ever-changing opinions, confounded by trials and tests. Reconnaissance and only reconnaissance emerged as a perfect fit to aircraft potential, with observations made aloft wanted to supplement those of the cavalry. All Europe agreed. German planners started work on a series of Army-funded Taube designs centered upon observation needs.

The ever imaginative French thought that an additional aerial function might be served: that of artillery spotting. However, the Germans judged artillery ranging as too futuristic to be of real concern. In the spring of 1913 they assigned a total of only three officers[1] to aerial ranging work – faint support indeed.

What of the British? As seen by Colonel J.E. Capper, known for his airship background[2], the prime British Army need was for a field-worthy machine – one easy to fly, highly reliable, able to both land anywhere and fly in high winds, all while offering great natural stability. As for desired performance traits, he could "sum it up in one word –speed."[3] It was speed that would permit evasion of enemy machines, "for it must be remembered that an aeroplane must not fight."

His refusal to consider combat reflected personal knowledge of the extremely light construction required for airship flight. Applying this finding to airplanes, he reasoned that the slightest blow meant total destruction. Fighting implied hits on both opposing machines, in turn suggesting mutual suicide. In similar fashion, ramming was impossible, for it meant the

Tractor or Pusher?

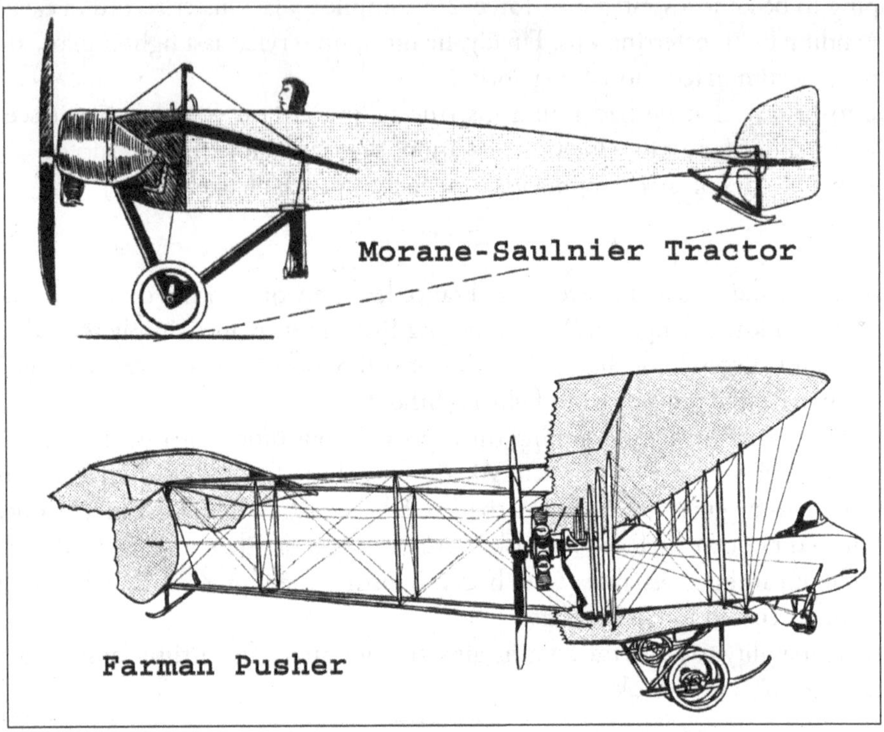

Each had problems. For circa 1913 tractors, especially severe were those of adequate vision below, plus that of providing a usefully large shooting sector. Competing pushers were slow. Choice depended on the machine's purpose. Source: (top) *Flight*, May 24, 1913, p.562; (bottom) *Flight*, October 19, 1912, p.941.

certain end of the aggressor aircraft. What then was to be done about enemy aircraft? Evasion seemed the only correct answer.

As for firearms, they were to be employed, if at all, as a last resort, in a desperate type of self defense, in much the same manner as an officer's side arms. Apparently uneasy at this decision, taken so early in the game, he then opted for a clear field of fire to the front of the aircraft. In practice, this meant that the pusher was wanted rather than the tractor. After all, he might be wrong about firearms and the human trait of hedging uncertainties is always a powerful driving force.

The pusher against tractor choice was not easy. The tractor was clean and fast, enjoying a perfect form for racing machines. In contrast, the pusher was inefficient, clumsy and slow. Yet, with its pilot located at the extreme front of the machine, the pusher offered two powerful advantages for military application: superb vision and an enormous field of fire to the front, all without propeller blockage.

Consider the successful and popular pre-war Morane-Saulnier tractor. The pilot could see everything located at a higher altitude, but vision down and forward was blocked by the wing presence. Unfortunately this very view – down and forward – was the one prized by military observers. Next, imagine a gun placed atop the cowling. Firing forward, or straight ahead, was prevented by that enormous propeller. Even pointing it in oblique fashion, and accepting some loss of accuracy, was not truly practical. The propeller was simply too large, forcing the use of a huge oblique angular offset–and resulting in correspondingly dreadful accuracy.

Next consider the Farman, a successful contemporary (1913) pusher design. The pilot, immediately behind the windscreen (extreme right), could see everything to his front–up or down. Given a gun, he was able to fire to his front or obliquely as he wished, without concern for the propeller. Clearly, there was much to be said for the pusher.

There were disadvantages. They were indeed slow – top speed for the Farman was all of 55mph.[4] Vision to the rear was awkward. Accurate shooting to the rear was difficult indeed. Rumors of murderous spin characteristics clung to the pusher concept and not the tractor. However, all things considered, pushers were a better bet – if guns and shooting were to become an important part of the aerial task. Would they?

Management was hesitant. The uncertain approach to guns was universal. Summing up 1912's official British opinion was the General Staff's Major Radcliffe:[5] "For practical purposes the aeroplane was invulnerable from the ground and had little to fear from hostile aircraft." However, a weapon should be provided "to guard against eventualities."

One's backside must be covered.

German doubts were even greater, for in 1912 experiments with rifles and pistols fired from aircraft made clear "they were unfit for use in aerial combat."[6] Commanding General of the Air Service Ernest von Hoeppner also noted that the obvious next step – employing water cooled machine guns – was rejected for aircraft use owing to gun weight. As light weight air cooled machine guns were not manufactured in Germany at the time,[7] the door was closed on air combat. Instead, evasion was seen as the only proper way to handle hostility in the air. The German conclusion came as a most important support for the widely held British view.

Struggling with their own uncertainties over air combat, the British felt it useful to spell out their airplane needs and hopes in a clear form, on the way to developing practical machines. Could it all be done with a single type? No, not really. Knowledgeable people pointed to a few basic designs as necessary to form up a useful air service. To influential pilot/manufacturer Claude Graham-White, a believer in the reality of air combat, at least two types were required. The first was a fast reconnaissance machine, and the second a "destroyer" capable of protecting brother aircraft from "hostile air patrols circling above the enemy's lines."[8]

This far-sighted view was backed by the well known tailless designer J.W. Dunne. He was certain that air fighting would come about; a certainty so strong as to question the practicality of any tractor airplane for military use. The resulting up front propeller would "impair its fighting value, for it impeded the line of fire straight ahead."[9] In short, only pusher type machines should be considered for the air service.

At the center of these arguments was engineer Mervyn O'Gorman, effective head of the Royal Aircraft Factory and as such, design impresario over all Army, i.e. Royal Flying Corps machines. It was O'Gorman who had the power to initiate a fresh design, either through his own Factory, or through outside contract. Always expansive, he contemplated designing fast and slow scouts in addition to "a small and large aeroplane for gun carrying."[10]

First though, came the BE2. Here was an Army cooperation vehicle, designed to serve as an observation machine and hack. Carrying a non-com pilot and officer observer, the goal was an all purpose machine capable of spying out a battlefield and then landing anywhere to turn in the observer's report. High speed was of importance in arriving quickly; low speed for both a good view and a safe landing on an unprepared field. It wasn't planned as a fighting machine. Should air fighting become significant, other designs would carry the load.

The BE2

De Havilland's sturdy design was prepared for an Army cooperation role.
Source: F.W. Lanchester, *Aircraft in Warfare* (NYC: Appleton, 1916) plate 1.

As a non-fighter, the tractor configuration was chosen rather than a pusher. Experience showed that mounting a propeller up front eliminated the serious propeller blockage experienced by pushers; blockage caused by the physical bulk of the fuselage and wings. The blockage effect was to restrict propeller inflow, cutting thrust. Merely moving the propeller forward, freeing up the inflow, meant that a significant increase of top speed could be expected. Given the tiny engine available to O'Gorman, a French Renault offering 70 h.p., any measure serving to increase efficiency was prized. The other readily available engine, the rotary Gnome, was despised by many[11] as unreliable. In short, designer Geoffrey de Havilland's instincts were

Seat Assignment, BE2a

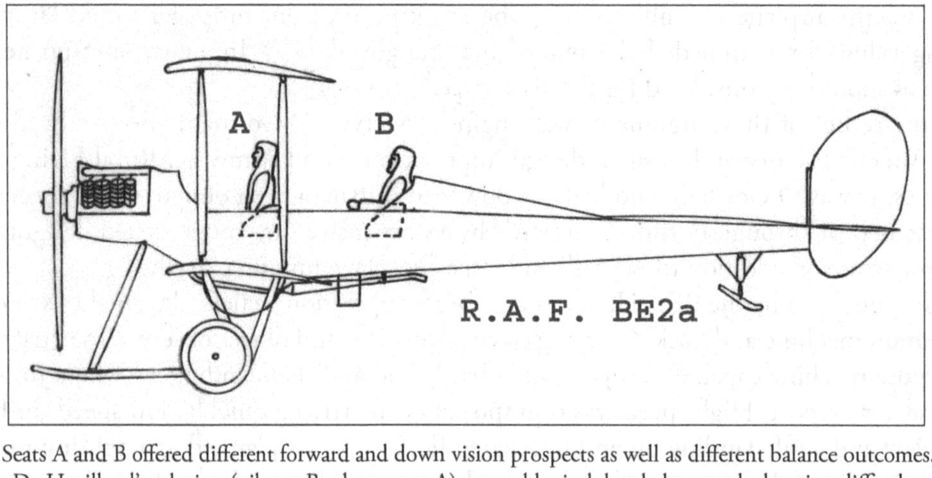

Seats A and B offered different forward and down vision prospects as well as different balance outcomes.
De Havilland's solution (pilot at B, observer at A) seemed logical, but led to much shooting difficulty.
Source: Original sketch prepared by author from official 3-views, *Flight*, November 16, 1912, p.1062.

good and the BE2 tractor versus pusher and engine decisions were sound. Unfortunately, the wartime implications would prove vastly troublesome.

Positioning the crew followed logically from considerations of vision and balance. Placing the observer in front (A) permitted a far superior down-and-forward view as compared to that of the rear seat occupant (B). As this perspective was critical, the observer was located at A and the pilot in the rear, at B.

Another consideration was that of aircraft balance. In a rough sort of way, the balance point of the entire machine in flight was close to that of position A. As a result, flying without the A occupant didn't change the balance–the aircraft felt much the same, though a bit lighter. On the other hand, removing occupant B drastically altered the balance, making for difficult flying. As Army missions were frequently short-handed, flight capability without an observer was a realistic requirement. Once again the practical solution was to put the observer in the A seat and the pilot in B.

This decision, like that favoring the tractor format, though logically based, would yet haunt the RFC. Their unfortunate effect was to make gun use difficult.

The BE2 was to become more than the first aircraft in wide use by the RFC. It also provided a means for full-scale experimentation, important not only for perfecting the machine, but for improving the breed at a time when little was known about design. An example of O'Gorman's endless experimentation with the BE2 is shown below.

The issue was aircraft stability and his hope that of easing the pilot's task. Could something in the way of modest design changes help? Specifically, what would the effect be of increasing the forward lateral or fin area? This was achieved by adding cuffs to the upper end of the wing struts. In the experiment shown, a total addition of 6 square feet was tested. The resulting

Flying Guinea Pig

Small fins placed at the upper ends of struts tested for stability effect. They helped find the correct angle of bank. Source: O'Gorman, M. *Technical Reports of the Advisory Committee for Aeronautics, Reports & Memoranda # 86* (London: HMSO, 1913) fig. 15.

Aileron versus Warp

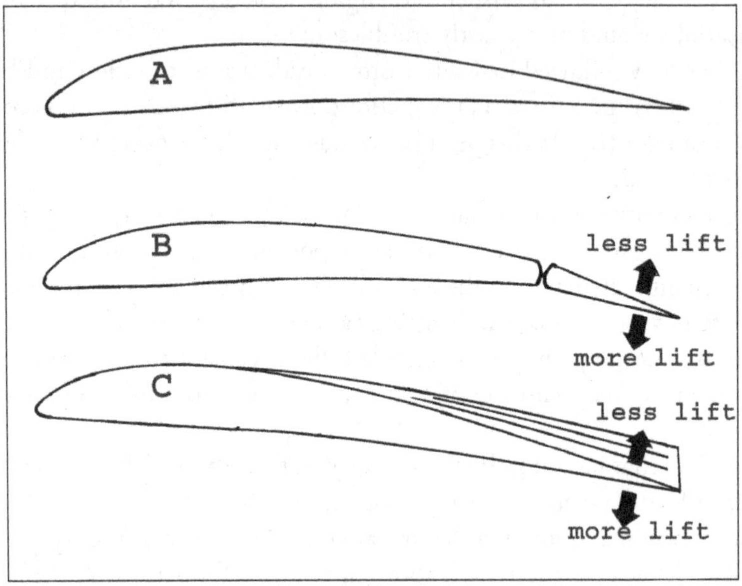

To alter local lift output, the Wrights learned to modify plain wing A by warping as in C. The modern equivalent is the aileron B. Over time, the BE2 design was changed, reluctantly, from warp to ailerons. Source: Original sketch by author.

machine had a slight tendency to bank automatically on turning; a feature well-liked by his test pilots. No disadvantages were noted.[12] However O'Gorman was disappointed–the gain was too slight; it wasn't good enough. Someday he would tackle the problem of truly automatic flight, but it would have to wait, for much more than a few cuffs were required.

Another, much studied problem was the twisting or warping of wings. If we examine the usual airplane's wing cross-section (A), somewhere near the wingtip we will note an aileron (B), a device satisfying today's piloting needs for local lift modification. It consists of a hinged wing portion able to swing down, generating more lift, or upwards to yield less. Starting with the Wrights, much the same result was achieved by warping the wing (C) in flight; a business of twisting it to vary the resulting lift until the desired value was reached. Warp was a time-tried process eliminating the need for the aileron's hinged and separate flying surface. Conservative designs employed warp, rather than ailerons. De Havilland chose warp.

However, warp had its problems. For one thing, wing structures incorporating warp were never truly at rest. Any passing gust, encountered either in flight or when simply sitting on the runway, served to twist the wings. In effect, the wind itself became an unwanted co-pilot, modifying the lift capability of the wings as it saw fit. In contrast, an aileron's controls could be locked when on the ground and made insensitive to gusts when in the air. Unfortunately, easily twisted wings could not. As a result, flight under gusty conditions was exhausting, requiring the pilot to fight against his virtual wind co-pilot at all times.

O'Gorman was that special engineer with a strong interest in difficult details. As an overall designer he was limited, and was wise to employ de Havilland as his chief designer. Granted sufficient self-knowledge to understand that his own strength was in the handling of tricky details, O'Gorman turned to the warp problem. What could be done to remove the sensitivity to wind?

As he saw it, some deflection when under gust loading couldn't be prevented. What could be done was to vary local wing stiffness so as to change the type of deflection that resulted. He sought to eliminate changes in lift owing to unwanted twist and untwist, by encouraging simple up and down wing movement instead, as a harmless substitute.

Here was a tall order indeed. Gusts could come from any direction–front, back or side–and were of most any strength. Furthermore, wing resistance against twist depended on such difficult to control factors as the weave of the cloth covering the wing, the precise varnishing treatment given the cloth and the amount of weathering and exposure experienced by the wing.

Not discouraged, O'Gorman had a test wing built to his own design. He was pleased to report much progress[13] in 1913. Mounted on a BE2 chassis and flown in wind, "the self-warp was small." On the other hand, "the force [required] on the warp lever was heavy." In short, the unwanted piloting force originating in gusts had been cut back. However, there was a price to be paid: larger warping lever forces in ordinary flight. There were other difficulties, for stability had worsened; i.e., "the aeroplane tended to overbank."

O'Gorman shrugged off the bad news. He felt that employing a different wing section would alter matters favorably and looked ahead to further tests. However, another larger issue loomed and captured his attention, that of wing fatigue failure owing to twisting and untwisting.

We have each learned to be wary of bending a light structure back and forth. After enough tries a fracture is likely. We each make practical use of this failure type to break off thin pieces into something smaller. Known as work hardening and fatigue, this form of breakage is one that lies in wait for the unwary, defying calculations. If ever a seemingly perfect subject for fatigue failure existed, it was the very warping and unwarping of wings that had captured O'Gorman's attention. Over time, wouldn't these wings fall apart owing to their own accumulation of back and forth stress? Newsworthy just then, in 1912-1913, were numerous inexplicable airplane accidents involving monoplane wings. For no obvious reason, the wings had simply fallen apart in flight. Was the root cause one of too many warps and reversals?

The ever energetic O'Gorman moved to find out. Needed was a machine capable of twisting and untwisting wings automatically, attached to a BE2 wing. By December 1912, the test wing had withstood 120,000 cycles of twists and untwists, each a sizeable 4½°. By May 1914, the figure stood at 360,000 tries.[14] All was well. He had shown that wing warping of a sturdy wing need not lead to fatigue failure, even after the equivalent of many years of use.

The wing twist episode supplies a sense of O'Gorman at work. Compared to today's lot, he was a very different sort of CEO. His employee de Havilland, destined to become famous as a designer, described him as "no yes-man".[15] Instead he was a solid administrator with a mind very much his own. Though reasonably adept at soothsaying and politics, O'Gorman's special abilities were those of an analytical engineer with enough egotism to prefer his own evaluation to those of any outside expert or committee. Once convinced that logic was on his side, he could be very difficult to move. Furthermore, he was driven by a longing to solve design problems that were generally regarded as hopeless; a tendency to relish the difficult rather than the practical. De Havilland sensed the undesirability of his own task – making O'Gorman's dreams real – and left the Factory before the war, in early 1914. His Factory design experience taught him a bitter lesson about people and ability.[16] There was such a thing as too much ability and pride in that ability; O'Gorman type engineers placed in positions of top level responsibility guaranteed failure. In short, the O'Gorman type had best stick to details.

The FE2

British fighting pusher, as flown in 1913. The two-seater had a gunner/observer up front and pilot immediately behind. Source: W.F. Lanchester, *Aircraft in Warfare*, (NYC: Appleton, 1916) plate 6.

Unfortunately for the British, de Havilland's departure removed the overall balance of outlook necessary in designing an airplane. O'Gorman was free to have his way. In time, the RFC would pay the price. Before moving on, de Havilland had much to do with the BE2's brother aircraft, the FE2 pusher; designed as a fighting machine.

A close relationship existed between the two aircraft – initially the wings were interchangeable – though other details were quite different. For one, the known inefficiency of the pusher

Rearward Shooting: FE2b

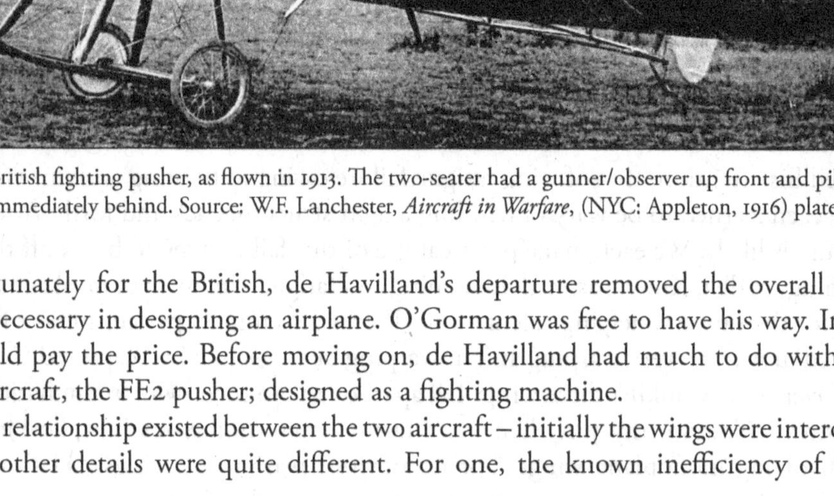

A pole mounted Lewis gun permitted the gunner to fire at enemies diving from the rear. Source: Original sketch by author; dimensions from A. Fage & H.E. Collins, *Technical Reports of the Advisory Committee for Aeronautics, Reports & Memoranda # 305* (London: HMSO, Jan.1917) fig.2.

configuration plus the weight of arms to be carried dictated employment of an engine much more powerful than that in the BE2. Years of testing five different engine possibilities led to the 120 h.p. Beardmore, admittedly "copied directly from the [European] Austro-Daimler engine"[17] but manufactured locally by British Daimler. Relatively reliable, stationary and water-cooled, the engine pushed the FE2 to a top speed of 81 mph, a respectable speed about 10 mph faster than its contemporary BE2a.

When serving as a fighter, the process of shooting to the rear offered problems for all pushers. The FE2 solution made use of a telescoping pole between pilot and gunner. Placing a Lewis gun on top of the pole, the gunner was to raise it as needed and then stand within his cockpit to aim the gun over the top wing. Doing so, he might hope to fend off an attacker diving from above. Should the gunner prove to be too short, yielding only a high angle of fire, height could be gained by standing on the contents of the ammunition locker: sturdy wooden boxes holding extra Lewis gun drums, carried in the gunner's cockpit.

When standing, most of the gunner's body was exposed to the passing wind. At 70 mph the drag load alone pressing upon his body could exceed 50 pounds.[18] Taken together with the G-forces produced by maneuvering, the total load was enough to eject an unwary gunner from his cockpit. A wise gunner saw to it that plenty of restraining straps and hand holds were available. As for the resulting shooting accuracy – firing to the rear was hopelessly inaccurate.

Certainly the aids given the gunner – a telescoping pole and ammunition boxes – were primitive, even when measured by the crude standards of the time. Why was so little thought given to the problem? In part, the machine's unhappy history served as a damper, discouraging all-out development.

Standing Tall

Substituting for the FE2's gunner, the standing preacher makes clear the position's instability, one buffeted by every gust. Source: *Flight*, September 26, 1918, p.1075.

When under test, the freshly completed FE2 prototype crashed, spinning in and killing the passenger sitting in for the gunner.[19] Many old wives' tales associating pushers and spins were brought out once again, adding to the loud criticism of the FE2 design, and especially of its nacelle, containing gunner and pilot. Particularly bothersome was its length and considerable side area, unbalanced by any comparable side area located at the machine's rear. To many British designers, the FE2 required a fresh approach, "for those who have done much flying on the pusher type [know] that a big fuselage tends to take charge and cause a spiral dive."[20] To some designers, ignoring the matter would only lead to more spinning accidents. To their annoyance, little was done.

FE2 designer de Havilland was generally well regarded. However, the reputation of the remaining O'Gorman designers was not the best. At this very time, one critical aero journal dismissed them as a "pernicious, obnoxious and deleterious gang of brain pickers".[21] True, the critic (C.G. Grey) was a professional scourge with a profound disrespect for the Factory's staff and products. Still, the criticism had a certain appeal – to many readers, there was little to be expected from the Factory. To these, FE2 drawbacks were sensed as inevitable, and not as readily correctable.

Finally, the crucial period of early 1914, like that of 1912, offered many doubts about the reality of fighting in the air. Unsure that a fighting aircraft was even wanted, it was impossible to argue convincingly for the money and effort necessary to eliminate technical difficulties. Instead, there was a human tendency to simply sweep the FE2, along with its problems, out of sight.

The many doubters included Major Sefton Brancker, destined to achieve high RFC rank in the coming war and post-war retirement as an Air Vice-Marshal. Here was a most effective seer and doer, and yet in the spring of 1914 Brancker[22] argued against the likelihood of air combat. As he saw it, the very process of arming an airplane necessarily lowered its performance owing to added weight and protuberances. If we imagine an encounter between a fast reconnaissance machine and a similar but heavily armed aircraft, the reconnaissance machine's best tactic would be to flee, leaving its armed pursuer far behind. His startling conclusion: *guns aloft prevented air combat*. In short, aerial fighting was unlikely.

And yet, despite the performance handicap, the arming of some aircraft might be useful, enabling[23] "the attack of troops, ships and important buildings." As for actual fighting between airplanes, it was at best "tentative ... within the range of possibility at the present moment." Again the backside was covered, and yes, it might happen, but don't bet on it.

Perhaps the most useful task for aerial fighting machines would be that of sentries, guarding some critical ground site against enemy observation. Here too, actual combat was unlikely; the presence of guns being sufficient to drive away interlopers.

In agreement was Major F.H. Sykes of the RFC, also destined for high rank. In 1913 he saw the fighting machine as necessarily heavy and the lighter scout as having[24] "various advantages over the heavier type" – those of speed, climb rate and ease of piloting. The inability of fighters to close with scouts would result in open skies above the battlefield: "both sides will know a great deal as to what their opponent is doing."

Finally and most important was the view of reconnaissance expert General David Henderson, who would head the wartime RFC. He expressed doubts (April 1914) over the ability of any aircraft to destroy another. Doing so required a position:

> … within short range of the adversary and herein lies the difficulty … until a fighting machine is produced which will equal the unarmed aeroplane in speed, climbing power and handiness [maneuverability] … an enemy can very quickly return to the safety of his own lines.[25]

Once again, air combat was sensed as most unlikely. True, someday things might be different … but someday would take care of itself. To those struggling with the FE2 combat airworthiness and gunnery issues, these official RFC views amounted to disinterested lack of support. As for shooting backwards–useful only for air combat–why face up to the difficulties of solution when shooting forwards in the ground attack role was one attribute that was actually wanted – and simple to achieve?

Furthermore, there was the FE2 spinning issue, likely requiring the reduction of that considerable nacelle side area. Unfortunately, this need was opposed by the demands of improved rearwards gunnery – sheltering of the gunner from wind blast was vital – in turn leading to an increase of side area, rather than a decrease. The conflicting design demands made simple solution most unlikely. It was all too much for the Factory. The FE2 went to war, largely unaltered.

Yet another factor serving to dampen the reality of aerial combat was the development of a truly fast scout – an aircraft moving at so high a speed that nothing could catch it. De Havilland and the Factory prepared their own entries in the race for speed. Wanted was much more engine power – not merely squeezing out a bit more–but a truly generous gain – at least twice the old h.p. figure.

One way of achieving great power was to add engines in Siamese Twin fashion. Wanted were engines capable of being stacked, something like cards. Not stationary engines, for they were too long and heavy. Rotaries appeared to suit the notion. Light and thin, they could be joined one engine immediately behind the other, and arranged to drive a common output

Fast Scout Hope

High speed was the design goal of this neatly streamlined, high-powered SE-4. Bedeviled with imperfections, it was not to become a production machine. Source: W.F. Lanchester, *Aircraft in Warfare* (NYC: Appleton, 1916) frontispiece.

shaft. Available at the time were the Gnome 80 h.p. rotaries and the Monosoupape (single valve) 100 h.p. engines. Each seemed a good candidate for stacking.

Designers were intrigued. With twin 80's, a total of 160 h.p. seemed within easy reach. If as much as 200 h.p. was possible, why not press for all out speed, say 130 mph, or some 50 mph beyond the usual, and simply scoff at enemy aerial fighters? The concept's appeal was enormous, especially so to Flying Corps intellectuals resistant to the notion of air combat. To these, any scheme for eliminating meetings between fast reconnaissance machines and enemy fighting machines was worthy of heavy investment.

Stacking two Gnomes seemed fairly straightforward and the Factory spent several pre-war years pursuing this end. Of those aircraft resulting, the SE-4 was most promising, but this neatly streamlined and speedy aircraft never came out of development. Too many issues remained unresolved. For one, there was the sticky issue of engine reliability.

Rotaries were inherently less reliable than stationary engines. Rotary spark plugs tended to foul with carbon deposits; in large part owing to the burning of that lubricating oil mixed together with fuel. The result was a tendency for plugs to misfire or even stop firing entirely, leaving the aircraft with a windmilling propeller – and no power. In addition, exhaust valves jammed up when deposits of burnt carbon prevented proper closing, producing the same result – a dead engine. Pilots accepted such rotary disadvantages reluctantly. Fortunately, the extreme lightness of the rotary offered a compensating advantage: better performance. However, pilot tolerance for stoppages was extremely limited at best and offered little room for bargaining.

Experience with stacked rotary engines showed increased reliability problems as compared to the usual rotary, for there were twice as many cylinders, spark plugs and valves; i.e., there were twice as many things to go wrong. In addition were the new problems created by the stacking process itself. Properly done, an extreme precision of manufacture and assembly was required, not easily achievable at the time. All things considered, stacked rotaries were doomed, unless some compensating piloting advantage arose.

Rather than an advantage, pilots sensed a disadvantage in their new high-powered rotaries – a mysterious new force – gyroscopic – threatening to override piloting input. The problem's nature – that of a physically complex detail – was exactly right for O'Gorman's skills, and he quickly produced a mathematical solution, along with experimental agreement.

Gyroscopic force arises when a rotating mass, say a propeller, is moved at right angles to its axis either horizontally–right or left–or vertically up or down. The force produced is directed at right angles to the new motion and can be disturbingly large, if the rotating mass is large and the new motion quick. The stacked rotary with its many rotating cylinders, moving together with a propeller, amounted to a great spinning mass capable of generating "a sideways twist … which *appears* to be very significant."[26] (O'Gorman's italics.)

Uncertain as to the load's practical significance, he queried veteran French race pilot Jules Vedrines. To old hand Vedrines, who had tried stacked 50's, rotary gyroscopic force effects were real but came well within the usual range of handling problems, being "much the same sort of thing as a gust."[27] Perhaps, but to Factory pilots the more powerful stacked rotary powered SE-4 was unacceptable. Its tendency to overheat[28] was the last straw. A rumored top speed of 135 mph notwithstanding, the SE-4 never went into production. There would be no speeding away from interceptors.

What could be done within the skeptical atmosphere of 1914 was to improve the existing and well-liked BE2, altering a good machine into a truly superb cooperation vehicle. O'Gorman

BE2c designer E. Busk

His design efforts converted the BE2 into a stable machine, after which his life was ended by a strange accident. Source: *Flight*, November 13, 1914, p.1114.

turned to the task, first dealing with the departure of designer de Havilland. A successor was chosen: recent science graduate E.T. Busk.[29] He seemed of the O'Gorman persuasion; thoughtful, mathematically inclined and willing to try most anything. Soon a competent pilot, he flew his own BE2 modifications and was thus able to spot problems without the usual test pilot/engineer arguments and delays. Here was a highly competent designer with only one significant drawback–an eerie personal carelessness suggesting a suicidal nature.

Two major changes were planned: more power and great automatic stability. The need for greater power was obvious; certainly, the old 70 h.p. offered a sadly minimal performance. Furthermore, dependency on Renault, or any foreign manufacturer for delivery, was unwise for a British war machine. Better would be a much larger engine manufactured under the direct control of the Factory itself. As for the format, the Renault design itself – stationary and air cooled – was fine, for it eliminated many of the headaches associated with rotary and stationary water cooled types. In time the new design emerged from Factory development as a 90 h.p. engine, reliable as any of its time. There was even a bonus: it resisted overheating and was well able to withstand tropical temperatures.

As for the 90 h.p. output, it was to 1915 as 70 h.p. was to 1912: a ticket to modest performance and no more. Though it served to improve the BE2 breed somewhat, 1915's competing aircraft were far more powerful. In the event of air combat, the BE2's ability to flee would be unimpressive.

Full inherent stability for aircraft had long been an O'Gorman goal and understandably so, for there was much to be said for it. Today's pilots are pleased to employ devices to this end, and those of 1915 had an even greater need for relief, for at the time piloting was a study in exhaustion, with the usual two hour mission demanding fresh control input every second of

The BE2c

Stable and effective, but lacking in maneuverability. Source: Original sketch by author.

the way. In war, with some pilots suffering from wounds or high altitude oxygen deprivation, the need for a largely self-flying machine was all the greater.

Busk's approach was one of bit by bit solution, with much cut and try, all guided by a sophisticated understanding. Fore and aft stability requires an extra large horizontal tail and a forward balance point located just so – these were achieved. Lateral stability and its demand for upturned wing tips (dihedral) were met, and so on. O'Gorman's wing twisting approach, despite his arguments and supporting experiments, were abandoned in favor of ailerons. All went well, as per plan. When complete, the resulting BE2c was capable of many minutes of automatic flight, not only reducing the pilot's burden, but permitting him to act as an observer, or to work a wireless set.

Finding this hard to believe, Major Brancker checked the inherent stability feature by flying for half an hour at about 2000 feet on a gusty day[30] – without touching the controls. All went well; Brancker was convinced.

There was a catch. Fully stable machines resist any call for a new flight path. The aircraft senses change of any sort – either those unwanted changes resulting from gusts, or those wanted from control action – as equally undesirable, and responds by altering course reluctantly. For most peacetime flights, this oddity is acceptable. Once accustomed to the slow control response, the pilot learns to think ahead. However, the need to escape bullets in war required an immediate response, and this was impossible with the BE2c.

Another aspect of the super-stable trait was the aircraft's flat refusal to pursue flight paths sensed as undesirable. For example, steep dives were ruled out. A strong pilot could supply enough control stick force to produce a shallow dive, but no pilot was strong enough to create a steep dive. Again, this was not a problem in peacetime, but to a desperate pilot seeking to escape aggressive pursuit, this limitation was painful indeed. Not only the BE2c, but two other RFC machines were officially declared[31] non-divers as well – when too late to permit change – the FE2 and the de Havilland fighter DH2.

BE2 Design Changes

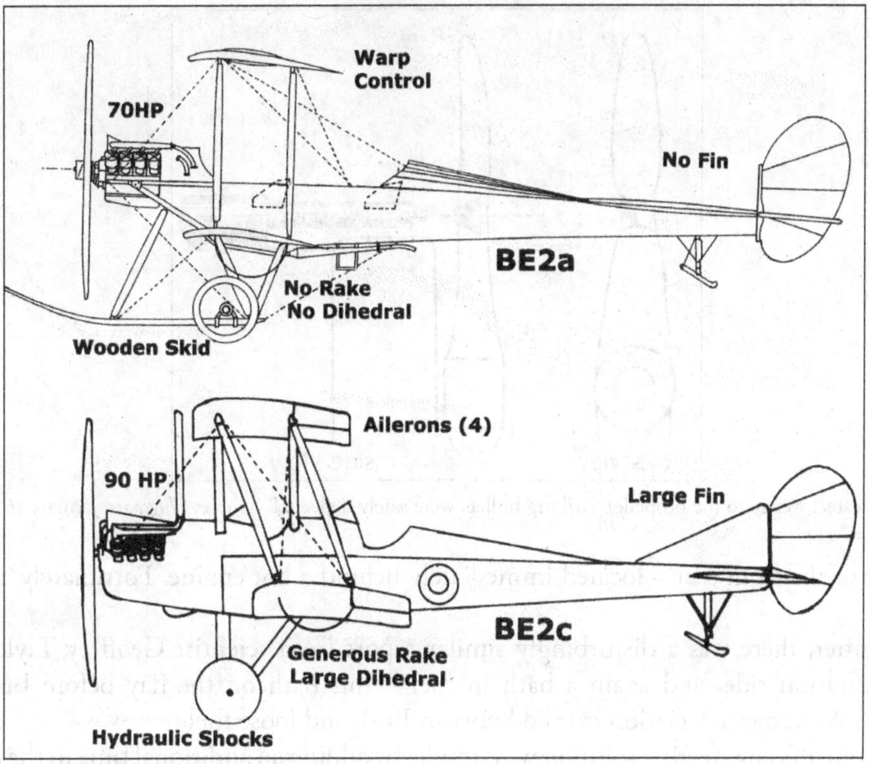

Profiles of the BE2 as it altered from the pre-war (BE2a) to its definitive wartime (BE2c) version.
Source: (top) *Flight*, November 15, 1912, p.1062; (bottom) TNA file # AVIA 14/5/2/29.

After the war, aerodynamicist L. Bairstow noted sadly,[32] "the will of an aeroplane is not a fortuitous characteristic." Wartime pilots used earthier expressions to denounce this trait. The consequences were to prove profound – for both the RFC and Richthofen.

Working up the BE2c took many months, a process continuing through the early period of the war. Just as predicted by RFC brass, the opening phase of the war proved a relatively peaceful period for aircraft, with negligible air combat despite an active ground war. Wanted for operations was exactly that machine being prepared by Busk: an easy-to-fly Army cooperation machine, and Busk drove himself hard to complete the project. However, something went terribly wrong and in November 1914, *The Times* (London) reported[33] his death:

> a biplane [BE2c] piloted by Mr. Busk caught fire … for three quarters of a mile the aeroplane, blazing more furiously every second, traveled down a slanting glide until it fell headlong to the ground …

Flying in formation with de Havilland, flames suddenly shot out of Busk's engine.[34] There was no chance whatever. It seemed a typical catastrophic engine fire of 1914, and yet odd stories began to circulate. There was Colonel J.E.B. Seely's report[35] of a flight demonstration in which he had served as a passenger. In flight, Seely's face was suddenly splashed with fuel. Busk had overfilled the small overhead gravity tank and the excess was simply dumped on him, as the

How to Shoot Forward on a Tractor

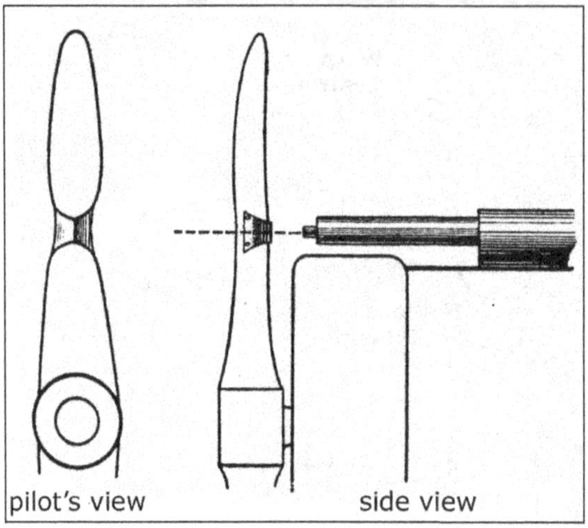

By bolting a steel wedge to the propeller, striking bullets were safely deflected. Source: *Flugsport*, January 16, 1918, p.30.

occupant of the front seat – located immediately behind a hot engine. Fortunately, there was no fire.

Soon after, there was a disturbingly similar report from scientist Geoffrey Taylor. Again a demonstration ride, and again a bath in fuel – this bath on the day before Busk's final accident.[36] A strange association existed between Busk and loose fuel.

The problem's engineering solution was simple: by adding an additional tube to the overhead gravity tank, excess fuel would be piped safely back to the main fuel tank. Busk's own solution – dumping the excess on the front seat – was strange indeed. Adding to the strangeness was O'Gorman's defensive, embarrassed comment:[37] "He merely took all the precautions of a clever engineer." The facts were exactly the opposite: Busk's neglectful actions were those of a twisted man bent upon suicide.

After Busk, the fuel problem was corrected. There the matter rested.

The BE2c had arrived and soon become the mainstay of the RFC. Several thousand were manufactured and served in its heyday from 1915-1917. Performance was modest,[38] requiring 20 minutes to climb to 6500 feet, where it flew at a maximum official speed of 72 mph. For its protection, there was the FE2b, offering a nearly identical performance[39] (19.5 minutes to 6500 feet and 73 mph once there) and the same super stability. Costs were typical, with the total BE2c airframe + engine cost at 1600 pounds in 1917,[40] and the FE2b at 2345 pounds, also 1917.

Even as the BE2c was prepared for service, a new factor entered – the birth of real air combat. Major F.H. Sykes reported[41] a "certain amount of fighting", starting in October 1914. The object was to blind opposing artillery by knocking out the enemy's seeing eye guidance, i.e., shooting down those enemy aircraft engaged in observing and correcting shell hit locations. Actual combat was rare, just as predicted by the pre-war doubters. When attacked, "as a rule the German made for his own lines."[42]

The next step was one of shooting more bullets when attacking. This came from a French concept relying not on pushers, but on fast tractors with propellers protected with steel wedges. The prospect of air combat had suddenly become real. Should the French propeller protector be perfected, ordinary liquid cooled machine guns would become devastating aerial weapons.

Germany had a gifted inventor available and interested – the self-taught Dutch engineer Anthony Fokker. He set to work.

The basic RFC premise: "air combat is unlikely" – a belief underlying the design of its key machines, the BE2c and FE2b – was about to be turned into so much nonsense.

3

Fokker Fodder

Air combat came about as the direct result of infantry demands. The lives of ground troops were made miserable by endless shelling, much of it guided by enemy observation aircraft. Troops pressed for an end to the menace. If enemy cannons couldn't be destroyed, surely something could be done about the eyes of the artillery: slow observation aircraft or balloons hovering above the frontlines. Why not shoot them down, thus ending shelling accuracy? Shelling without accuracy would lack profit. Artillery fire would become a pointless exercise. As an important result, fewer infantry lives would be lost. The argument was convincing.

First to act were the French. Together with the British they manned a Western Front hundreds of miles in length, subject to the shells of German cannoneers. Repeated French

The Wedge at Work

Pilot Roland Garros flying a deflector-equipped Morane N. Source: Oswald Boelcke, *Hauptmann Boelcke's Feldberichte* (Gotha: Perthes, 1917) p.161.

infantry pleas resulted in action by the French Air Service. Most every type of aircraft and gun was tested, seeking the best combination.

To pre-war racing pilot Roland Garros, the optimum was a single-seat tractor airplane,[1] equipped with a standard issue light machine gun and a propeller armored with wedges capable of deflecting bullet strikes. His choice had its good side: a speedy and highly maneuverable aircraft aimed simply by positioning the machine. However, there was a bad aspect as well, for the gun employed was the official French clip-fed machine gun (St. Étienne), notorious for misfires and stoppages.[2] Overall, the system was workable but crude and accident prone. Pushed into combat starting in February 1915, Garros successfully downed three German observation machines by mid-April. Not only the French Air Service, but the German Air Service was impressed. There was something more important here than merely the fate of one more weapon: perhaps enemy artillery observation could really be stopped.

Wedge Details

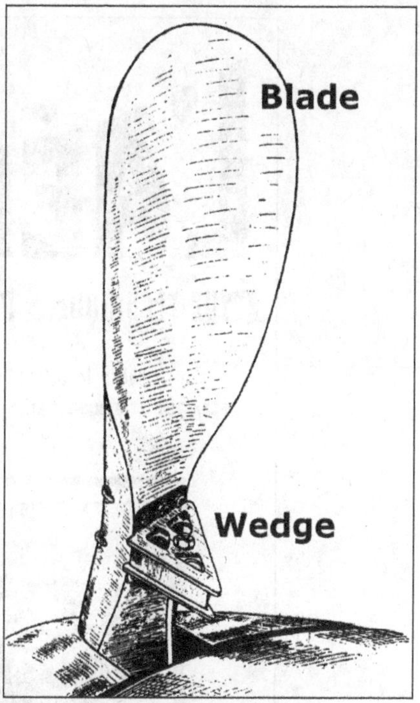

Pilot's view of a propeller blade equipped with a deflector wedge. Source: Auguste L. Masmejean, *Les Avions Allemands* (Paris: Librarie Aeronautic, 1917) p.14.

On April 19, Garros was caught with an engine stoppage over German-held Courtrai. Lacking altitude, there was little choice. The operational plan was to land, set fire to his machine and attempt to escape. His forced landing went well, but the airplane did not burn properly. Garros was captured. Even more disturbing was the loss of the deflector secret, for bolted to each propeller blade was a perfect working sample; the result of months of effort. To knowledgeable Germans, the intended use of the propeller's steel wedges was obvious. Wanted immediately were copies for the German Air Service. Seeking immediate action, the wedges were turned over to Anthony Fokker's aircraft firm.

Balzac noted that there are but two paths to great success: that of genius and that of corruption. Anthony Fokker employed both. In part a skilled airshow pilot and small-scale manufacturer, he had the searching imagination of an inventor. Though an original thinker, he was content to appropriate the inventions of others as starting points for his own efforts. As for payment, assigning credit or royalties to other men was not one of his strong points. Of all possible inventive abilities, his specialty was a shrewd assessment of what the customer really needed. He then moved energetically to supply it, without troubling himself over the intellectual property rights of others. Reflecting this trait, his early designs owed much to machines he admired; for example, the Fokker M.5 owed more to Morane-Saulnier's design department,[4] than to Fokker's.

Handed a Garros deflector, he saw it as useful but flawed; i.e., not a complete answer to shooting needs. Its fundamental drawback came from the impact and destruction of about 10% of all rounds fired – those hitting the wedges. This wasted percentage was turned into flying bits and pieces of lead forming a metallic spray about the aircraft nose, sometimes acting to smash windscreens or clog engine air breathing intakes. It would be much better to eliminate

Deflector Flight Takeoff

L'AÉROPHILE

REVUE TECHNIQUE & PRATIQUE DES LOCOMOTIONS AÉRIENNES

DIRECTEUR-FONDATEUR : GEORGES BESANÇON

Publie le BULLETIN OFFICIEL DE L'AÉRO-CLUB DE FRANCE

RÉDACTION ET ADMINISTRATION : 35, Rue François-Ier (Champs-Élysées) PARIS (VIIIe) — Téléphone PASSY 66-21

Un des derniers vols de Roland GARROS
sur son parasol "MORANE-SAULNIER", armé d'une mitrailleuse

(our translation) "One of the last flights of Roland Garros on a Morane Saulnier Parasol, armed with a machine gun." Source: *L'Aérophile*, front cover, May 1915.

bullet strikes entirely, with its wasted rounds and destructive bullet spray. Could this be done by interrupting the machine gun's fire whenever a blade passed in front of the gun muzzle?

Accomplishment was difficult. Engines and propellers of the time turned over at about twenty revolutions per second. This meant that the blades of a two bladed propeller passed by at about forty times per second. Machine guns fired at a rate of about ten times per second. There was no match. Furthermore, both propeller and machine gun rates could vary considerably. To detect the presence of a blade when in an undesirable position and prevent the gun from firing, all at a rate of many times per second was a tough challenge. Nowadays the task would be assigned to fast responding electronic devices. At the time, only mechanical devices were available, and these were usually too slow to cope.

One who tried was engineer Franz Schneider. His patent of July 1913, with drawings openly featured by *Flugsport* [5] just after the war's start (September 1914), drew startled interest from every nation. The concept employed a cam mounted on the aircraft propeller shaft. As it rotated, the cam blocked access to the trigger whenever the blade passed in front of the gun.

When the firing path was clear, free access to the trigger was provided for the shooter. In principle this was fine, but the extreme speed of operation was too much for Schneider's slow moving components. Pre-war trials of the device were unsuccessful.

Fokker assigned several of his own employees – machine designers – to the problem. Their backgrounds happened to be strong in the area of metal stamping or punch press operation, a business of fast moving parts and violent accelerations. Exactly this experience was crucial to a solution and within weeks Fokker had a working "interrupter" consisting of Schneider's concept, properly executed. Ignoring Schneider's contributions and those of the Fokker company's own machine designers, Anthony later announced that he alone had invented and

How to Fire Between Blades

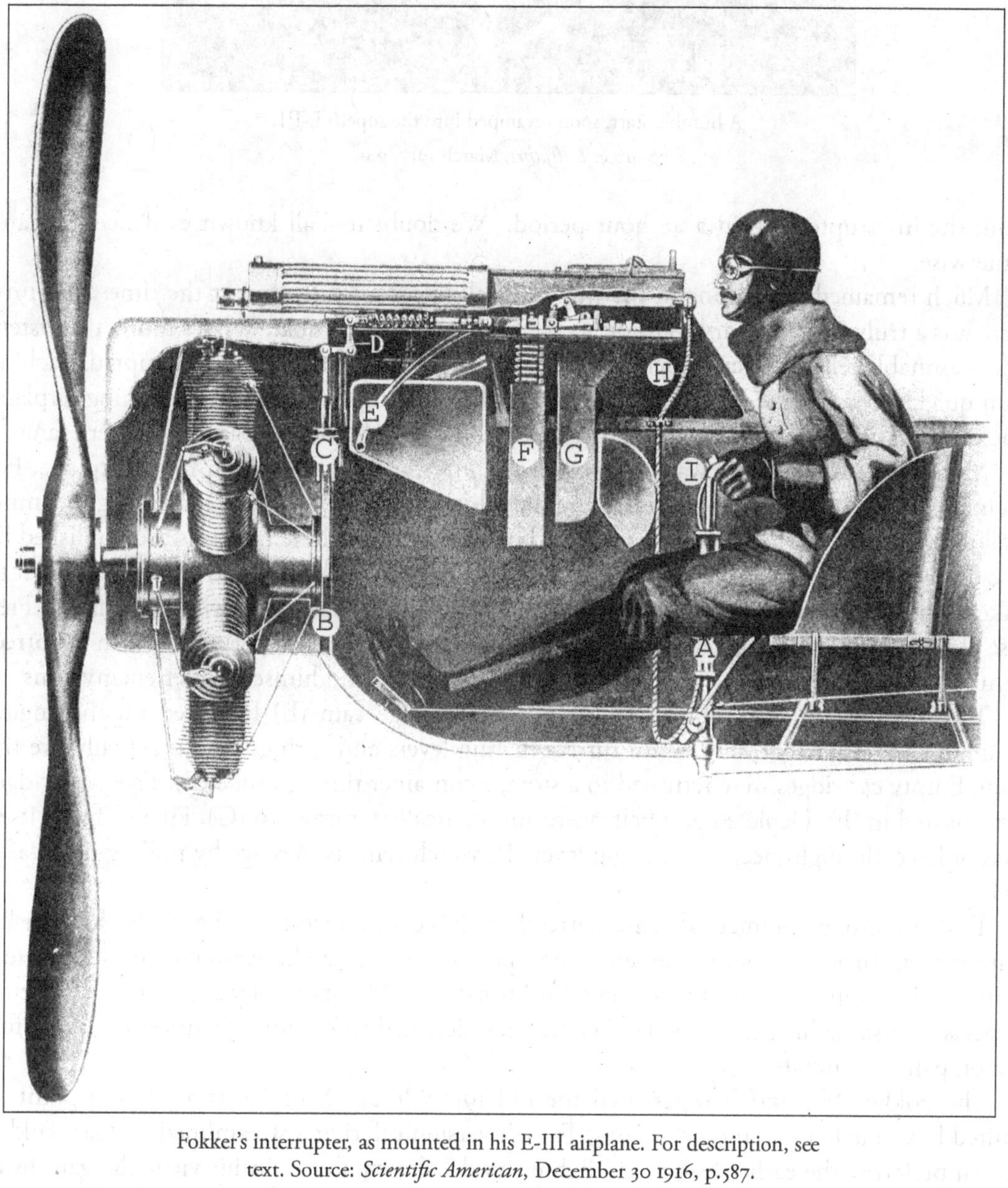

Fokker's interrupter, as mounted in his E-III airplane. For description, see text. Source: *Scientific American*, December 30 1916, p.587.

Anthony Fokker and his M-5

A humble start, soon revamped into the superb E-III.
Source: *Luftfahrt*, March 1917, p.9.

built the interrupter within a 48 hour period.[6] We doubt it – all known evidence indicates otherwise.

Much remained to be done in the way of small improvements, but at the time (mid 1915) here was a truly revolutionary solution to the problem of air combat. What's more, the system was reasonably reliable, even under conditions of inept maintenance. The interrupted machine gun quickly became the fighter pilot's basic tool. Taken together with its matching airplane, the combination became the world's first true fighter aircraft and the basis of Fokker's fame.

More than just shooting was involved in the interrupters' application to an airplane. For example, there was the problem of helping the pilot clear those inevitable machine gun jamms – all to be done while he flew. In the case of Fokker's E-III machine, this was accomplished by use of lever (A) at the pilot's inner left thigh, which locked the elevator and enabled the pilot to take his hands off the control stick. He was then able to clear stoppages with both hands. Free use of the rudder bar remained, as did lateral movement of the stick, permitting him to correct aim with his legs, or even to turn out of trouble should he find himself under enemy guns.

The gun portion of the interrupter employed a huge cam (B) mounted on the engine crankshaft to drive follower (C), in turn actuating levers and springs (D) to actually fire the gun. Empty cartridges were returned to a storage container through tube (E). Fresh cartridges were stored in (F). Depleted gun belts were automatically returned to (G). Finally, firing itself was ordered through mechanical firing lever (I), which sent its message by pulling on a cable (H).

Fokker's strong commercial sense correctly pointed to a fortune to be made through his interrupter. There was more – he sensed an opening to sell matching aircraft: those designed with the interrupter in mind. Starting with his factory's M.5 monoplane, he turned its better aspects into something new: the Fokker E series, destined to become the interrupter's perfect accompanying aircraft.

The Fokker M.5 and E types used the old 1912 Morane-Saulnier as a starting point. It suited him. He ignored the later (1914) French version offering a streamlined format. Fokker much preferred the earlier leaner and lighter model shown above. In his view, the gain from

E-III Derivation

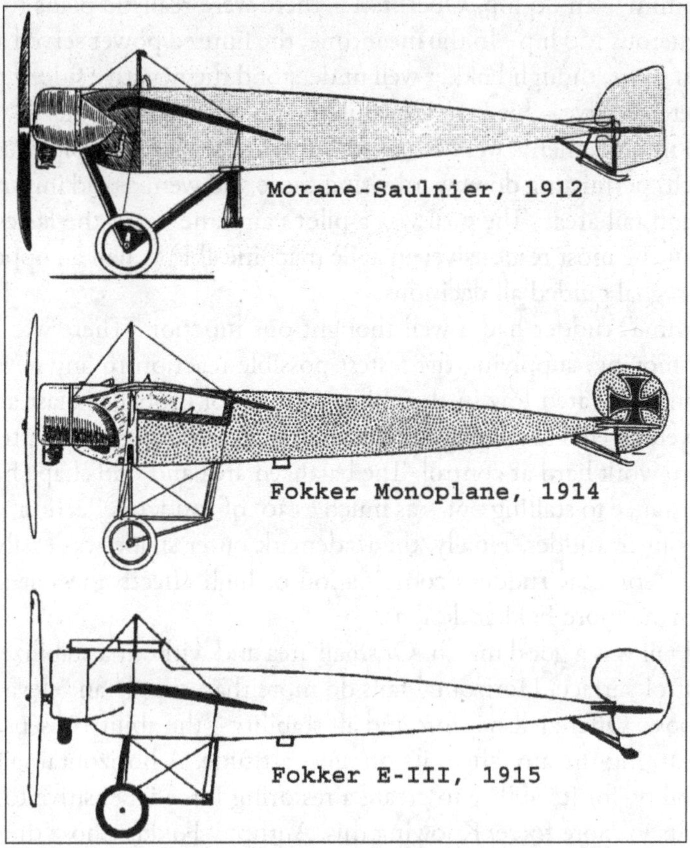

Initially a French sport plane (top) Fokker converted the design (middle) into an early war Army co-op machine, and finally (bottom) into the revolutionary fighter. Sources: (top) *Flight*, May 24, 1913, p.562; (middle) *Aerial Age Weekly*, January 17, 1916, p.429.; (bottom) *L'Aérophile*, August 1917, p.277.

streamlining was less important than its cost: added weight. Better a low weight fuselage than a heavier, rounded fuselage.

As for the aircraft's rotary engine and associated gyroscopic force issues – matters that had given O'Gorman pause – Fokker refused to worry. Yes, strange forces did arise in rotary engine operation but fortunately: "experienced pilots carry out corrective control action instinctively, without understanding the reason for it."[7] He did admit to exceptions; i.e., difficult gyroscopic force areas. One example was flight at extreme altitudes, when little surplus control power remained to prevent flight path problems. Another was flight within a tiny circular path. However, as neither appeared significant in 1915, they were dismissed.

No rotary enthusiast, he properly assessed the rotary as "tricky, unreliable and difficult to operate."[8] His grim view reflected personal experience with the Gnome. Pilots generally agreed and British experience was much the same. Airplanes employing rotaries would not find easy acceptance.

Of course, there were positive features and one useful characteristic was the lack of water-cooling, with its need for extensive warm up. A rotary powered airplane could take to the air faster than one with a stationary engine, and was invulnerable to the curse of holed or frozen radiators.[9] More important was the rotary's low weight per horsepower –far lower than that of stationary engines-making for a reduced overall weight. As for the modest output of the engine made available to him – an 80 h.p. Oberursel – there were realistic plans to quickly upgrade the engine to a generous 100 h.p.. In the meantime, the limited power served as a goad to make every bit count. In short, though Fokker well understood the negative side of the rotary, weight considerations were decisive – his E series would be powered with a rotary.

E series design improvements were achieved through a trial and error process. A plastic side window (see sketch) permitting downward vision came and went as did innumerable redesigns of wing pinions and tail areas. The goal was a pilot's airplane – not the fastest, for the engine was too small – but the most responsive; an agile machine able to nail an opponent engaged in close combat. This goal guided all decisions.

Even that "comma" rudder had a well thought-out function. There was no fixed fin area. Instead it was all-moving, supplying the fastest possible reaction to any new input. Without a fin and quite small, it rated low in the ability to control propeller blast at low speeds – as in takeoff. However, given a small engine, the rudder area was big enough to do its job if the pilot was willing to work hard at control. The balanced area and odd shape had the additional virtue of great resistance to stalling out – as much as 30° of rudder deflection[10] could be applied without running out of rudder. Finally, the trademark outer shape was easily bent from steel tubing. In all, the "comma" rudder's combination of high effectiveness at a low cost would carry it through many more Fokker designs.

The horizontal tail was a good match. Of small area and without a stabilizer, it too made for a demanding control surface. Horizontal tails do more than supply an "elevator", though that is their main purpose. Offered also is fore and aft stability – the ability to sense a gust and react automatically, returning the aircraft to its pre-gust attitude. A horizontal tail needs plenty of area to create stability, for its ability to create a restoring force is sensitive to surface area; i.e., more surface results in more force. Knowing this, Anthony Fokker chose the smallest possible horizontal tail area – he didn't want stability. He had learned much from his earlier too-stable Spider design: stability had its problems.

For one, there are times when great stability could actually produce a crash. A stable reaction to a gust might well include a good deal of roll, useful in restoring heading. At appreciable altitude, roll was fine. However, when landing too much roll meant striking the ground with a wing tip – and an accident. Of course, an alert pilot could override the sometimes suicidal wishes of a too-stable machine, but then where was the profit in stability? Yes, it permitted pilots to relax once altitude was in hand. Once there, the airplane almost flew itself. However, this feature counted for little in Anthony Fokker's plans – relaxation was not his goal.

Stable designs offered another and more serious drawback – they placed a heavy restraint upon wild maneuvers. The resulting inability to dive steeply mattered in a warplane. Through their stable BE2c and FE2 aircraft, the British had learned the same lessons, but had shrugged off corrective action. Instead, there was always the hope that there would be no air combat, and no need for wild maneuvers.

Unlike the British, Fokker was not misled by wishful thinking. If O'Gorman thought stability a fine idea, interrupters mounted in the right aircraft would soon change his mind. As for the right aircraft, Fokker pushed for all-out maneuverability – wanted were aircraft with the ability to stunt their way into a dominant shooting position. He was content to counter the enormous BE2c horizontal tail with the E-III's much smaller unit.[11] At a time when stable designs[12] were usually given a tail size equal to 16% or more that of wing area, the BE2c[13] was granted 17%, while the FE2b[14] tail area was set at 17.3%, Fokker's unstable E-III[15] was given less than 12%.

Once committed to a demanding aircraft and a hard working pilot, other design decisions fell into place automatically. The aileron versus warp choice that had proven so difficult for the BE2 and O'Gorman led to a very different solution: Fokker chose warp. As always, his case was logical.

The E series monoplane wing would necessarily be of greater span than the same area, arranged in biplane form. When warped, the planned longer wing resulted in less drag than an equivalent shorter wing biplane, employing ailerons.[16] The superior wing efficiency – i.e., less drag – resulted in a pro-warp decision. As for those special warp drawbacks – a sensitivity to gusts producing an ever-moving control stick, along with an increase of piloting load – these counted for little in Fokker's planning. Combat effectiveness ruled. Better low drag than a genteel machine.

When all was done and the E-III emerged, foreign designers were not impressed. Contempt prevailed, guided by the "not invented here" philosophy. For example, one important change introduced by Fokker was the substitution of steel tubes for wooden members. Not only the fuselage, but much of the wing and all of the tail and rudder were fashioned of steel. As compared to the usual improperly dried wartime lumber, steel tubes represented a tremendous advance in strength and durability. Yet one British review saw only drawbacks; for example, the kinking of a tube by the dropping of a heavy tool when under construction and subsequent

The E-III Weighs In

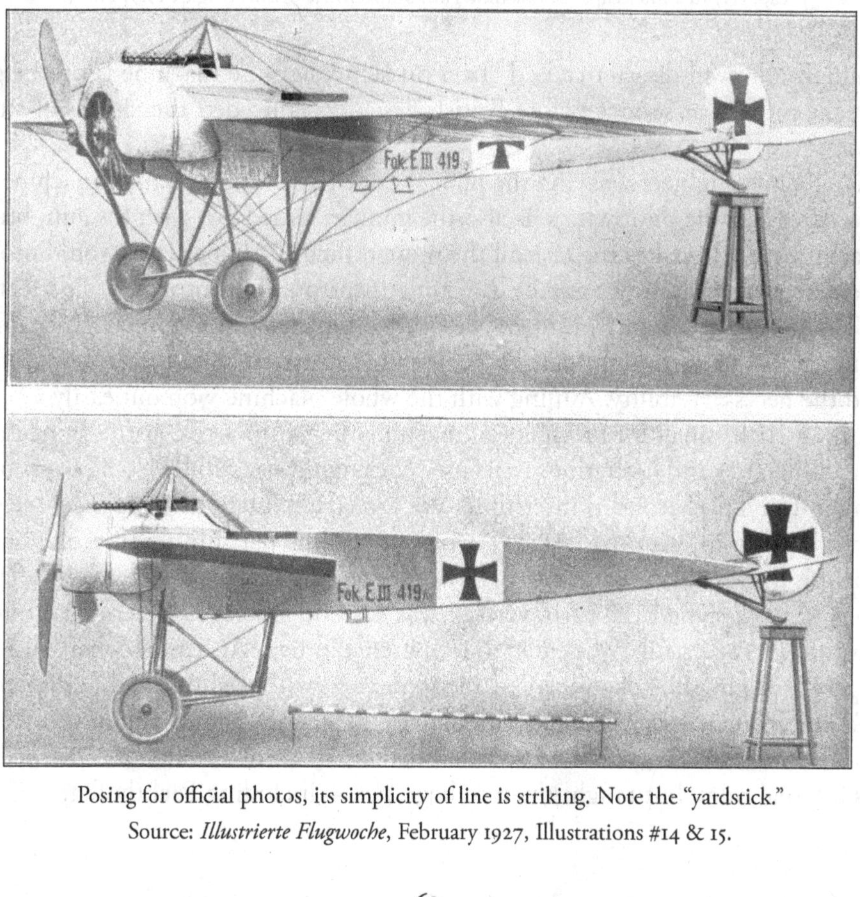

Posing for official photos, its simplicity of line is striking. Note the "yardstick."

Source: *Illustrierte Flugwoche*, February 1927, Illustrations #14 & 15.

Pilot's View of E-III Cowling

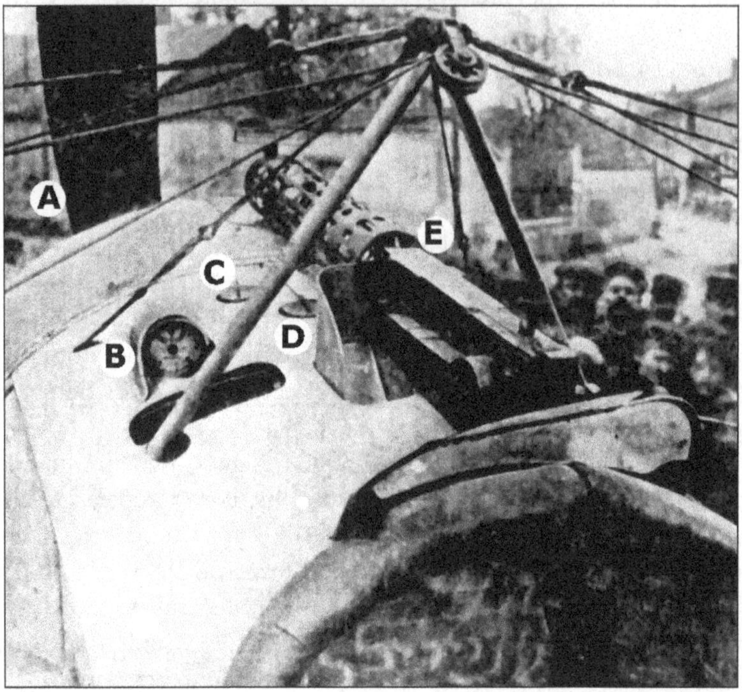

A French crowd examines a downed aircraft. Details: (A) propeller; (B) fuel gauge; (C) oil filler cap; (D) fuel filler cap; (E) machine gun. Source: *L'Aérophile*, August 1917, p.279.

failure in flight, or even disaster caused "by a misstep when the machine is on the ground."[17] It would take much war service before British designers conceded the virtues of steel tubing over wood.

To some French engineers, having the pilot shoot by pointing his entire machine seemed a poor idea. After all, "the pilot who was also the gunner, aimed not with his gun, but with his whole machine, which makes the task all the more difficult."[18] Experience would prove exactly the opposite to be true: aiming a gun by directing its surrounding airplane is a perfectly natural process. Though many sought profit by shooting from flexibly mounted guns aimed at an angle to the airplane's own flight path, accuracy proved extremely difficult; few men and gun sights had the necessary ability. Aiming with the whole machine won out easily.

With the E-III in small lot production, machines began to arrive at the front in mid-1915. There were difficulties and hesitations in its use. The engine was still the 80 h.p. version and not the promised 100 h.p.. Secondly, interrupter use forced a reduction of the machine gun firing rate from a basic uninterrupted cyclic rate of 600 rounds per minute to a safe but sluggish 400.[19] Was this modestly powered and slow shooting machine capable of effective fighting?

Among those assigned the early version was Oswald Boelcke, a German frontline pilot with a history of successful two-seater shooting encounters. At a time when all air combat knowledge was slight, Boelcke accepted his ignorance with a shrug and addressed his new machine's employment with a rare combination of energy and thoughtfulness. His E-III experience would serve to write the book that defines air combat. He not only spelled out air fighting's internal rules, but taught them to beginners – including Richthofen.

Pilot's View of Controls

Left and right straps secured the control stick when parked. Details: (A) control stick; (B) shock cord to restrain landing gear; (C) gun trigger; (D) blip switch; (E) tachometer. Source: *L'Aérophile*, August 1917, p.278.

For example, in order for fighting in the air to occur, it's necessary for the aggressor to fly at a speed sufficient to overtake his adversary.[20] Only the faster machine's pilot can decide: yes, I will fight, or no, I will flee. The slower machine offers its pilot no choice. At issue is not only the usual horizontal speed, but vertical speed as well, for it is possible to flee by climbing away, or even by diving away from an opponent. In short, combat can be ordered only by the pilot who has the necessary performance edge on hand. This basic rule is logical and was obvious at the time. For those lacking in performance, the design of combat tactics – especially aggressive tactics – was a matter of defying common sense; of substituting shrewd schemes for the rules. Fabricating successful schemes became Boelcke's role.

He realized that one way to achieve that necessary edge in speed was by diving. If sturdy and unstable, a slow airplane could be dived at a steep angle, quickly building up speed. Achieving a high velocity, the aggressor aircraft could be leveled off within shooting range of its target. Using its momentum, the attacker could then easily dominate its prey. Should the attack fail, there was a fair chance of repeating the event-first climbing, and then diving as before.

As Boelcke and his protégé Max Immelmann worked to perfect the sequence, they realized that there were other advantages to the scheme. For one, there was the matter of unlikely or late detection by their prey: mostly artillery observation or photo reconnaissance machines. In performing their task, the French or British aircrew looked downwards as they searched for frontline positions, artillery strikes and mapped check points. Looking upwards was something done occasionally and reluctantly. In time the enemy would learn to reverse his priorities, but until then a diving attack from higher altitude – typically 2000 feet higher and of a dozen seconds duration – was unlikely to be detected until too late for an effective response.

The dive granted the E-III attacker another odd virtue: it made his nationality uncertain. Carefully painted with German insignia, E series wings and fuselage crosses seemingly offered clear identification. However, diving put the aircraft into a largely "head on" attitude, where no insignia could be seen by the prey. Instead of an E-III, target crew-members detected what appeared to be a French Morane-Saulnier aircraft complete with its well known monoplane wing and unusual nose. The first mention of the E-III in an official RFC communiqué (August 22, 1915) noted this very problem: " ... the observer mistaking the machine for a Morane did not fire ... "[21] No easy solution would emerge. Fokker's borrowed format was not only aerodynamically sound, but offered a "wolf in sheep's clothing" form of disguise as well.

As for the shooting itself, when should it start? If used in the dive, it would likely alert the prey. Was the probability of success while diving high enough to warrant the risk of early disclosure – and possible escape by the prey?

The chances of hitting the target aircraft while diving were poor. Making for difficulty was the target's own speed and trajectory. It was necessary to aim well ahead of the target to get a hit – perhaps 30 feet ahead – and to continuously change the center of aim as the dive proceeded. Bringing this off correctly was most unlikely. Yet despite the odds, there were hits. These resulted, not from brilliant shooting, but from the enormous scatter produced by airborne machine guns. The soft, springy mount offered by wings and air yielded a spread of bullets so great that the possibility of a hit, no matter how unlikely, could well occur.

As the working rule governing shooting in a dive, E-III fighter pilots learned to start shooting when the supply of bullets on hand was large, and the enemy clearly aware of one's presence, as proven by a sudden change in position or flight path. In these circumstances, there was little to lose by shooting. However, if only a few bullets were on hand, or should the target aircraft seem oblivious to the impending attack, it was better to hold off shooting in favor of

A Deliberate Widening of the Pattern?

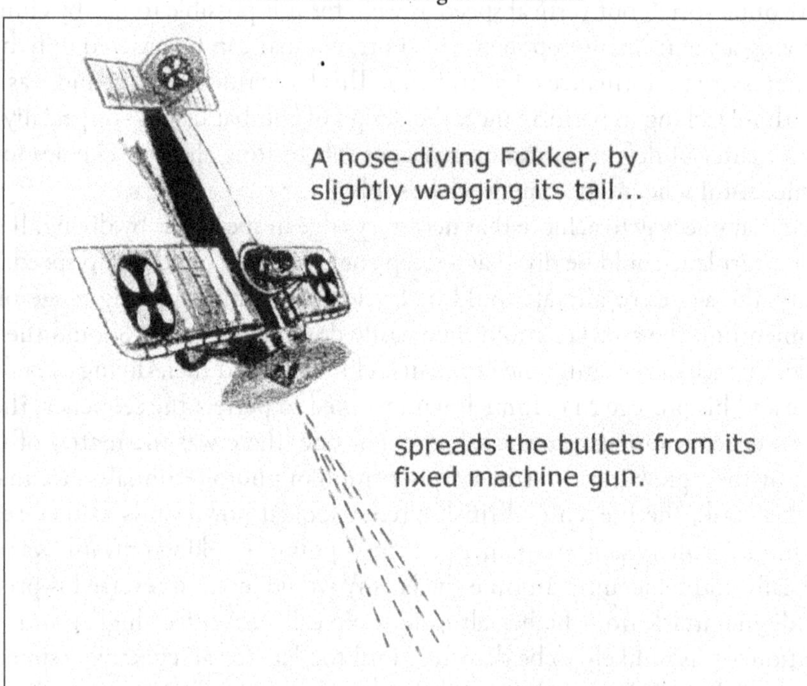

An erroneous German explanation of the too wide bullet dispersion produced by diving E-IIIs. Source: *Die Luftflotte*, September 1916, p116.

the flattening out, closing-in period following the dive. Shooting then offered a much higher probability of a hit.

Effectiveness was generally ignored by those with an ample supply of bullets. In the early days of the E-III, some dove repeatedly, saturating the air with bullets sent towards a remote target – a tactic seen as both safe and acceptable. Coming from a single gun, expenditures of 300 to 400 rounds per engagement were known, with total shooting times approaching the best part of a minute in duration. Puzzled British on the receiving end of far too scattered a set of bullet sprays believed they resulted from deliberate E-III pilot action; i.e., pilots hoping for a hit were slamming tail and rudder controls back and forth to spread the gun pattern. In reality the huge dispersion was inherent in shooting from a light aircraft at a great range. Research would yet show that on a bumpy day, at a reasonable range, an airborne Vickers machine gun placed its bullets anywhere within a huge circle, one larger than a wingspan in diameter.[22] Rather than working to increase the pattern's size, E-III pilots needed the opposite: some means of reducing the dispersion. Their only effective solution was to decrease range. This was accepted reluctantly owing to the obvious catches: shortening the range meant that fewer bullets could be fired by an overtaking, speedy aggressor and also made it easier for the enemy to strike back accurately.

Even as Boelcke and Immelmann struggled to optimize Fokker's weapon, Anthony worked to improve the breed. The 100 h.p. version was delivered at last. Next, company representatives went to the front to upgrade the interrupter with the latest improvement: a restoration of the pre-interrupter Maxim type machine gun firing rate of 600 rounds per minute. Suddenly the E-III was both speedy and powerfully armed.

Anthony himself appeared at the front to serve as a demonstrator, and equally important, to make friends for his company. A superb stunt pilot, he put on a striking show guaranteeing immediate acceptance. Then, to assure future respect, there was always a bribe. In the case of Immelmann, Fokker's offer took the form of a post-war job as an engineer, complete with a personal cut for every machine sold.[23] A suspicious Max was reassured when the offer was repeated before witnesses. From Anthony's point of view, it was worthwhile – a generous offer might prevent public damning of those inevitable Fokker lemons that came Immelmann's way.

And lemons there were. One grew from the attempt to stack two standard 80 h.p. rotaries into a package yielding 160 h.p.; a premise that excited Fokker as well as O'Gorman. It seemed the perfect replacement for the E-III's original, too modest engine. Offered was not merely a boost, but a truly commanding amount of power, neatly contained within a lightweight package format. The resulting machine would not only be faster but could carry two guns, and just possibly three.

The usual rotary pluses and minuses were expected to continue, as usual. Yes, gyroscopic forces would be larger, but Anthony was unconcerned. Pilots would cope. They always had. True, there was another force issue as well – engine torque effect – but here too, Anthony was confident. Wasn't this just another standard piloting problem, warmed over?

Every engine must generate sufficient torque – or twisting action – to drive its propeller. The aircraft reacts oppositely to the torque, employing its ability to roll as a means of action. For conventional engines, aircraft tend to roll left wing down as seen from the pilot's seat. Control was easy; a matter of warping a bit more lift into the left wing and using some rudder to counter the resulting yaw. For experienced pilots, then and now, the corrective process was

Anthony Fokker, circa 1914.

Both an innovator and scoundrel, he did much to shape Great War air combat. Source: *Flight*, November 2, 1916, p.963.

automatic. However, complications arose from one of the rotary engine's advantages – use of a blip switch.

The rotary lent itself to a temporary halt in the delivery of power. A simply cut in ignition would do. It then coasted. The huge momentum – all those spinning cylinders – made it easy to start up again. As gas vapor continued to enter the cylinders while coasting, merely turning on the ignition was enough to produce full power. After a few barks and misfires power was restored, and all was as before. This method of temporarily cutting power had tactical merit. In a diving attack, if coming in too high, simply hitting the switch; i.e., "blipping" it off and on, served as a delicate means of altitude control. If under attack, blipping the switch could reduce height quickly, fooling enemy gunners. In landing, if coming in too high, blipping was the easiest and quickest way of reducing altitude. So important was the blipping function that the E-III's blip switch was placed immediately above the trigger at the top of the control column, in easy reach of either thumb.

As always, there was a price. With the ignition cut and the engine coasting, engine torque was no longer developed. Yet the controls, previously set, continued to generate a corrective roll – a roll suddenly unwanted. Fortunately, the undesired roll was small and the pilot could easily intervene – unless he was saddled with an engine twice as powerful as the usual. Then he was faced with a problem. Even so, the difficulty could be handled. However, there was another problem as well.

Those gyroscopic forces developed with the massive rotating engine were also proportionally greater. Matters reached a point where Boelcke found it necessary to work the blip switch, cutting RPM, in order to make a sharp turn.[24] Only by doing so was he able to control the gyroscopic forces liberated by the turn. However, working the blip switch unleashed the torque imbalance. He then had two nasty control forces to regulate. In an airplane intended for ordinary wartime fliers, this wouldn't do; the combination of torque and gryroscopic force problems was too much. The 160 h.p. E-III was dead.

Even so, the 100 h.p. version was very much alive. General von Hoeppner's E-III summary was fair: "The first real combat plane … an extraordinary gain in speed, maneuverability and ceiling … a terror to our foes."[25]

There was another novel tactical aspect to E-III employment. With the fate of Garros and his deflector secret still fresh in German Air Service thoughts, steps were taken to prevent a repetition with the interrupter. Von Hoeppner noted: " … in order not to fall into the hands of the enemy [the E-III was] ordered not to fly over the hostile front."[26]

This prohibition produced a combat-free sanctuary for British and French aircraft, starting at the frontline and extending homeward. Ending of pursuit by E-IIIs at the frontier pushed both sides into altering tactics. British fliers had been granted a useful, safe zone; and the Germans sought to prevent entry.

Boelcke's basic prey, Allied observation aircraft, made full use of the new incentive, usually fleeing when up against the E-III. Their departing move came as a dive, serving to increase speed while heading for home. Once reaching the frontline vicinity, some Allied pilots would even shut down their engines and glide to a forced landing on the safe side of the lines.[27] Though an inglorious end, those who felt they had no chance preferred it to trading bullets.

As E-III pilots learned to use their aircraft for shooting, fleeing from them became ever more difficult. Testing many shooting attitudes and positions, Boelcke realized that the best was located 50 meters behind, and directly in line with his prey.[28] Once in this spot, no aiming corrections were required for the speed or trajectory of his enemy. So close a range meant that allowing for bullet drop owing to gravity was unnecessary. Indeed, no special gun sight settings of any kind were needed. He simply fired, much as in the practice gun pit at the home field. If this sweet '50 and behind' position could be held and enough bullets fired, the result was an almost certain victory.

Allied pilots reacted with new emphasis upon maneuver, hoping to shake any pursuing E-III. However, the Factory's BE2c was too loaded with stability genes to maneuver quickly. An E-III pilot in a trailing position could read BE2c tail and rudder movement signaling a new maneuver to come. Able to predict the BE2c's next move, and blessed with a fast maneuvering machine, E-III pilots were not easily shaken off.

As for the basic performance figures, all the numbers favored the E-III. A captured E-III was found able to climb to 6500 feet in 13 minutes; a task requiring 20 minutes for the BE2c.[29] Once there, maximum speed equaled 83 mph for the E-III, while the slower BE2c achieved 72 mph. In short, pushed into combat, the BE2c had no easy way out. It couldn't speed away, climb away, or dive away from a determined E-III. Something else was required. Interest focused upon a better means of shooting.

Factory engineers worked up new schemes for shooting backwards. Their design goal: blasting any E-III holding a trailing position. The BE2c had always been armed with a single flexible Lewis machine gun. The task was to make the gun potent. One approach was to improve the old mount system consisting of a group of small pylon tower supports surrounding the gunner/observer cockpit, front and back, into which the gun could be dropped as required. Rearward fire deserved something better–a smoothly moving swivelling mount controlling shooting.

BE2c Rearwards-Firing Gun Mount

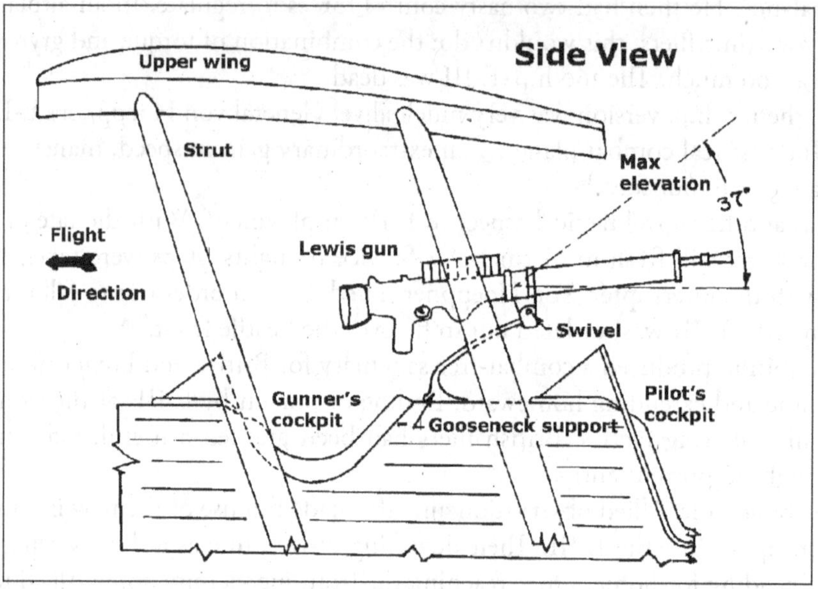

Kneeling on his seat, the gunner fired to the rear, immediately over the head of the pilot. Source: Original sketch by author from Royal Aircraft Factory working drawings, dated Aug. 1915; TNA file #AVIA 14/5/1/67.

The improvement achieved was one of better gun balance and diminished vibration and creep, useful in achieving long range accuracy. Even so, rearwards shooting remained sadly inaccurate. The gunner faced backwards, kneeling on his seat, with his upper body exposed to propeller blast. Constrained by struts, wings and the pilot, his vision was limited. He fired immediately above the pilot's head, knowing that a moment of carelessness would put bullets into his own rudder. When used at maximum elevation against diving E-III's, proper gun sight alignment required the gunner to drop to the cockpit floor. In this position, he was blind to events occurring anywhere other than high above his aircraft.

In addition to these drawbacks of apparatus, the BE2c gunner's task was inherently more difficult than shooting from an opposing E-III. As we've noted, shooting with the E-III's gun bolted down along the aircraft axis eliminated any need for correction of aim owing to gun angle. Bullet direction was roughly the same as aircraft direction. Not so, for the BE2c's rear gun. Unless corrected, when shooting at a diving E-III with the observer's gun set at high elevation angle, serious aiming errors resulted – errors of roughly 40 feet at a range of 250 yards. In theory it was possible to apply gunsight corrections eliminating the error; however, the lack of time and continuously changing size of the correction made elimination in practice most unlikely.

Added to the above error – that resulting from angled fire – was a second major error, that resulting from guesstimating the necessary lead, or the moving target error. We have seen this problem before from the vantage point of diving E-III pilots, facing the likelihood of 30 foot errors in predicting target position at the time of bullet strike. BE2c gunners were faced with similar uncertainty as to target location a second or two after firing – when their bullets arrived. Merely aiming at what could be seen wasn't good enough and applying the right amount of correction was a fine art that few possessed.

Sharing the Gun

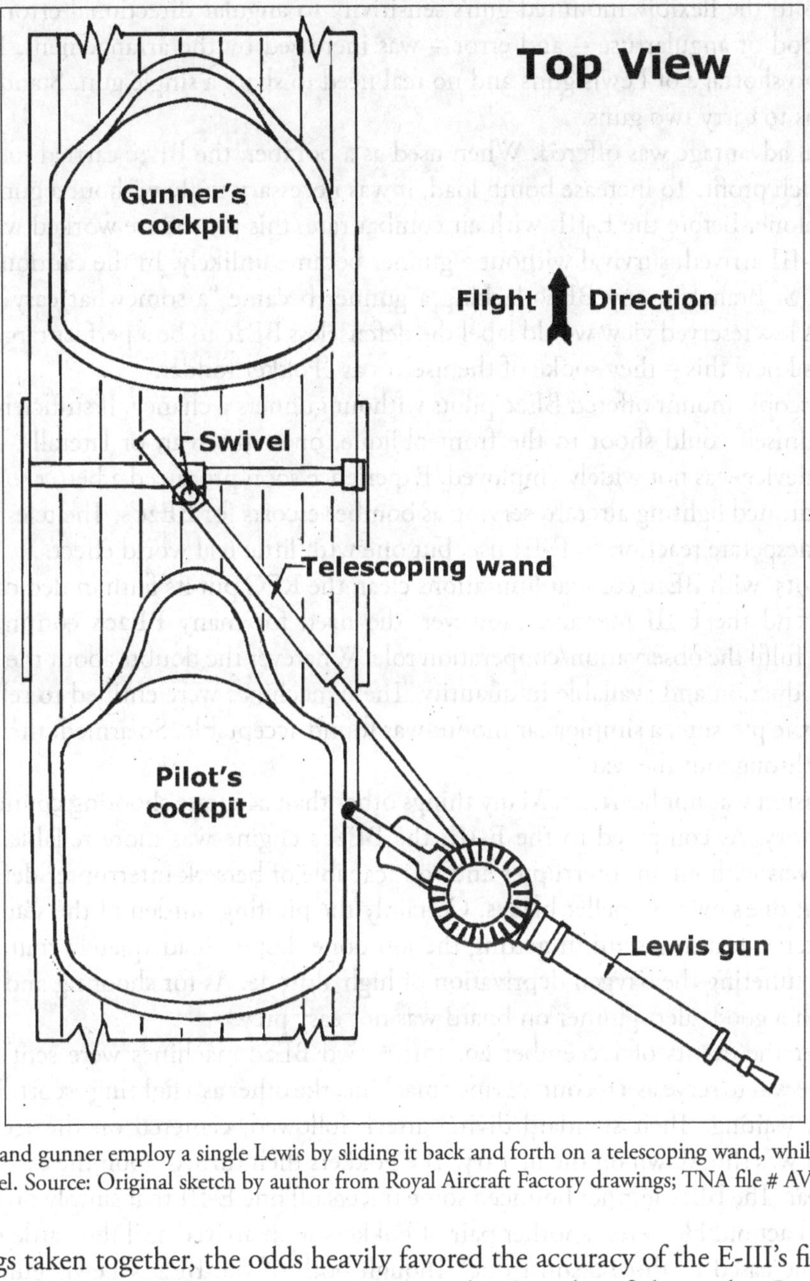

BE2c pilot and gunner employ a single Lewis by sliding it back and forth on a telescoping wand, while turning it about a swivel. Source: Original sketch by author from Royal Aircraft Factory drawings; TNA file # AVIA 14/5/2/26.

All things taken together, the odds heavily favored the accuracy of the E-III's fixed Maxim over that of the BE2c's flexible Lewis gun. As given by Canadian fighter pilot Captain Vivian Voss in 1918, " … the observer's [flexible] gun was never so deadly as the pilot's [fixed] gun."[30] Much combat experience was summed up in Voss's simple conclusion. However, in 1915 the issue was still uncertain. To some, there seemed a winning chance for a flexibly mounted Lewis, if given the right gun mount design. Factory engineers tried again.

The resulting telescoping, swiveling mount was a most ingenious arrangement offering a gunning partnership to a pilot and observer. Each could shoot the same gun, passing it back and forth as required. For the pilot to seize the gun and fire, use was made of the BE2c's inherent stability, with the pilot simply releasing the controls when necessary. No solution was offered to the flexibly mounted gun's sensitivity to angular directional error. If anything, the likelihood of angular use – and error – was increased by the arrangement. Furthermore, there was no shortage of Lewis guns and no real need to share a single gun. Standard wartime practice was to carry two guns.

One real advantage was offered. When used as a bomber, the BE2c carried too few bombs to yield much profit. To increase bomb load, it was necessary to fly without a gunner; i.e., the pilot flew alone. Before the E-III, with air combat rare, this procedure worked well. However once the E-III arrived, survival without a gunner became unlikely. In the cautious judgement of General S. Brancker, any BE2c lacking a gunner became "a somewhat easy prey for the Fokker."[31] A less reserved view would label the defenseless BE2c to be a perfect target. Resentful BE2c pilots knew this – they spoke of themselves as "Fokker fodder."

The telescopic mount offered BE2c pilots without gunners a chance. If sufficiently dextrous, the pilot himself could shoot to the front oblique, or to the rear, or laterally. However, in reality the device was not widely employed. Experience soon produced a better solution in the form of dedicated fighting aircraft, serving as bomber escorts for BE2c's. The telescopic mount signaled a desperate reaction to E-III use, but one with little real world effect.

In late 1915, with BE2c combat limitations clear, the RFC put its faith in dedicated fighting aircraft to end the E-III menace. However, the need for many BE2c's continued; aircraft required to fulfil the observation/cooperation role. Whatever the doubts about the BE2c, it was in mass production and available in quantity. These machines were entitled to self-protection. Bowing to the pressure, a simple rear mount was found acceptable. So armed, the BE2c was to soldier on throughout the war.

The decision was not heartless. Many things other than accurate shooting count in deciding air war victory. As compared to the E-III, the BE2c's engine was more reliable. The BE2c's Lewis gun was without an interrupter and so incapable of berserk interrupter defects, such as shooting off one's own propeller blades. Certainly the piloting burden of the stable BE2c was much lighter; a feature useful in getting the job done despite inadequately trained pilots, or with pilots suffering the oxygen deprivation of high altitude. As for shooting and self-defense, a BE2c with a good, alert gunner on board was not easy prey.

Consider the events of December 29, 1915.[32] Two BE2c machines were sent to Cambrai, France. One was to serve as a reconnaissance machine, the other as a fighting escort. Two Fokkers were there, waiting. Their standard diving attack followed, centered on the reconnaissance machine. It was shot down on the first try. The Fokkers then turned upon the escort, attacking from the rear. The BE2c gunner bounced some tracers off one E-III that simply dived away, out of sight and action. However, another pair of Fokkers soon arrived and the battle odds against the BE2c increased to three against one. Though both of the BE2c's Lewis guns were used, resulting intermittent jamming and desperate, fumbling clearing attempts acted to reduce return fire. Fleeing towards the frontlines the BE2c dumped altitude, diving as best it could, trying for a bit more speed and reaching for a height so low that the Fokkers would be unable to employ their standard diving attack. At times flying at an altitude of 15 feet, the BE2c fought off the E-IIIs for more than 20 minutes, finally crossing the lines to safety.

The incident showed the BE2c at its best and worst. In the first attack, the single machine working at reconnaissance was caught out by surprise. Its escort could do nothing. In the second, the fully alerted and determined escort defended itself in fine fashion. Given adequate warning, the BE2c could put up a sturdy fight. While in no sense an air superiority fighter, neither was it doomed to become "Fokker fodder." Much depended on the BE2c's use, aircrew skill – and operational luck.

Most BE2c trauma resulted from the efforts of Boelcke and Immelmann. Their tactical work had gone well. Not only were there many victories, but important lessons were learned and passed on to fellow fighter pilots. For example, repeated tries convinced Boelcke that a face-to-face or head-on shooting approach was ineffective.[33] He learned that head-on closing speed was so high that too few bullets could be fired before it was necessary to turn away from the target, preventing collision. The numbers supported him. Opening fire at 250 yards permitted the firing of less than 30 bullets before survival itself demanded taking evasive action. To Boelcke, whose combat encounters frequently required the firing of hundreds of bullets, 30 wouldn't do. Something better than head-on combat was necessary. What?

The diving form of attack was indeed superior to head-on. Among its virtues was a relatively slowly changing event yielding a longer shooting opportunity and a reduced likelihood of collision. However, the shooting dive lacked a good second act. If the prey survived, a circling contest usually followed with no certainty as to who would win – certainly an acceptable business, but one lacking in tactics assuring victory. In a few weeks of trial and error, Immelmann evolved a promising second act possibility: a maneuver leading to a repetition of the original diving attack.

Consider a diving attacker at the end of his run, as below. His excess speed is easily converted into a half loop. Once on his back, he rolls right side up. He need only dive slightly to restore

Classic Immelmann Turn

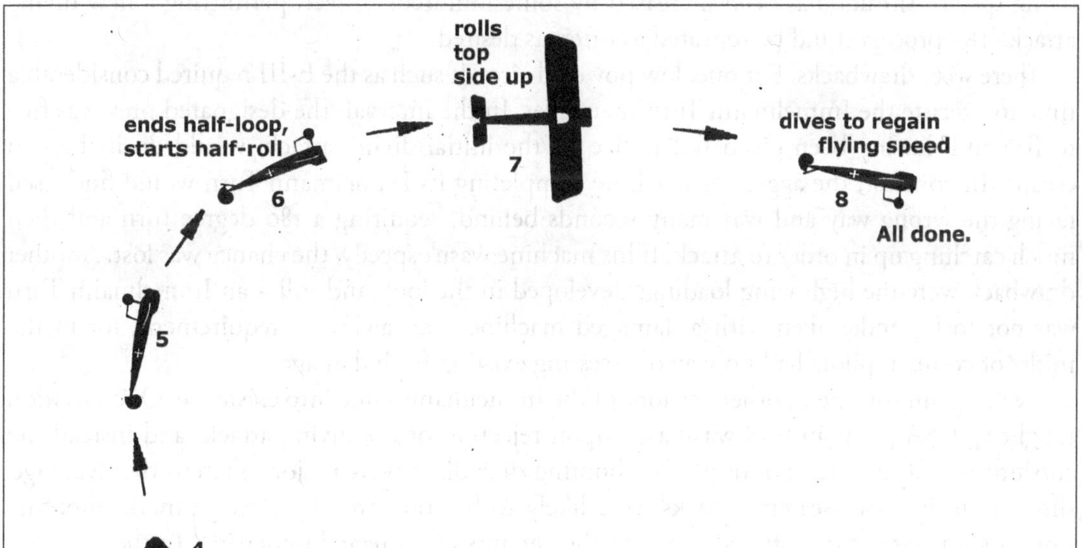

This maneuver could add altitude quickly; useful in preparing for a diving attack. Source: Original sketch by author.

A Variation on Immelmann's Theme

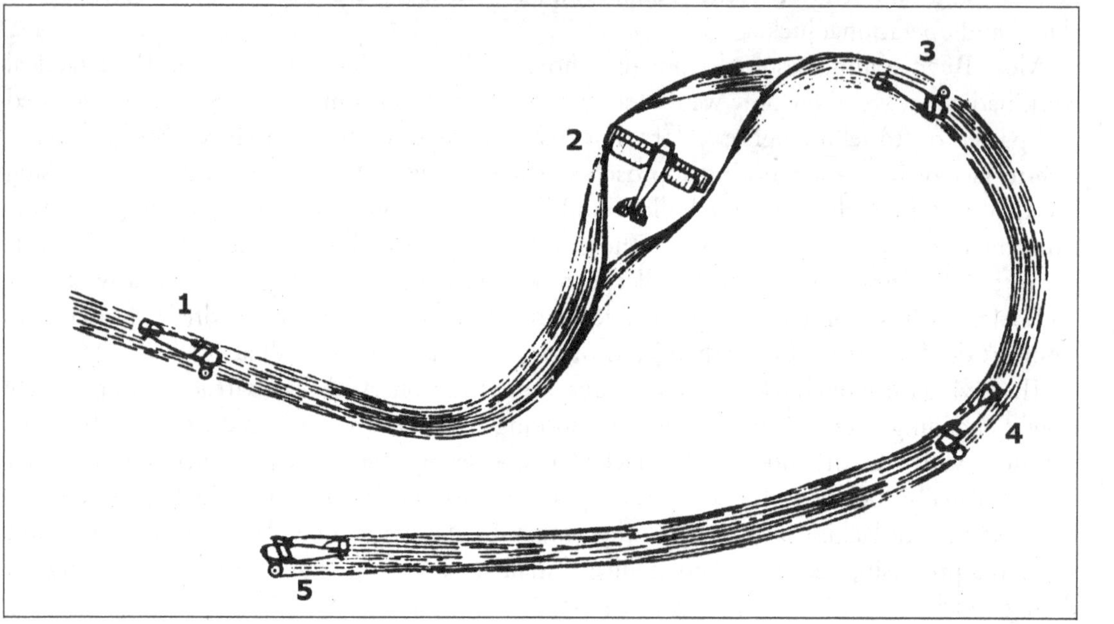

Shallow diving aircraft (1) half rolls and zooms (2), then does an inverted half loop (3,4) to end the maneuver in a shallow dive (5). Source: *Aerial Age Weekly*, June 24, 1918, p.727.

flying speed. Altitude has been increased by some hundreds of feet, permitting a new diving attack. The process could be repeated as often as desired.

There were drawbacks. For one, low powered aircraft such as the E-III required considerable time to execute the Immelmann Turn maneuver. In the interval, the designated prey was free to flee and, having been given full notice by the initial diving attack, would do its best to escape. In contrast, the aggressor machine completing its Immelmann Turn would find itself facing the wrong way and was many seconds behind, requiring a 180 degree turn and then much catching up in order to attack. If his machine wasn't speedy, the chance was lost. Another drawback were the high wing loadings developed in the loop and roll – an Immelmann Turn was not to be undertaken with a damaged machine – an awkward requirement, for in the midst of combat, pilots had no way of assessing existing fresh damage.

Seeking improvement, other versions of the Immelmann came into existence. One variation taught to USA pilots in 1918 was based upon rejection of the diving attack, and instead the substitution of upward shooting. The shooting dive did have a major inherent disadvantage: directed against two-seaters, attacks were likely to be countered by alert gunners. Shooting upwards was safer, for it offered access to the enemy's unprotected underside. In the variation shown, upward shooting was to occur at about position 2. A net gain in altitude wasn't the goal, and even a loss was acceptable. Experience proved the maneuver itself to be useful, even when performed without a target. Its twisted path made pursuit difficult, and the directional change was frequently that sought. This variation became a useful part of the fighter pilot's repertoire, and went on to acceptance by British WWII leading ace Johnny Johnson as the true Immelmann Turn.[34]

Sound Boelcke and Immelmann tactics led to growing British casualties. By the end of 1915 losses were disturbingly large; large enough to give the British sensational press an issue: that

Flying Gun's Advertising Debut

An E-III downs a Farman 20 in Fokker's announcement of his new weapon.
Source: *Deutsche Luftfahrer Zeitung*, January 1916, p.24.

of a "Fokker Scourge" decimating Allied aircraft. With nearly 50 pilots and observers lost in a two-month period[35] (early November 1915 through early January 1916) something new in the way of British tactics was essential.

Politicians reacted with comforting half-truths and lies. Under-Secretary for War H.J. Tennant admitted to a certain success by the Fokker, but noted its serious disadvantages. For one, it was incapable of crossing over the frontlines because its tiny fuel allowance made it unable to spend much time in the air – this was nonsense, but pleasing nonsense. As for the main duties of military aircraft; i.e., reconnaissance and artillery guidance, he saw the single-seater machine as obviously unsuitable and therefore not much of a war machine. Not so; it was simply another, novel type of war machine; one concerned with different goals. Finally, concerning the heavy British losses: "the Germans can hide their own whilst advertising ours

… my military advisors are satisfied that our Flying Service has given a good account of itself in recent fighting."[36]

The awkward fact was that losses were indeed severe. As most casualties consisted of reconnaissance aircrews surprised in ambushes, RFC General Hugh M. Trenchard ordered escorts for all reconnaissance flights. These were to consist of a minimum of three fighting machines for every reconnaissance machine.[37] If this meant many fewer frontline missions, so be it.

In turn, Boelcke and Immelmann were faced with a new problem: fighting against enemy formations. Moving into spring 1916 they grappled with many new issues, from the aging of the once dominant Fokker, to questions of Air Service staffing and aircraft types suited for a tremendous expansion of size of fighting units. There were new fighter aircraft to be assessed and many new pilots to instruct in the tactical arts. For example, there was Baron Manfred von Richthofen, a tyro fighter pilot of uncertain merit.

4

After the Fokker

Good air fighting tactics are those that lead to many victories. However, tactics do not exist alone – they must be paired with machine performance. Early in the game, the order was in dispute: did the machine or tactics come first? Bitter experience showed the importance of accepting the fighting machine with all its quirks as a given, and then developing the right tactics to suit. Any attempt to reverse the order was likely to produce only empty hopes, for designers were unable to come up with an aircraft filling a list of requirements. In short, realism demanded the construction of tactics based on those fighters one had on hand. As a major complication, the aircraft kept changing.

Promising new ideas were plentiful. Instead of the standard bolted down gun, why not two machine guns for the Fokker E-III? Why not angle the gun slightly to do away with the tricky aiming correction required in a diving attack? If biplanes really climbed better, why not give

Team Leaders

(left) Capt. Oswald Boelcke, key air combat thinker and doer; (right) Lt. Max Immelmann, a most able practitioner and his E-III. German caption translation: "The Best One!" The machine gun has been painted out to meet censorship requirements. Source: (left) *Osterreichische Flug-Zeitschrift*, December 1916, p.275; (right) *Die Luftflotte*, April 1916, front cover.

(from the original) "The Deadly Fokker"

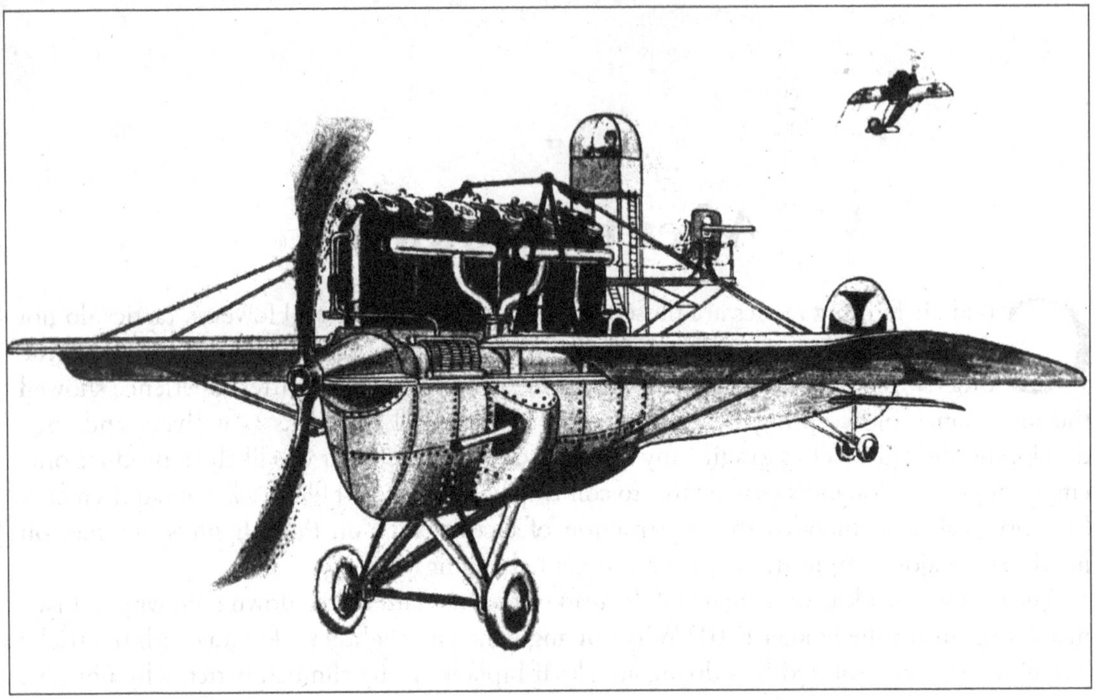

Tiring of false "revelations" this scornful British sketch offers us the Fokker's secrets: an enormous engine, nautical cannon and body armor. Source: *Flight*, February 3, 1916, p.103.

the Fokker two wings? If two entire wings seemed too much, what about a compromise: say, a wing and a half? Though all these notions were tried, little success followed – to truly improve fighting aircraft was far from simple. The art of devising superior tactics was no easier.

Into this quagmire moved Boelcke, determined to control the design of fighting machines and serve as a fighting pilot, all while developing new tactics and teaching those tactics to beginners. His chosen role was large and cut through the normal chain of command. Certainly his Captain's rank was too low for the task. He made the mission feasible by trading on his personal fame. Even the USA, then neutral, became intrigued as his score mounted, with his seventh victory widely reported in blow-by-blow fashion as seen from the ground.[1] A French challenge, questioning the honesty of his score keeping was inevitable, and it came with the official German report of his 40th victory (April 30, 1916) – a claim damned as fantasy by the Allies. Offered instead were French corrections to the total, pointing to a score of 29. Whatever the true number, whether 29 or 40, his was a huge success. Boelcke not only invented much of air combat tactics, but risked his life on a daily basis to verify the truth of his beliefs. In a world of straw men, he was a most impressive achiever.

Boelcke entered 1916 sensing that the days of E-III dominance were numbered. The French, regarded as Europe's best pre-war designers, had produced the formidable Nieuport 11 'Bébé' as competition. Then there were the British designers, working up improvements to their FE2 and DH1 machines – variations rumored to be successful. Without doubt the E-III's interrupted gun, extreme lightweight, pilot only aircrew, and ability to dive steeply had changed the game, but for how long would its features dominate combat? Boelcke pushed for new, greatly superior fighters as crucial.

Nieuport 11

Effective against the E-III, the "Bébé" pushed Boelcke to seek a better fighter. Source: Original sketch by author from 3-views, *Luftfahrt*, February 1917, p. n/a

Consider the opposing Bébé. Powered with an 80 h.p. Gnome rotary, it made the most of its modest thrust by outdoing even Fokker's miserly approach to the spending of weight. At a gross weight of 1056 lbs.[3] it weighed less than 80% of the E-III's 1340 lbs. The result was a much better climb rate, in addition to a speed advantage of roughly 10%. The Bébé not only offered greater performance, but was also superior as a dogfighter – especially in the deadly circling match.

Here circling radius was everything, for the fighter on the inside circle could hope for a 'straight ahead' clear shot at his outer circle opponent. The unfortunate fighter on the outer

Circling Duel

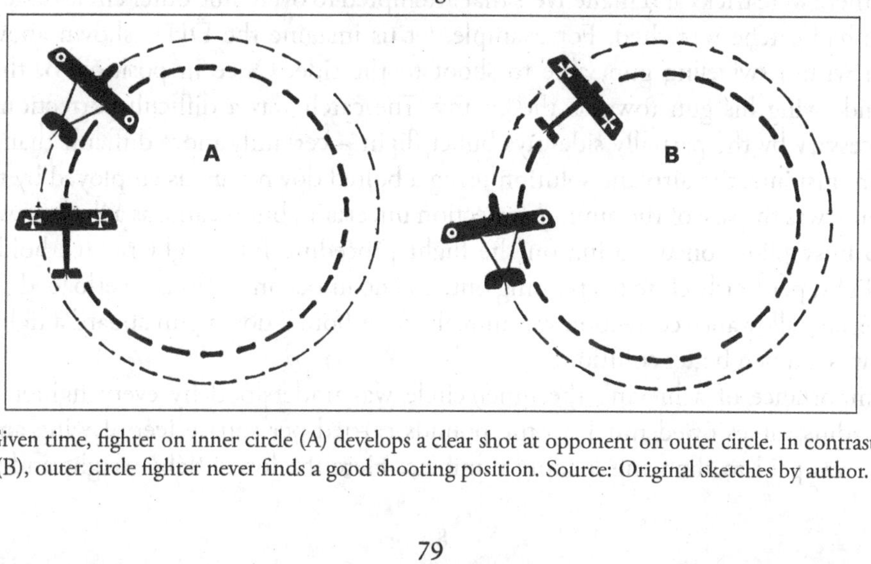

Given time, fighter on inner circle (A) develops a clear shot at opponent on outer circle. In contrast (B), outer circle fighter never finds a good shooting position. Source: Original sketches by author.

Nieuport Gun Controls

To reload: pull A and butt swings down, permitting access. To fire: yank B. Source: *La Guerre Aérienne*, March 1917, p.306.

circle never had the same opportunity: no matter where located along the outer circle, whether faster or slower, his gun never pointed at the enemy.

True, there were tricks and maneuvers that attempted to overcome outer circle disadvantages, but these had catches attached. For example, let us imagine the DH2 (shown above) to be equipped with a swiveling gun, able to shoot to the side. Once in position B, the British pilot could swing his gun towards the enemy. The catch was a difficult correction for aim made necessary by the partially sideways bullet flight – certainly more difficult than the zero correction, just-aim-the-airplane solution using a bolted down gun, as employed by the E-III.

Not only was the size of the aiming correction uncertain, but it came as a 'last straw' burden for a too busy pilot concentrating on the flight procedure for a tight radius: holding near stalling flight, perilously close to spinning out. To encumber an anxious, overloaded pilot with a complex aim allowance correction was unrealistic. A bolted down gun aboard a tight circling airplane was a much better solution.

The importance of achieving the inner circle was understood by every fighter pilot. As circling radius values owed much to the pounds carried per square feet of wing area,[4] great attention was paid to the wing loading numbers. Here the lower Bébé weight and generous sesqui-plane (wing and a half) area meant a tighter circle – and a simpler shot at the occupant of the outer circle.[5]

The Bébé did have drawbacks. Our sketch of the aircraft shows one: the pilot was blind to many events located above the top wing. Just as we are unable to see the pilot for reason of upper wing blockage, he was similarly incapable of seeing an enemy located in front, at a higher altitude. In contrast, the E-III vision upward was superb.

Another drawback consisted of the gun location. Set upon a tripod above the top wing, it occupied a remote spot that didn't lend itself to reloading or the clearing of a gun jam. To reach the gun, it was necessary to rotate the butt downward by pulling on a lanyard. The pilot then half stood while leaning into the prop blast above the cockpit to work on the gun, all while flying the machine in combat. For comparison, the E-III pilot's gun was within reach, leading to easier performance of gun tending chores.

Another Bébé disadvantage consisted of the fewer rounds fired before the necessity of reloading, as compared to the E-III's Maxim gun plus interrupter. The Maxim employed lengthy belts containing hundreds of rounds, while the usual Lewis drum held only 47 bullets. Attempts to introduce a larger Lewis drum – the "double" with 96 rounds – were troubled by the high arm strength and skill required for replacement. Pilots usually had only one hand available, the other being on the control stick. For most men, one arm wasn't equal to the task. As a result, Lewis gun users accepted the lighter, lower drag 47 round standard drum as the only practical solution, only to curse the limited number of bullets available when in combat.

As a final Bébé drawback, the half-sized lower wing was weak, and known to fail occasionally when in a steep dive. As a result, anything approaching a steep dive was out – a serious limit upon combat maneuverability.

Despite these negative aspects, the Bébé was capable of holding its own against the E-III in every flight condition other than diving. Above all, given a circling duel, the Bébé was more likely to emerge as winner. Coming at a time of E-III dominance, the Bébé generated respect. Its core concept would appear again in a stronger and more powerful version – the Nieuport 17 – destined to become one of the most successful Great War fighters.

However, in early 1916 the Bébé seemed just one more flawed fighter design. Boelcke believed its defeat to be simply a matter of the right tactics. His thoughts on the problem were assembled and published as part of the "Dicta Boelcke" – a set of rules for winning aerial combat. These were: [6]

1. Put yourself into a superior position before attacking. Try to get the sun at your back.
2. Once initiated, carry attacks through.
3. Shoot only when the range is close and the enemy is properly in your sights.
4. Beware of trickery. Never take your eyes off the enemy.
5. Nail your enemy from behind. Frontal attack is useless.
6. Don't attempt to evade a diving attack. Instead, rise to meet it.
7. If fighting over enemy territory, keep an escape route in mind.
8. (For the entire *Staffel*) Attack in groups of 4 to 6. Should the attack break up into individual combat, avoid piling up on single opponents.

The advice was good. Even if a Bébé pilot sighted a diving attacker early enough to take evasive action, he was prevented from diving away by that weak lower wing. Nor could he

Start of a Circular Duel

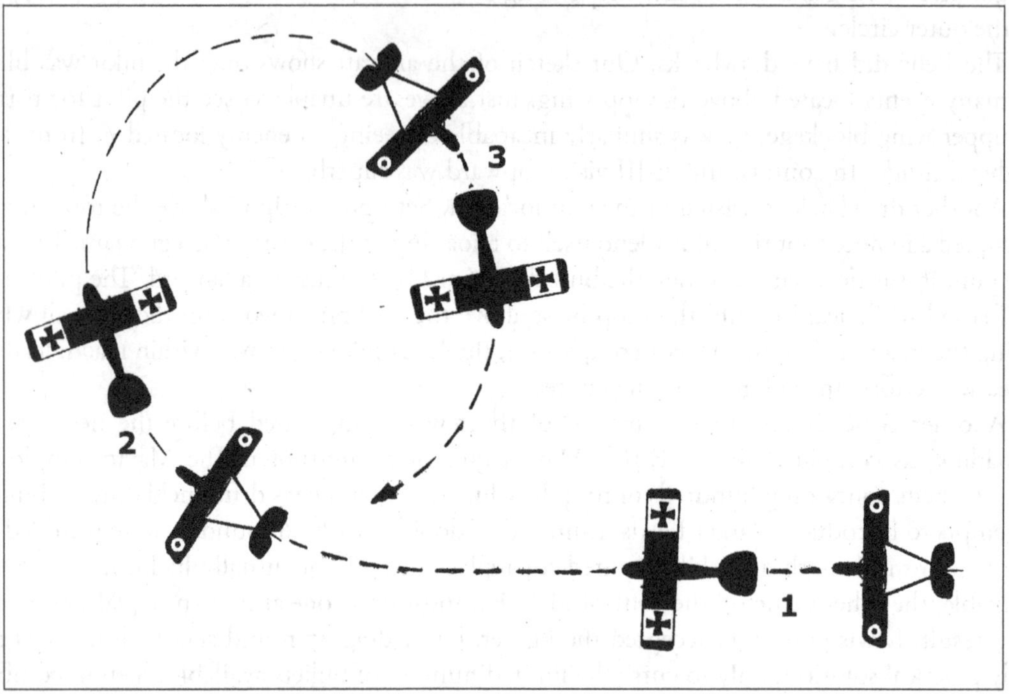

(1) German fighter under attack turns, hoping to face attacker. (2) However, aggressor continues to turn tightly, foiling German hopes. (3) Joint path spirals into a tight circle. Source: Original sketch by author.

hope to speed away on the level, for his attacker likely had a speed bonus on tap – the profit gained from diving. With a safe exit for the Bébé ruled out, German victory through a diving attack was likely.

However, the attackers also faced a challenge, though of a different type – that of piloting the right aircraft. Offensive machines necessary for the Boelcke type of attack were strong, high-speed divers, and yet capable of offering a fast climbing rate. The combination was difficult to achieve – good divers tended to be strong and heavy, while most good climbers were weak and light. Compromise machines were notorious for failing to offer either desired feature. Developing the right fighter was Boelcke's concern over the 1915-16 winter. With several promising candidates on hand, he hoped to replace his aging, low powered Fokkers and move into a productive 1916.

Not all his plans were realistic. Even battle against the Bébé type fighter remained unresolved. Consider a German fighter pilot's possible moves when surprised by an attack upon his tail – what then? Dicta #5 called for never running away from an enemy fighter. Instead, one was to turn, directly facing the enemy.[7] There was a certain logic here, for the planned German single-seater fighters were tractor types with forward firing guns. To fire effectively, such aircraft must face their opponents.

The difficulty with this advice was failure to picture the enemy's response. Rather than face the German fighter, a sensible enemy would most likely attempt to remain on his opponent's tail. Given circling radii of roughly equal size, and equally skillful pilots, there was little possibility of changing places. In other words, the German pilot had little chance of facing his enemy. Instead, as shown, the machines would trace a spiral, growing ever tighter as they

Fokker Successors: Albatros DI and DII

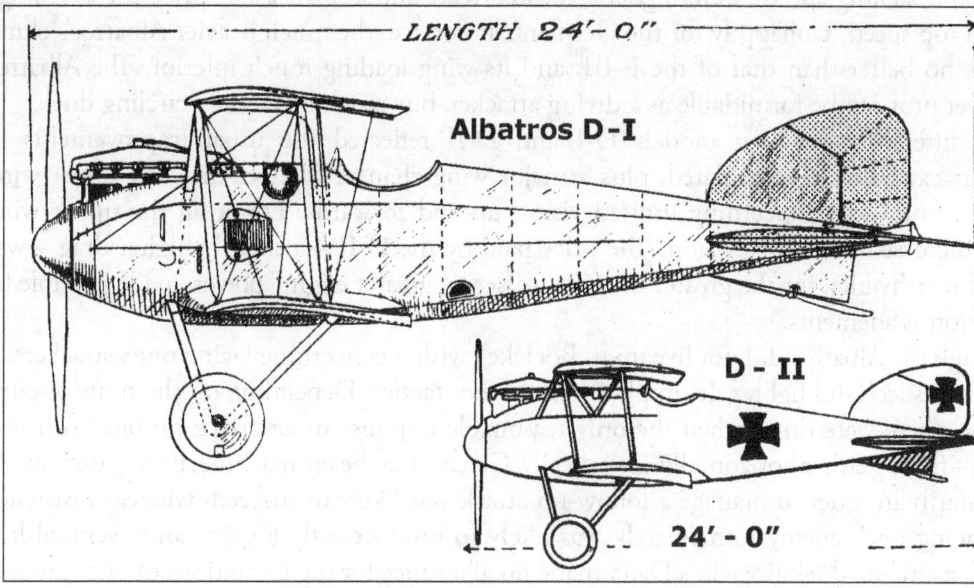

More powerful and sturdier, these fast, formidable divers were worthy of Boelcke's elite squadrons. Source: DI: *Flight*, June 28, 1917, p.639; DII: *L'Aérophile*, February 1917, p.51.

moved from positions (1) through (3). This special path came about from the lead pilot's hope that tightening his turn would result in arrival at the highly desired trailing position. In reality, the spiral would probably end in a circling duel, with outcomes as noted previously.

Of course Boelcke hoped that his new fighters would display outstanding circling characteristics, tight enough to turn inside their Allied opponents, thus proving the soundness of his tactics. However, fighter flight characteristics are one of man's less predictable areas. On this occasion, Boelcke faced life's uncertainties with a certain amount of wishful thinking. Perhaps his new fighters would really out-turn the Allied competition and all would be well – but perhaps not. In reality, when the crunch of 1916 air combat came, they did not.

Formidable in many ways, the impressive features[8] of the new Albatros D-I and II fighter planes carried a penalty – they were heavy aircraft. At a time when 90 or 100 h.p. seemed adequate to many designers, the Albatros offered 160 h.p., and that in the form of a most reliable Mercedes liquid cooled engine, as against the miserably undependable rotary 100 h.p. Monosoupape going into RFC service. The catch? The Mercedes was much heavier.

There were two machine guns instead of the usual one gun – an arrangement better able to pour out more bullets within those few seconds when the gun sight and enemy were in proper alignment. There was also the hope that a jammed gun would leave its remaining twin able to fire, permitting survival.

Finally there was an inspired fuselage. Instead of the usual sticks and cloth, layers of thin wood veneer were bonded to produce a curved, streamlined and strong form. Here was a solution both sturdier and aerodynamically superior to the conventional arrangement. Unfortunately, it was also heavier.

Where speed was concerned, the increase in power was large enough to offset the added weight. As compared to the Fokker, maximum speed was increased by a handsome 25%. French criticism[9] of a limited "speed range" as compared to their own lighter machines – i.e. Albatros takeoff and stalling speeds were higher – was correct, but seemed a fair price for that huge boost in top speed. Unhappily for the German Air Service, the much heavier Albatros's climb rate was no better than that of the E-III, and its wing loading much inferior. The Albatros would yet prove to be formidable as a diving attacker, but much less so in a circling duel.

The differences between models D-I and D-II reflected the usual improvements in details as experience accumulated, plus a major wing change. The original D-I upper wing brought complaints concerning limited vision up and forwards. Lowering the upper wing greatly increased the pilots' vision. The price paid by the D-II – a slightly higher drag – was deemed worthwhile, for the greater drag was offset by greater engine power, made possible by production refinements.

Though the Albatros did not live up to Boelcke's wishes concerning facing one's attackers, it was a most successful fighter. It simply favored other tactics. Depending on the traits of one's machine, there were times when the only reasonable response to an attack on one's rear was evasion – fleeing either horizontally or vertically. Given a fast, heavy machine, fleeing downward momentarily in order to manage a follow-up attack was likely to succeed, whereas insistence upon facing one's enemy immediately was likely to produce only a spiral and eventual loss through a circling duel. Boelcke's Dicta made no allowance for the limitations of one's aircraft. Nor did he accept holding a losing position, even one held only momentarily. For example, he refused to consider the need for fleeing, even that limited evasion required to bring about an ultimate victory. The necessary sophistication would come with experience.

Much as he spelled out future tactics with a combination of brilliance and wishful thinking, just so Boelcke planned his corps of fighter pilots. In the special case of his own squadron, he took one extra step by using personal interviews to both attract and then measure the quality of recruits. This odd use of his time seemed worthwhile because 1916's needs for skilled, aggressive fighter pilots had turned desperate.

Junior partner Max Immelmann was dead. His body was found amidst the remains of an elderly, crashed E-II in June 1916. Whether he was vanquished in combat, as claimed by the British, or brought down by a defective interrupter shooting off his own propeller has never been clarified. Boelcke lost more than an able fighter pilot: his hand-picked successor was gone.

In July 1916, the enormous Somme battle pointed to still heavier piloting demands ahead. A new Somme fighter squadron was wanted immediately. Boelcke toured frontline squadrons seeking recruits from Army co-op, observation and artillery guidance units. A pilot's ticket and the right spirit were his only requirements. He met and accepted Richthofen. Few would have supported the choice.

With his father as a serving officer, and many cousins enlisted in the wartime cavalry, the Richthofens[10] were a military family. Generations of ancestors had prospered from farming, horse raising and land management. In Manfred, his parents sensed a quick, lively, daredevil type. Never a gifted student and clearly unsuited for the scholarly professions, he was good with horses and dangerous stunts. It was Manfred who tied his handkerchief to the top of a tall steeple by climbing it at the risk of his life; a performance without ladders or an audience.

To the family, his affinity for horses and relish for danger smacked of a future cavalry officer. At age 11, with no enthusiasm on his part, he was sent off to a proper cadet school. A previously free soul, he found the discipline painful. He reacted by doing as little studying as

Richthofen, 1917

A proud and most successful fighter pilot displays his new Blue Max award. Source: Manfred von Richthofen, *The Red Air Fighter* (London: *The Aeroplane* and General Publishing Company, 1918) frontispiece.

possible. Inevitably, his teachers saw him as slow-witted. Only sports and hunting made his life worthwhile.

Aged 20 at last and commissioned a Lieutenant in the cavalry (1912), horses were all important. Jumping and galloping at prize-winning levels exacted a price, and Manfred accepted falls and broken bones as necessary for rising above the competition. Racing through a tricky, 40 mile long course for the Kaiser Prize (1913), he won despite a tumble and broken collar bone. His single most important trait emerged: a fierce determination to take home the top prize, no matter what the cost.

With the war's start his long planned cavalry role was suddenly made uncertain, with the very concept of horsemen acting as the "eyes of the Army" foundering, owing to new weaponry. Given a machine gun war, cavalry units had little chance when used against entrenched infantry. To drive the point home, his cavalry cousins – the entire group of six[II] – were quickly slaughtered without any useful result.

Richthofen's reaction showed another important personal trait: though brave enough, he rejected service or causes that appeared silly by his own lights. Where no logic existed, neither would he. Officers with the right background were always able to transfer, and his was certainly the right background. When facing pointless or dumb orders, he made full use of the right to move on.

And so, enough of the cavalry. If the Army was to have eyes, those eyes would be airborne, rather than horse borne. He transferred out, volunteering to serve as an observer for the Air Service.

He found flight and airplanes to be fine indeed, but became restless serving a Germany uncertain of flight's proper wartime application. Initially an observer/gunner on the Russian front, he drifted into a heavy bombing unit based in Belgium. There he fought several encounters with French machines – combat that left him surprised at his own inadequacy as a marksman. The very survival of his opponents meant that few of his bullets hit home; an odd result in view of his considerable hunting experience. For some inexplicable reason shooting in the air was different, and much more difficult.

Seeking answers, he felt himself fortunate to bump into the already famous Boelcke one day in October 1915. They shared a train ride and much conversation. Boelcke stressed one major point: to fire accurately, get close before shooting (Dicta #3). Richthofen decided that Boelcke's special means for doing so consisted of his Fokker. In contrast, Richthofen was unable to close with the enemy owing to the lack of maneuverability displayed by his clumsy "apple barge" aircraft. Deciding that his own training and aircraft were unsuited for the fighter pilot role he sought, he determined to make a fresh start. He would become an E-III pilot.

One more transfer and he was undergoing flight training. Then a disturbing development: he proved to be a mediocre trainee, with little natural feeling for the piloting process. Sent up on his first solo, he was fearful but willing. Made lighter by the absence of his instructor, the machine handled a bit differently, offering more than the usual amount of buoyancy. Every student pilot goes through this experience, first sensing and then correcting for the different feel of the machine. There's a new tendency to float along, without the usual altitude loss, especially evident when landing. Natural pilots take it in their stride. Less gifted pilots, flying mechanically, have difficulties in adjusting. Richthofen's reaction was extreme: his solo landing ended in a somersault crash.

His always patient instructors shrugged and continued their efforts. When solo flight was finally mastered, he moved on to figure eights and repeated takeoffs and landings. Feeling adequate at last he was given a check ride, only to flunk and undergo repetition of his training. Progressing to aerobatics, he showed no flair at a time when maneuvering skill, in the Immelmann fashion, was viewed as the key to air combat success. Reacting to his lack of skill, a reluctance to perform tricky aerobatics became a permanent Richthofen trait; one he defended with a sour grapes form of denial. As he put it: "The decisive factor does not lie in trick flying, but solely in the ability and energy of the aviator … aggressive spirit is everything."[12]

Whatever the doubts about his flying ability, there was no question about his aggressiveness. Assigned to a permanent station near Verdun, he improved his two-seater's firepower by adding a remote machine gun, Nieuport-style. What's more, he sought combat with his home made lash-up, and claimed a victory over a hapless French machine. The German Air Service was pleased to announce the victory, but refused to credit it to Richthofen, for the only witness was his observer. Serious scoring had arrived and independent witnesses were required.

In August 1916, Boelcke's recruiting tour came through. He sought new combat pilots to staff elite squadrons dedicated to wiping out aerial opposition. As Germany's best fighter pilots, they were to receive the latest word in weaponry – machines certainly better than the old E-III. Richthofen was quick to volunteer and Boelcke, who remembered him well, was pleased to sign him up, despite Richthofen's excessive number of transfers, weak record as a student pilot and lack of subsequent victories. Boelcke saw something more important – Richthofen's furious need for recognition and fame. It was the best of starting points, matching his own.

What of British plans, moving into 1916? Reacting to the E-III, and hindered by the lack of a competing interrupter, the British still had some obvious fighter plane possibilities. For one, they might prepare a fresh design employing the conventional pusher gunship concept. Given enough performance, this might well be the proper answer to the E-III. Or, they could improve their existing line of tractors; those aircraft carrying flexible or remote guns, such as the BE2. New arrangements of multiple outrigged guns were under study and a winner might just emerge. Finally, they could assume that a British interrupter would come about shortly and design a suitable matching tractor fighter while waiting. Given the desperate need for a resolution of the E-III menace, all these possibilities were pushed simultaneously.

Designer de Havilland, freed of O'Gorman and the Factory, had started work at the new, privately owned Airco firm. First off the drawing board came the DH1, designed along the usual pusher 'gunbus' lines. Testing proved it to be merely one more sluggish two-seater pusher. It wouldn't do.[13] Instead, officials favored Airco's light weight, single-seater pusher design, powered with the new and larger 100 h.p. Monosoupape-Gnome engine.

At last, a formidable E-III competitor for the RFC was under way – the DH2. True, its wing loading figures suggested a circling radius a bit larger than the E-III's. A drawback, yes, but one compensated by both a faster speed and a superior climb rate. Even so, the DH2 was not a clear winner. There was the awkward issue of diving, or more accurately, non – diving.

The ability to dive is obviously important to a fighter aircraft. However, diving comes at a price – one must accept reduced stability – and so a painful trade-off was required. How much stability is necessary? Unhappily, there is no simple answer. Great stability makes for an

DH2

A lively single-seat pusher, this British fighter did much to end the E-III menace. Source: (large sketch) *The Aeroplane*, August 23, 1916, p.309; (inset) original drawing by author.

easy-to-fly aircraft. If nudged by a gust, an ultra stable airplane will automatically return to its old course. As less pilot input is required, an inept, or wounded, or oxygen deprived pilot flying a highly stable aircraft is more likely to survive despite poor quality piloting. This was an important advantage, for wartime piloting skills were reduced not only by misadventure, but by the lack of time available for training.

The lack of stability – or instability – also has its virtues, of which permitting steep dives is but one. In general, maneuverability is eased by instability. Whatever must be flown every second, without the possibility of relaxation, has the right genes for a highly maneuverable aircraft. A mean, tricky machine best fits combat needs.

British design was hung up on stability considerations. Before the war, extreme stability seemed best. Pilot strain was reduced. Accidents were fewer. The resulting relaxed pilot could take on the duties of observer. Pilot training was short. As for combat and maneuverability, much existing sophisticated planning denied the likelihood of aerial fighting – and if so, why worry about maneuverability? The resulting case for positive stability was strong and designers responded with a series of stable machines – aircraft with no ability to enter a steep dive.

Should a steep dive be attempted, even the strongest pilots were unable to push the control stick forward with sufficient force to produce more than a shallow dive. As expected, maneuvers of any kind were executed slowly: the ultra stable machine was a hesitant dogfighter.

Military machines fitting this category were officially spotted and called out as the result of careful testing performed a few years later – in 1918.[14] Prominent were the BE2c, the FE2b, and the DH2 – the main RFC machines employed to engage Boelcke's fighters in 1916.

BE2c Gun Mounts

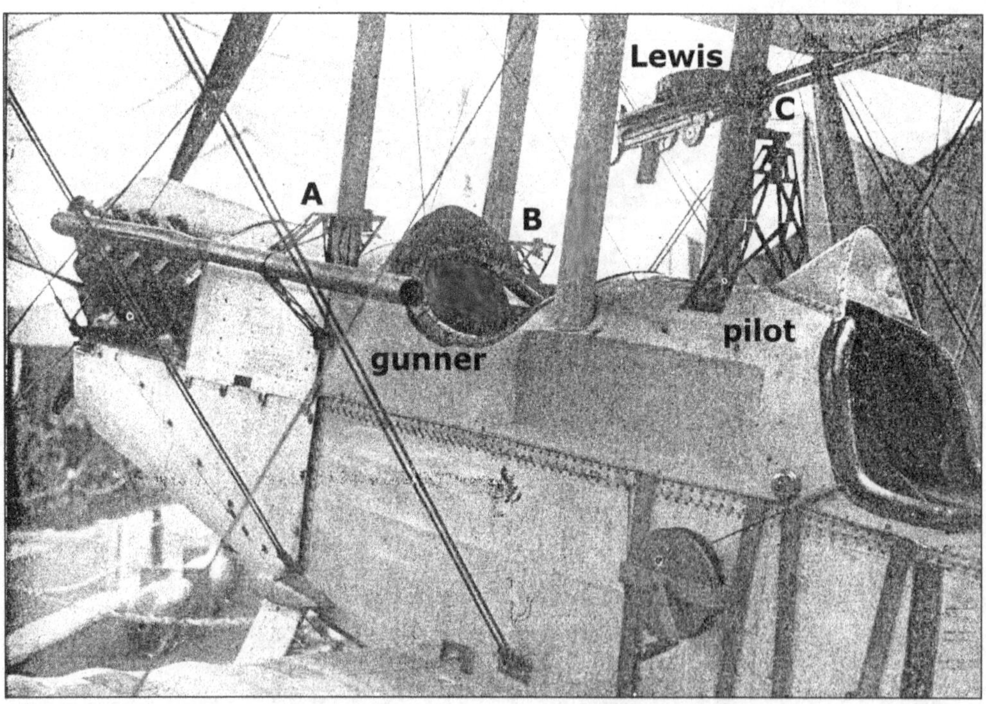

To hold aim on a circling enemy, it was necessary to move a BE2c's Lewis gun from front oblique mounts (A and B) to rear mount (C). Gunners were understandably furious.Source: *Flugsport*, January 19, 1916, p.38.

Handicapped by the limitations of excessive stability, their British pilots would not find aerial combat victories to be easy.

The BE2c struggled with another serious limitation: one of clumsy shooting arrangements. The varied gun mount arrangements forced upon the BE2c through lack of an interrupter were a trial for every gunner.

Consider an enemy machine passing from left to right directly ahead of a BE2c. To avoid putting bullets into the BE2c propeller, it was necessary to interrupt shooting and shift the gunner's Lewis gun from its left oblique gun mount (A) to the right (B) – a painstaking process at best, and one requiring neat timing – all to be done in the midst of combat. This was a maddening drawback. The rear gun mount (C) was also highly useful, but moving the gun there required another interruption. The very number of spindly gun mounts, each resembling a trellis, promoted a "flying Christmas tree" image, one that quickly turned into a sneer following the BE2c everywhere.

The unsatisfactory BE2c shooting arrangements led to endless attempted improvements. Inevitably came the question: why not use the pilot to increase the level of firepower? One method was to give the pilot a separate, bolted down Lewis gun aimed along a forward oblique, angled to clear the propeller arc. In principle, only the pilot's left hand was required. Pressing a thin cable attached to the trigger was enough to fire the gun. Reloading while flying was obviously difficult, but no more so than with the Nieuport Bébé.

Shooting at an angle to the aircraft path led to aiming problems. Emerging bullets follow a path reflecting both the bullet momentum and that change produced by the angled

BE2c Pilot as Gunner

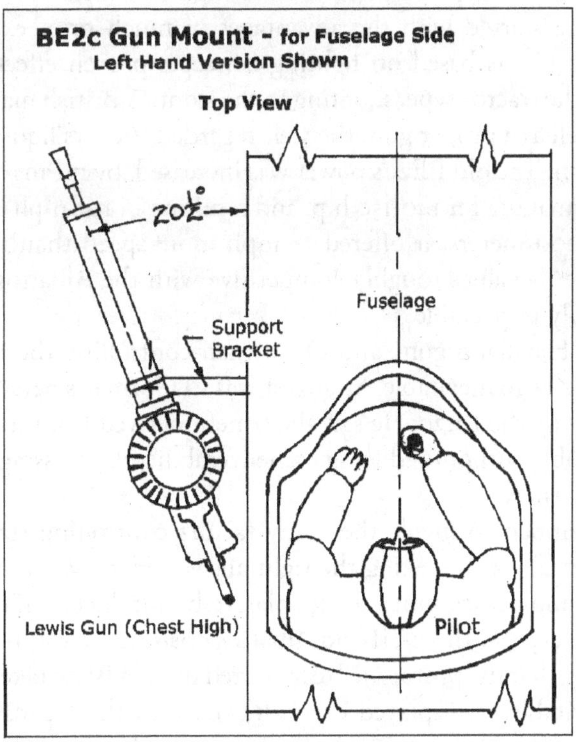

The angled, fixed gun position permitted the pilot to shoot forward without hitting the propeller. Aim was not simple. Source: Original drawing by author from data TNA file #AVIA 14/5/1/82.

mount. Boelcke had tried it on a Fokker and quickly returned to the 'straight ahead' option. However, BE2c pilots didn't have the attractive, alternate E-III possibility of shooting through the propeller. To many BE2c pilots, even angled shooting was better than serving solely as a chauffeur, leaving the observer/gunner to do all the shooting. Many such conversions were fitted, despite its "Christmas Tree" implications, and despite official RFC steps to limit the "impedimenta" to be carried.[15]

The need to respond – to shoot back – drove many pilots. RAF Marshal Sholto Douglas, then a BE2c pilot, noted an occasion when his observer's Lewis gun jammed in the midst of combat. Douglas then opened fire with his pistol, firing six shots in an obviously futile attempt to continue the action, noting only: "I like the idea of blazing away at the Hun."[16] Once aroused, men are aggressive beyond the call of logic.

Whatever the clumsiness of the shooting arrangements and inability to dive, in 1916 the BE2c was viewed as necessary by top RFC General Hugh Trenchard. It was easy to fly, landed most anywhere, and, above all, was in good supply through mass production. In Trenchard's view, need for the BE2c would continue[17] "until the RFC is in possession of a machine as good as or better than the German Fokker." A practical man above all, he correctly pictured the difficulty of continuing the air war without it. In short, despite its unsuitability for aerial combat, the BE2's fine performance as an observation and light bombing machine made for continuing demand.

A sense of the significance of any aircraft is reflected by its losses. In the last half of 1916 (July-December) Germany claimed[18] a total of 49 BE2 types as downed; a number slightly larger than one quarter of their entire Western Front claims. Clearly, the BE2 series was in widespread use, and was of a type that lent itself to high casualties.

The follow-on BE12 started with the advantages of much prior experience. Designed as a single-seater fighter, it was based on fighting concepts proven effective by the E-III. The machine was to be of the tractor type, shooting to the front. A British manufactured interrupter was ready at last, as well as a proper gun: the well-regarded Vickers liquid-cooled machine gun, suited for bolting down. The old BE2c's power was increased, by means of four cylinders added to the standard eight, making for 140-150 h.p. and resulting in 102 mph at sea level. At a typical combat altitude of 2000 meters, it offered 25 mph more speed than the BE2c and climbed at twice the BE2c rate[19] – values roughly competitive with the Albatros. In short, BE12 basic performance was highly respectable.

However, with de Havilland gone and O'Gorman controlling the Factory design process, aircraft design oddities were inevitable. Strangest was O'Gorman's determination to retain the ultra stability featured by the BE2c. He saw the benefit derived from stability – easy piloting – as a key virtue, achievable without reducing maneuverability. In pressing this decision, he went against all BE2c experience.

Given time, he planned to juggle the many factors controlling stability – airfoil choice, engine location, tail area, etc. – seeking the right answer. Here was a search ideally suited for O'Gorman's patience and dedication; a design plan to be conducted in the same manner as his wing warp study. However, in the E-III and Albatros crisis, there was no time.

Time was so lacking that the prototype BE12 started life as a BE2c taken from the production line and rebuilt. Inevitably, it displayed every drawback of the BE2c. With about the same weight and wing area,[20] it offered roughly the same wing loading and circling performance

BE12 under Unfriendly Eyes

Exhibited to a curious German public, this captured BE12 was a sensation. Source: *Flugsport*, March 1917, front cover.

– yielding too large a dogfighting pursuit circle. As for maneuverability, it was as stiff and reluctant to change trajectory as its parent. The result was one more dreadful fighter aircraft.

There were virtues. Despite its awkward side mounting, the Vickers machine gun itself was effective. Unfortunately, working on a jammed gun was made difficult by its location. A remote gun was added to serve as an alternate. The two guns together – neither of which permitted easy access – were reasonably successful.

The BE12 was sturdy, fast and offered acceptable shooting characteristics. That it was no fighter became only too apparent after it reached the front in quantity, in 1916.

Its end might have been different: a cry from the front[21] for the development of a single-seater BE2c suited for long range observation had seemingly been answered. However, it was not to be the BE12.

For the BE12, as in Boelcke's injunction to first face the enemy, there was a huge gap between a seemingly reasonable plan and actual performance. General von Bernhardi's pre – war rule[22] putting tactics first, "in order that the airships may be built accordingly" was precisely wrong. Conclusion: tactics must follow and guide real life performance, rather than lead.

Boelcke and his elite squadron would welcome the BE12 with the necessary dose of reality. His Albatros fighters were ready.

5

Richthofen versus Two-Seaters

The Somme battle speeded Boelcke's approach to air fighting. His new fighter squadron, *Jagdstaffel* 2, was listed on the books and staffed as of August 30 1916.[1] Responding to the crisis atmosphere, the Air Service sent a full complement of brand new Albatros fighters within an additional two weeks. Boelcke attempted the complete unit's first patrol a few days later (September 17) with a sweep directed towards the Cambrai vicinity. Richthofen was part of Boelcke's group.

More than a beginner but less than truly knowledgeable, we might expect Richthofen's career to follow the usual trainee path, one stressing the building of experience under a flight leader's protective wings. However, there was no time for careful nurturing within the shadow of the Somme battle. Even this test-the-waters patrol soon stumbled upon a sizable formation of BE2's rigged as bombers, protected by FE2b's. In all, the Germans faced 14 British two-seater fighting machines. Boelcke's awkward decision: attack or flee?

Boelcke's flight of 5 pilots were of a mixed background. More to the point, none had significant Albatros fighter experience. Attacking a strong defense group with a raw flight team manning unfamiliar aircraft could appear unwise, and even foolish, to chair- bound Generals. Without a workable means of communication between pilots, attack could only result in an 'every man for himself' melee against a greater number of enemies, with each enemy likely to be more experienced. At issue was not only the fate of his men, but the future of an ingenious tactic – one based on employing fighting aircraft in specialized squadrons, each hopefully capable of wiping out enemy aircraft by the handful instead of the usual one at a time, now and then.

Nothing shakes an uncertain high command as does steep, unexpected losses at the very beginning of a new combat approach. If anything, the German Air Service had exhibited unusual risk taking ability in accepting Boelcke's plans for separate air fighting squadrons. From the political/administrative viewpoint, avoiding severe losses in the opening phase of his planned expansion was the obvious move.

In short, common sense ruled against too early an attack; specifically those premature attacks conducted before the necessary lessons of aerial warfare were mastered. Many of the necessary how-to lessons already existed or would do so shortly. Only patience was required, permitting a gathering and learning process. However, Boelcke was a most impatient sort. He spent a few seconds, sorting odds, tactics and probability.

For example, how best to attack a FE2b? Why not simply employ the usual Fokker E-III method – the diving attack – as developed against the BE2 and other two-seaters?

Though the FE2 and BE2 designs shared super-stability and an inability to dive steeply, their very different shooting arrangements separated their degree of vulnerability and suggested quite different forms of German attack as superior. Specifically, the pusher FE2b's guns were

Diving Attack and FE2 Stall Defense

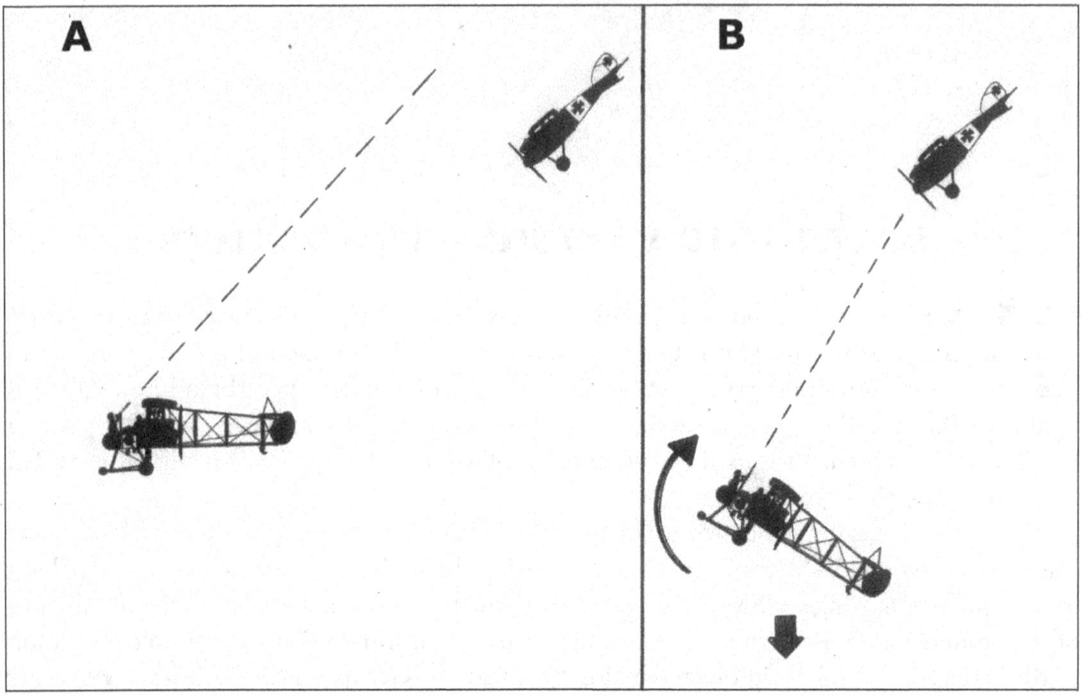

A standard attack (A) prevents gunner retaliation, for his field off fire is too limited. However, if suddenly stalled (B), the incidence change and altitude drop act to enlarge the gunner's field of fire. He can then hit back at the attacker.Source: Original sketches by author based on 3-views Flight, June 28, 1917, p.619 and A. Fage & H.E. Collins *Technical Reports of the Advisory Committee for Aeronautics, Reports & Memoranda # 305* (London: HMSO, Jan. 1917).

arranged to face an attack from a similar or higher altitude – front or rear. The wide-angle opening and unlimited fire to the front is evident. Shooting effectively at enemies diving from the rear took some doing, but was soon mastered by the RFC.[2]

The deliberate stall ploy, used to open the field of fire to the rear, was a shrewd move but one with drawbacks. The resulting loss of both speed and altitude forced a stalling FE2 out of formation, and increased the likelihood of it becoming a straggler, suited for mopping up. Then there was the gunner's nacelle itself, described by one gunner[3] as: "[an] aerial footbath that hardly reached my kneecaps." Precise shooting from so inadequate a source, all while standing within a howling wind was not easy – making the bringing down of enemies, especially those who were above and behind, an uncertain business.

Even so, Boelcke was impressed. He drew a careful, conservative conclusion: attacking an FE2b from above was not the optimum move. Instead, attack from below, and especially from the machine's blind spot located at its bottom rear was much to be preferred. Once occupying this spot, the attacker was relatively safe and well able to pour bullets into the FE2b fuselage, located forward and above. He passed this on. Given this slender tactical advice, Richthofen was considered ready for the pressure of battle and need for reinforcements permitted no delay. Evaluating the odds and needs, Boelcke signaled his squadron to attack.

The action was instantaneous and vicious. Choosing an opponent was straightforward – nearest was best. Using his height advantage, Richthofen first managed a diving attack and "took my aim and shot. He [the FE2b gunner] also fired … and both of us missed our aim."[4] Richthofen then swung under his opponent to occupy Boelcke's suggested back-and-below,

Blind Spot Attack

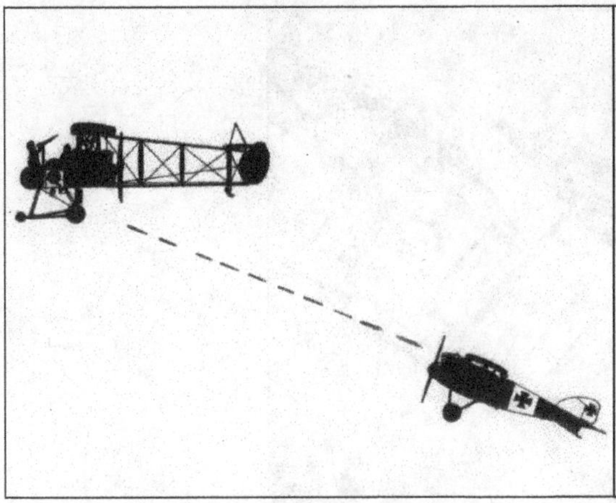

Once into the FE2's blind spot behind and below – it was possible to open a surprise attack without immediate counterfire. Source: Original sketch by author from same sources used for image on previous page.

Victory and Confusion

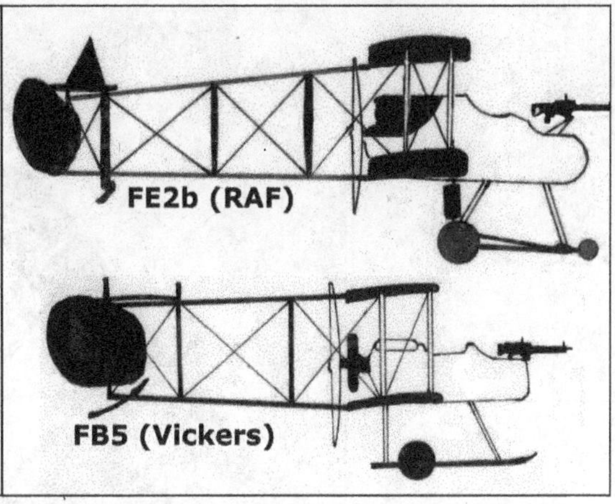

Shooting down an FE2b for his first victory (top), Richthofen incorrectly identified it as a Vickers Gunbus (bottom). Given the striking similarity, the error was understandable. Source: Original sketches by author from same sources as before and *Flight*, June 12, 1919, pp.760-761.

blind spot position. Once there, he increased his nose-up attitude, risking stall, to be able to fire directly at his target. Moving as close as possible, his target was unable to escape. Also, when at a negligible range, shooting subtleties or counter maneuvers no longer mattered. The official[5] combat report indicated that Richthofen " … fired several times at close range … ten meters … [and] the enemy propeller stood stock still … " The British two-seater descended in a long glide on the German side of the lines and it was all over. Richthofen had his first victory (September 1916), so excited by events that in landing alongside to gain confirmation, "I nearly smashed up my machine."[6] Both the wounded pilot and observer died before reaching medical aid.

There was the usual confused upshot. Another German pilot staked a claim for the same downed aircraft. However, all parties finally agreed: it was really Richthofen's victory. Then there was the matter of the downed aircraft's ID. Richthofen claimed to have shot down a Vickers – but his badly shot about victim was obviously a FE2b. Here he was confused by the similar appearance of the two machines – further proof of his lack of experience.

Plagued by an unreliable engine, the Vickers 'gunbus' had a short and unsatisfactory combat career. At the time of Richthofen's incorrect identification, the poorly regarded gunbus was no longer a significant combatant; however, it continued to exist in the imagination of propaganda artists, with a large sketch of a burning gunbus appearing in *Flugsport*, the semi-official German aviation journal just days before Richthofen's victory. Widely studied by German Air Service personnel, this sketch may well have influenced his mistaken judgement.

Oddly enough, convinced that the FE2b was a Vickers, Richthofen remained unshakable despite official correction and his subsequent increasing experience. In all he was credited with twelve victories over FE2 type machines, a total that peaked many months later in 1917's "Bloody April". He identified most of these – incorrectly – as Vickers types.

Despite his increasing expertise, the FE2 was never an easy target. If anything, its many virtues made for a formidable opponent. This judgement was widespread; for example, RAF

End of a Vickers Gunbus

This widely seen and easily remembered German propaganda sketch may have influenced Richthofen. Source: *Flugsport*, September 8, 1915, p.573.

Marshal Sholto Douglas, at the time a two-seater combat pilot, rated the FE2 as one of 1916's more useful fighting aircraft, though not the best – a position given to the Nieuport.[7]

Caught by an attacker occupying its blind spot, the FE2b's best defense was a fast turn.[8] Given a strong pilot, a quick turn could not only match that of an Albatros – just possibly losing him – but also forced a complex lead allowance shooting correction upon the attacker, likely preventing accuracy. It was straight ahead flight that offered a simple deflection allowance – turning alone could well be a good move, for shooting at a turning target was much more difficult.

Finally a turning FE2b, if given enough roll, permitted its gunner to see and hit an occupant of its old blind spot. Here was a potentially deadly counterattack, capable of destroying Albatros pilots too slow to assess the new FE2 prospects achieved by 'turn and bank' attitude.

To offset this form of FE2b defense, an attacking Albatros might shorten the range to near zero – as demonstrated in Richthofen's first combat victory. However, this could be difficult to bring about. Granted a seasoned and fully aware pilot, the FE2 became a fast jinking, shifting, and circling machine impossible to approach closely. Fortunately for German attackers, the FE2 was usually burdened with a guard assignment limiting free-form maneuvering. Certainly, holding formation with bombers or observation machines placed severe restraints upon a defending FE2's flight path.

In sum, a freely maneuvering FE2, in experienced hands, could well be a formidable foe. To an extent, Richthofen's many FE2 victories followed from combat with enemy pilots

Changing the Odds

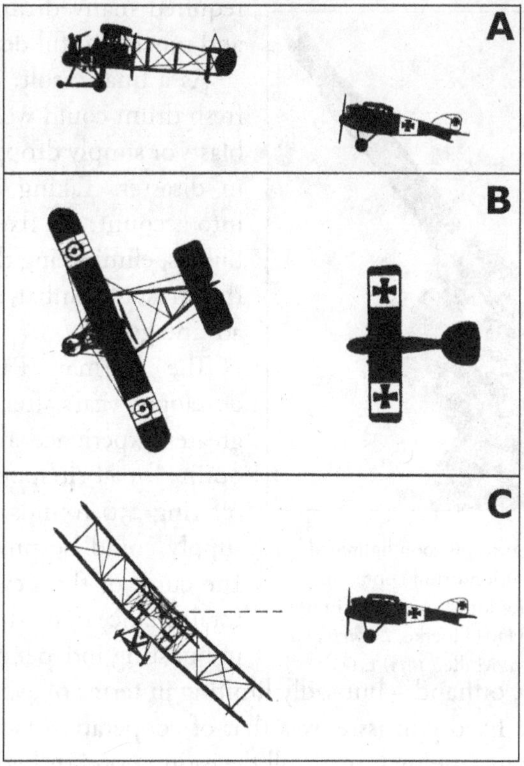

An FE2b could eliminate its blind spot sinecure (A) by a partial turn (B) taken together with a steep bank (C). The FE2b's resulting change permitted it to shoot down enemies responding too slowly to the maneuver. Source: Original sketches by author from sources used for diving attack.

deficient in either experience[9] or awareness, or those too slow to abandon their guard duty responsibilities in order to defend themselves.

Another factor boosting Richthofen's score was the superior gunnery available from his twin bolted down guns, as compared to an opposing FE2's two-seater flexible Lewis guns. In principle a flexible (movable) gun would seem a more useful concept, with last moment changes in aim possible as dictated by the gunner. However, in practice, the many drawbacks associated with flexible guns prevented this hope.

One catch was the need for clearance between the moving parts of the flexible gun mount. Simple hinges or pivots required clearance between components – small spaces and gaps giving rise to the complaint of Sholto Douglas[10] who saw himself as armed "with a rather wobbly Lewis gun … " Decreasing the clearances eliminated the wobble and tightened the resulting shot pattern, but made gun movement – always hampered by wind pressure – that much more difficult.

A second disadvantage was the limited number of bullets available to most flexible guns before reloading was required. The pause while removing an old drum and inserting a fresh one could well mean a one sided – and fatal – halt to combat. Starting with a fresh drum and using the recommended 6 rounds per burst, the Lewis gunner had less than 8 bursts on tap. Furthermore, despite the 6 round recommendation, combat bursts tended to run long, resulting in perhaps only 4 or 5 bursts as truly available. These were few indeed. Typical air fights

The Too Small Drum

Though this pre-war Lewis gun was soon lightened and streamlined, its ammunition drum containing only 47 bullets – a severe limitation – continued in use throughout the war. Source: Hans Floerke, *Deutchland in der Luft Voran* (Munich: Muller, 1915) p.145.

required many drums worth of cartridges – and much painful dead time while reloading.

As a final insult, in reloading the gun, a fresh drum could well be carried away by air blasts or simply dropped overboard, resulting in disaster. Taking all these disadvantages into account, the fixed gun's larger supply of bullets, eliminating the need for reloading in the midst of combat, counted as an important advantage.

The German Parabellum flexible gun, developed years after the Lewis, reflected the greater experience available to designers by opting for a belt/spool cartridge arrangement offering 250 rounds. Thus, a greater ammo supply could be provided for flexible guns. The curse of the Lewis design was one of a total reliance upon the drum concept – useful in boosting independence – indeed, the gun could even be fired freely, offhand – but sadly limiting in terms of available bullet supply.

A third flexible versus fixed gun issue was that of cooperation between gunner and pilot. In the case of the fixed gun, one man made all decisions, good or bad. For flexible guns, two men were usually involved – men who, while endlessly admonished to cooperate in their actions, were sufficiently human to frequently operate at cross purposes. Here, the lack of communication equipment was serious: hand signals, shouting and slaps had their limitations.

One disappointment in cooperation was that of vision and the sighting of enemies. Common sense suggested that "two men looking out"[11] must be better than the one set of eyes available in a single-seater. Reality proved exactly the opposite: "two heads were worse than one."[12] To an extent the problem arose from laziness – that is, depending upon one's partner to carry the load of searching the skies – and partly from the terrible FE2 sighting prospects available against those enemies employing an approach from the lower rear, behind the engine and propeller.

German Flexible Gun Solution

Accommodating 250 rounds, the Parabellum employed a tricky belt plus spool feed plugged in at (A). Immediately under the gun is the bag used to catch spent cartridge cases. Source: *Flugsport*, January 1918, p.32.

Another source of pilot and gunner cooperation difficulty was that of maneuvering in combat. To expect accuracy from an FE2 gunner while experiencing the stress of wild maneuvers was unrealistic: gunners needed a simple path offering a low G-loading to work effectively. Their pilots knew this, but were faced with the problem of forced maneuvering required to keep a canny enemy in sight. The solution required a truly shrewd pilot, able to anticipate his enemy's moves and then fly an intercepting course offering the shooting opportunities of a steady path. As the FE2 was much slower than the Albatros or other fighters used by Richthofen, this ability to anticipate and head off German fighters was far from easy. Indeed, predictive, forward-looking tactics were well beyond reach for many of the poorly trained and therefore mediocre FE2 pilots. What could be offered by such pilots was energetic maneuvering, and this was done, despite the gunner's curses.

When that rare combination of a gifted pilot and a skilled gunner flew as a combat team, the results could be impressive. In ace Captain James McCudden's view: "A two-seater in which the pilot and observer cooperate well is more than a match for a scout … "[13] It was Richthofen's good fortune to encounter few FE2 aircrews with the necessary skills. And of those who were skillful, still fewer achieved the proper level of working cooperation necessary to challenge his fighter.

A sense of the cooperation struggle may be gained from a single issue: which gun rules? In addition to the typical FE2 observer's two Lewis guns – one for frontal use and the other mounted on a telescoping pole for rear or lateral use – the pilot had yet a third Lewis, capable of being fired to the front over the observer's head. In principle, whichever gun was 'on the attack' controlled the priorities. If it was the pilot's gun, the pilot was in total charge and could ignore his gunner's needs. If the attack gun was one of the gunner's, the pilot was to accept a supporting role, flying the machine to maximize his gunner's chances.

Consider a frequently encountered combat situation. Let's say that the gunner is engaged in attacking a frontal enemy when the pilot notices a number of fresh enemy machines diving on his rear. Is the pilot to continue aiding his gunner's attack, or should he maneuver so as to prepare a strong defense? Which is most important here: attack or defense?

The official answer[14] was both too subtle and incomplete: if the two-seater was about to experience a potentially overwhelming attack, then defense took first priority. An example was given: should the number of fresh attackers amount to three, then certainly defense came first. Fine, but suppose there was only one fresh attacker? What then? How was the judgement to be made concerning whether the fresh attack was of the truly threatening type, and so deserved full attention? Under what circumstances was the gunner's attack on a frontal enemy to be abandoned in favor of immediate defense?

Officialdom offered nothing. It was all up to the aircrew. Inevitably, pessimistic aircrew members would see even one attacker as threatening, and optimists would not. Dissension and working at cross-purposes was certain. Instead of a practical resolution, RFC instruction[15] pointed to the happier, if "rare", times resulting when an FE2 would be able to dive on an enemy formation, "the pilot picking a lead machine and the gunner a following machine." In this way, two enemies could be attacked with one FE2. Well, yes.

The issue of gun jams further burdened aircrew relations. Certainly prevalent, two-seater reactions varied widely. At one extreme were the views of FE2 NCO gunner Arch Whitehouse. Starting as a ground force machine gunner trained to take apart and assemble Lewis guns until he could do so blindfolded, he automatically took whatever remedial action was necessary to clear stoppages. As a result, he flew Western Front combat missions for many months, enduring much combat and earning important decorations, all without a single "serious gun stoppage."[16] Given his unusual background, he was unable to sympathize with anyone experiencing of "a serious delay" in gun operation.

Few shared his training and subsequent good fortune. In particular, student pilots carried too full a schedule of flight instruction and were given little time with guns. As a result, many FE2 pilots were initiated into combat lacking the ability to cure jams. Gunners themselves varied widely in their training and ability. Most learned that taking remedial action in class was one thing, while doing so in the air under enemy fire was quite another. With their lives hanging in the balance, contempt and fury for a partner unable to take instantaneous corrective action was inevitable.

Richthofen had experienced exactly this form of aircrew dissension. Earlier in his career, serving as a two-seater gunner, Richthofen had fired and missed at an easy target. His previously friendly pilot,[17] "reproached me for having shot badly, and I reproached him for not having enabled me to shoot well." Equally bad British aircrew cooperation was a factor in many of his subsequent victories.

Even well functioning aircrews learned that some cover was necessary for time out of action. Should a gunner's Lewis jam or need a drum changing, FE2 pilots were encouraged to use the dead time to "either attack, or defend the machine by maneuver." Hopefully, the pilot was to attack using his own gun, for "a vigorous attack by the pilot is the best cover."[18]

If the pilot's gun was out of action, the recommended maneuver was to kick the rudder back and forth. This legs-only process freed the pilot's hands for work on the gun. Simultaneously, the gunner was to fire "accurate shooting, or not"[19] to mask the unavailability of the pilot's gun. For those highly skillful pilots able to direct the control stick with their knees, a better move was to bank and turn sideways,[20] offering a difficult target while freeing both hands for gun correction. Exactly this procedure was standard for the Fokker E-III.

With so much depending on the ability to fire at will, and gun jams prevalent, the possibility of using paired or twin guns was investigated. It was hoped that if one jammed, the other would be available. Twin gun advantages were real, and certainly the doubled firepower of paired fixed guns was important in combat. However, it would be learned that the foggy, freezing weather likely to jam one gun would likely jam its twin: gun duplication was only a partial answer.

For Lewis guns, pairing was generally unsuccessful. The resulting high gun mass slowed any desired shifting of the aiming point. Replacing two drums at a time was a severe nuisance. The greater air drag of the gun combination was also a negative point and most gunners agreed with Flt. Lieutenant F.M.M. West, who "preferred the single Lewis, as I could maneuver it with much greater ease."[21] As a result, twin Lewis guns were rarely employed.

Granted two fixed guns, Richthofen's fighters were usually opposed, not by the combined firepower of a FE2b's three Lewis guns, but by whichever single Lewis happened to be pointed in the right direction. To further increase the odds in his favor, Richthofen made use of the FE2b gunner's inability to fire accurately while maneuvering. Of the three guns, the one pointed upwards and rearwards was especially sensitive to airspeed and acceleration, for its gunner stood smack in the center of a high-speed slipstream. Shooting backwards while stalled at a low airspeed was one thing and worked well enough to be a serious option; however, firing accurately when engaged in a high-speed maneuver was quite another matter. Even the RFC conceded that " … once the machine [FE2b] can be forced to dive or stunt, the gunner can't stand up and use his gun."[22]

To Richthofen the proper tactics were clear: encourage the FE2b to dive. At best, the dive itself would be of a shallow type, easily overtaken by his own fighter. Furthermore, with the

FE2b Gunner's Guns

A downed FE2b offers the standard Lewis gun on post (A) for lateral and forward shooting, plus a second Lewis (B) for shooting towards the front. A third Lewis–the pilot's gun– has been removed. Source: *Luftfahrt*, October 1917, p.22.

gunner out of action owing to wind, a subsequent attack from the above/rear was not only safe but likely to be profitable. It remained only to induce the FE2b to dive.

There were ways. Much depended on FE2b aircrew fear and ignorance. One way was to open fire prematurely, at too great a distance and altitude. As much of the fighting occurred on the German side of the frontlines, within a few miles of the front, there was always a British hope of escape by fleeing across the lines to safety.

The concept of a safe zone for the British was backed by Boelcke himself,[23] who preferred the much greater profit gained by bringing down Allied aircrew members as prisoners – those flying on the German side of the lines – as compared to those brought down on the Allied side. The latter were mostly men who would fight again another day; however, if taken prisoner they were truly out of the war. This view discouraged German fighting machines from pursuing enemies across the Allied lines. More than a philosophical wish, orders were issued to this effect

In Memoriam – October 1916

With his Blue Max award prominent, Boelcke poses for one of his last photos. Source: *AVIA* (Netherlands) November 1916, p.207.

in 1916. Interviewed after the war, *Hauptmann* Carl Bolle, a member of Boelcke's squadron, said, "At the Somme, the pilots of single-seaters were expressly forbidden to cross our lines."[24]

To a set-upon, hapless FE2b pilot bent upon fleeing to safety, and desperately trying to increase his exit speed, diving seemed best. To cover ground in a hurry, jinking and maneuvering were dropped – straight line flight was faster. This worst possible combination played into Richthofen's hands, for the resulting high-speed shallow dive prevented accurate rearwards shooting from a fleeing FE2, and the straight line flight path eliminated Richthofen's problems of gunnery lead and deflection. To profit from FE2 limitations, it was only necessary that he create sufficient panic, leading to a desire for escape above all.

In using this process, as compared to close-in fighting, Richthofen expended many times more bullets. Many of these were fired to produce fear, rather than damage, and were fired from so great a distance that accuracy was impossible. He preferred it that way. True, his first victory had resulted from extremely close range and only a few bullets, but given some thought, he decided that close range was overly dangerous – a few well-aimed rounds might find him or, and far more likely, collision might result. As he put it: "I had gone so close that I was afraid I might dash into the Englishman."[25]

He had learned a profitable lesson: better than a struggle at 10 meters range was a distant engagement with a fleeing, diving FE2 located some hundreds of meters away. More profitable was a contest between a soft target unable to shoot back effectively, opposed by his twin fixed guns and a full complement of bullets – many hundreds of bullets. Given these conditions, it was just a matter of time and bullets until Richthofen triumphed.

In achieving FE2b victories, Richthofen officially reported expended bullet counts ranging from 200 to 300 to 400 and even 800 cartridges. Reflected was not sloppy shooting, but shrewd tactics: *it was much wiser to win by expending too many bullets at a long range than by employing too few bullets at a close range.*

Boelcke's October 1916 death through collision with his own wingman in the midst of combat – occurring within Richthofen's sight – reinforced the point. Flying in proximity to either friends or enemies had strong drawbacks. Yes, there were times when nothing else would work, but with the FE2b as enemy, other tactics were equally successful and much safer.

For one, deliberate loss of surprise when attacking could sometimes be useful – even against those FE2b pilots too wise to flee. Instead of attempting to sneak up on an enemy aircraft unseen, in the hope of inhabiting its blind spot, it could be profitable to announce one's presence by opening fire when far out of range. Experienced enemy pilots would then most likely settle into a circular pattern; one offering a sound base for maneuvering, and a difficult target as well. However, owing to circling, the always low FE2b speed over the ground was cut to almost nothing. The result was to make it that much easier to catch up with the FE2b. True, the enemy pilot had been alerted and warned that a fight was impending, but his near-zero ground speed meant that he was unable to reach a nearby safe zone, or friendly aircraft, or anti-aircraft guns. Richthofen's gain consisted of isolating the enemy. At times, when the sky held many British machines, the singling out process was profitable, despite its loss of surprise.

Thus shooting at an ultra long range had its uses, but when under pressure and shooting for destructive effect, Richthofen preferred to open fire at the close range of 50 yards.[26] Most gunnery experts preferred 100 yards, and RFC advice suggested even 200 yards as suitable.[27] Given Richthofen's concern about collision, why 50 yards rather than 100? There were some clear gains: for one, bullet spread was smaller as the range closed, increasing the probability of multiple destructive strikes on an engine or fuel tank. There was also a gain in accuracy, for smaller values of the always uncertain deflection allowance were necessary. Finally, a new and most useful factor promoting accuracy entered: tracers.

An FE2b on Display

On exhibit in Berlin as war booty, little damage is to be seen aside from the bashed-in nose, likely received upon its final landing. Source: *Luftfahrt*, March 1917, p.18.

Over great distances, tracers could be misleading. Optical illusions[28] arose to mislead and infuriate users. However, at his preferred short range of 50 yards, tracers accurately described bullet path. So perfect was its portrayal that deflection allowance and even gunsights could be ignored – instead, all aim was controlled by what was seen. In a fast changing gunfight, where no man could think quickly enough to do the necessary calculations required by deflection allowance, tracers were a superb solution. As for the short range necessary to make tracers practical, Richthofen was willing – after all, 50 yards was much safer than the 10 meters he had come to fear.

Even as Richthofen learned to cope with the well-regarded FE2, other two-seaters came under his guns – especially the ever plentiful, and generally despised BE2. When hunted by the E-III back in 1915, it proved an easy victim. Yet, unlike the Fokker, late versions of the BE2 managed to hang on, surviving to see the war's end. Though a poor fighter, other BE2 features were precisely those wanted in an artillery machine – it could land almost anywhere and had superb visibility. Especially well-liked as a long range reconnaissance machine, and fairly capable as a light bomber, it was too good a machine to discard.

As for fighting, there was always the hope that one those endless revisions of BE2 Lewis gun mounts might produce a winner – a machine able to shoot effectively – permitting survival when sharing the same sky as Richthofen.

Shown is one more gadgeteer's approach to shooting in the frontal direction. As given previously, the problem stemmed from that enormous four bladed propeller; efficient but offering severe blockage to shooting forwards. Lacking an interrupter, it was necessary to shoot at an angle to miss the propeller. This time around, the shaky "trellis" gun mounts have been eliminated in favor of mounts bolted, high up, upon the wing struts. Forced to stand, the

The Always Useful BE2c

Though a poor fighter, its simple, sturdy lines and superb vision helped it serve effectively as a light bomber and artillery observer. Source: Claude Graham-White and Harry Harper, *Air Power* (NYC: Stokes, 1917) p.241.

BE2–Dressed and Undressed

(main illustration) Uncovered fuselage skeleton with gunner up front and pilot in back; (inset) covered, largely with cloth. Sources: (main) F.W. Lanchester, *Aircraft in Warfare* (NYC: Appleton, 1916) plate 4. (inset) original by author.

BE2c Front Gun Mounts

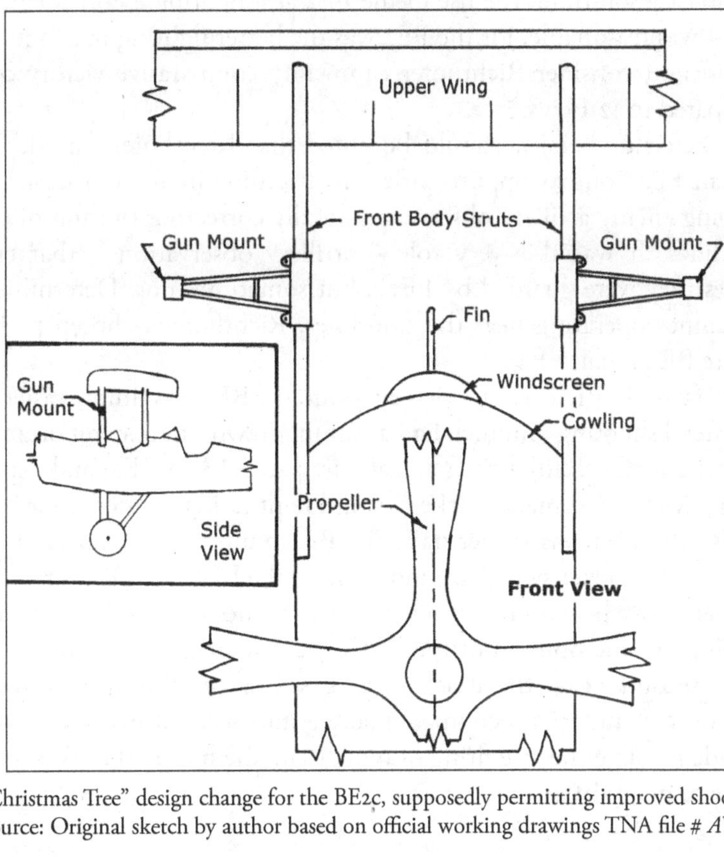

One more "Christmas Tree" design change for the BE2c, supposedly permitting improved shooting at frontal enemies. Source: Original sketch by author based on official working drawings TNA file # *AVIA* 14/5/2/33.

gunner fired at a safe, proper angle and then if required, transferred his Lewis gun between mounts as a frontal enemy aircraft passed from side to side. The advantages claimed were those of greater mount rigidity and a smaller aiming correction, owing to a decreased oblique aiming angle.

Drawbacks included: (1) the necessity for the gunner to stand with his upper body doused in the propeller blast; (2) the low shooting accuracy obtainable from any form of angled fire; and (3) the need for transferring the Lewis gun from mount to mount in the midst of action. Even RFC officials came to view the endless mount designs with contempt. For example, RFC General H. Trenchard upon inspecting a similar gun mount commented, "I never saw such ridiculous nonsense."[29]

Though shooting to the rear eliminated the propeller blockage problem, experience pointed to other difficulties, ranging from the distraction produced by shooting directly over the pilot's head, to occasional hits on the rudder or elevator. All things considered, many aircrews preferred lateral shooting, despite serious problems in estimating deflection allowance. In shooting to the side: (1) the gunner was able to crouch down, avoiding some of the air blast; (2) he was less likely to hit his own aircraft, over-excited or not; and (3) shooting took place a few feet distant from the pilot, rather than a few inches away, permitting him to concentrate upon flight rather than offer a cringing inattention.

In all, the BE2 was much inferior to the FE2 as a gun platform. While the FE2 had severe limitations, especially when shooting to the rear, it did offer superb frontal shooting. The BE2 was handicapped, front or rear, by blockage, propeller blast and gun mount problems that permitted no easy solution. The use of the FE2 as a fighting escort for the BE2 – rather than the reverse – was reasonable, for the FE2 was the better fighting machine. As confirming experimental evidence, consider Richthofen's 1916-1917 comparative victory count: 17 BE2's downed, as compared to 12 FE2's.[30]

In weighing these numbers, it should be noted that Richthofen's mode of fighting led to more BE2 than FE2 combat opportunities. To frontline infantry troops, nothing was as infuriating as flying enemy artillery observers, carefully correcting the aim of cannon located far behind the lines. It was this very role – artillery observation – that employed most BE2's. Sometimes they were guarded by FE2's, but sometimes not. Determined to eradicate observation machines operating near the frontlines, Richthofen's chosen path would come across many more BE2's than FE2's.

As a secondary factor in Richthofen's victory count, the BE2 was simply easier to shoot down. Even the BE2's lateral shooting gimmick had a painful drawback, one important enough to be fully detailed by the RFC.[31] Rather than actually fly parallel to a BE2, and expose themselves to lateral shooting, canny German attackers would feint doing so momentarily – for periods of a few seconds. The idea was to persuade the BE2 gunner to set up his Lewis for lateral shooting, all while the attacker swung around to sit on the BE2 tail. Of course, the exasperated gunner would then move his gun to a mount suited for shooting to the rear – but this would take still more time. In the opinion of the RFC, the time required "to react and realign the gun – perhaps 30 seconds" gave the attacker his "best chance." Given the usual machine gun cyclic firing rate of 10 rounds per second, and taking into account necessary pauses, the thirty second delay made possible the safe firing of more than one hundred bullets – enough bullets to decide the fate of many BE2s.

Even if a BE2 gunner was set for a rear attack, German fighter pilots soon learned a means of outwitting the defense. Rather than the usual direct attack employing a shallow dive, it was much wiser to dive vertically some distance away – too far for accurate defensive shooting from the BE2. Given the extra speed picked up in the dive, it was then possible to close in quickly under the BE2 tail, where its gunner vision and accuracy were poor, while those of the German fighter were fine indeed.[32]

Richthofen's combat reports[33] supplied highlights of his BE2 victories. His words were limited to unusual happenings, with ordinary fighting viewed as too humdrum to record. Even so, many of his tactics were revealed, as were those of the opposing RFC.

His first BE2 victory (# 8 of his 80-victory total) was gained over a machine attempting a light bombing mission, as signaled by the absence of a gunner. Here the desperate need for an increased bomb load led to eliminating the gunner to save weight, making it that much easier to down. Of all possible BE2 arrangements, the no-gunner version was the German fighter pilot's choice. However, such opportunities were rare.

More typical were victories # 19 and # 20, over BE2 machines carrying gunners. Here he was able to approach closely, unobserved, and open fire from his favorite 50 meter distance. When one of these targets proved inert, the result of a lucky early hit, he moved closer – to a distance of one aircraft length – and continued shooting. Given the right circumstances, his concern over collision was set aside. In this case, the BE2's inert behavior convinced him that there would be no erratic last moment maneuvers, and that a close approach was safe.

When a BE2 showed the presence of a gunner and plenty of life, but was cursed by a hapless desire to flee in a straight line, Richthofen employed his favorite FE2 tactic. Following at a great distance, he would fire many bullets in the belief that despite his range-limited accuracy, sheer numbers and better ballistics would win. In effect, he was betting his life on the supremacy of twin fixed guns as compared to the BE2's single flexible gun. He found the process to be both safe and generally victorious. To gain victory # 22 against a fleeing BE2, some 500 bullets were required. Essentially the same was true of # 29.

Long range shooting was not always the answer to those who fled. Some BE2 pilots attempted to use their flying skills to get down to tree top level and play a hide and seek game. Here the idea was to discourage the aggressor, for the game was equally dangerous to the prey and the pursuer – one wrong move and collision with a tree or house ended the game. Those pursued hoped that their aggressors would give up the chase – and many did – as not worth the risk.

Richthofen was well aware of his own limits as a stunt pilot. He had little natural feeling for aerobatics and for the most part flew mechanically, though with great determination. In the case of victory # 32, determination carried the day: his target, an observation BE2, flew into the ground when a tricky on-deck maneuver failed.

The rest of his BE2 victories, told in similar reports, indicate that his earlier lessons remained intact, with successful techniques used repeatedly. Typically, those attacked were artillery observation machines carrying a gunner, with the actual attack occurring near the frontlines. Always balancing the collision prospect against the needs for accurate shooting, Richthofen would approach closely if his target appeared unaware. If wide awake, he would open fire at a greater distance. Close or far, his twin fixed guns spelled the end for most of his BE2 victims, either through wounds or aircraft damage.

Two-seater German Claims

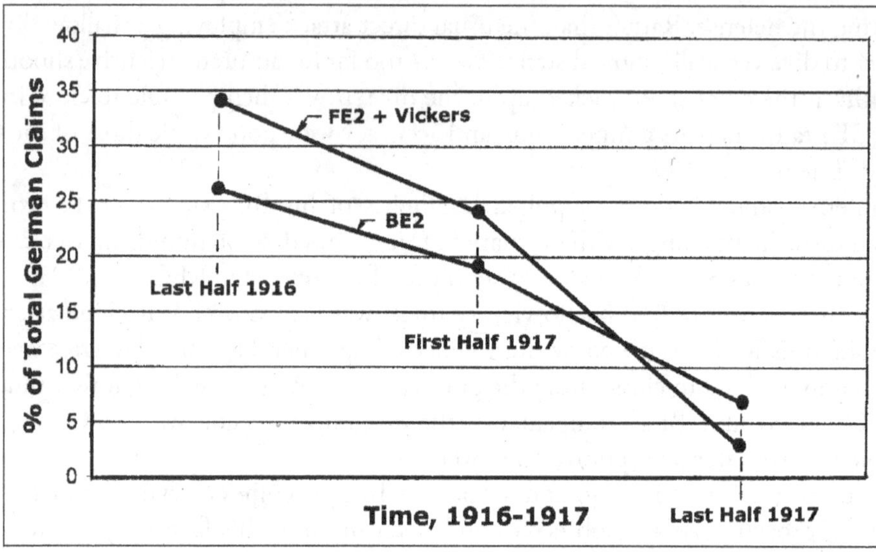

Moving into 1917, total German claims for downed FE2 and BE2 aircraft fell sharply as older types were replaced by newer designs. Source: Original plot by author from data, *Luftfahrt*, October 1918, p.16.

Next Generation RFC Two-seaters

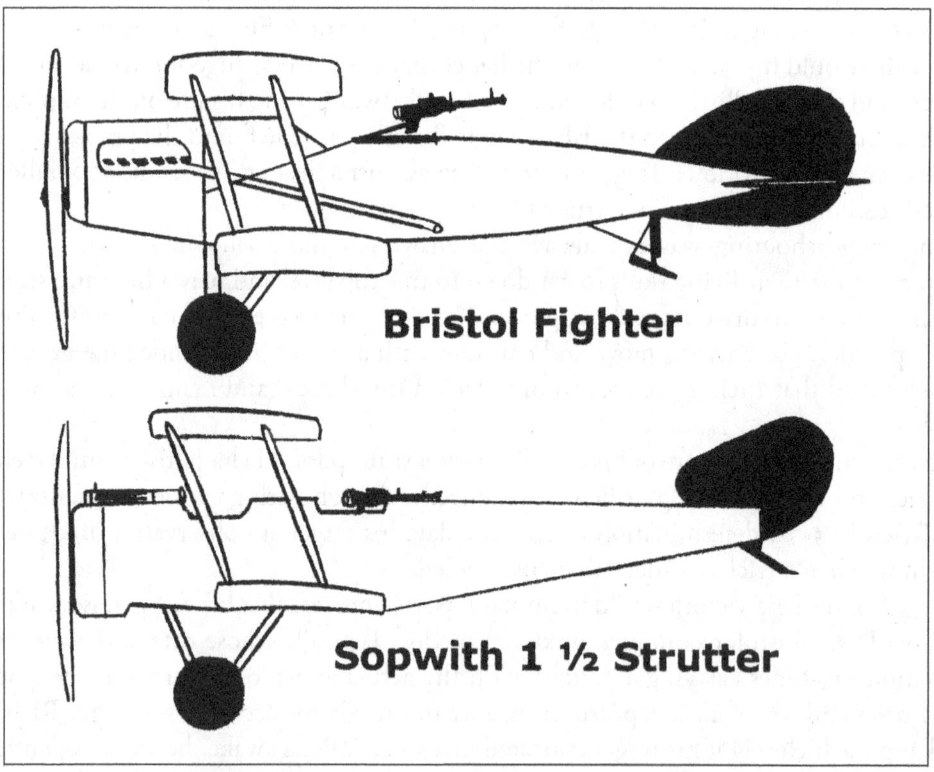

Despite improved performance and armament, they continued to fall victim to Richthofen's usual techniques. Source: Original sketches by author based on 3-views, *Flight*, February 6, 1919, pp.170-171, *Flight*, January 23, 1919, pp.102-103.

Over time, and especially after "Bloody April" of 1917, Richthofen's victories against both the BE2 and FE2 slowed and stopped. Richthofen hadn't lost his touch. Instead, having developed other two-seaters believed to be superior, the RFC had reduced the number of older two-seater types operating on the Western Front. The natural result was to cut all BE2 and FE2 losses sharply, as shown, and push Richthofen into a new learning cycle, centered upon the new machines.

Not only did the new two-seaters vary in their fighting abilities, but Richthofen's aircraft were updated as well. In effect, the same two-seater versus single-seater struggle continued, though it was played with new aircraft on each side. This time around, some of the RFC two-seaters had fixed, forward firing machine guns as well as the usual flexible Lewis guns. In another major switch, Richthofen's continually improved Albatros and Halberstadt series machines were traded in for the Fokker Triplane – a business of exchanging fast and furious aircraft for one that was slow and maneuverable. Inevitably, combat was influenced.

Did combat against two-seaters really change? Not really. Consider the Sopwith 1½ Strutter. At last able to shoot through the propeller, it offered the pilot a bolted down Vickers gun complete with interrupter. In addition, the gunner was given a Lewis gun set within an effective rear circular turret. Taken together, the resulting design would seem a sensible, up-to-date shooting combination. Yet in downing his first 1½ Strutter (victory # 23), Richthofen successfully used the same "long range + too many bullet technique" evolved to deal with the FE2. Once again, Richthofen fired 400 bullets towards his opponent[34] and the battle was over. His combat reports describing subsequent victories over 1½ Strutters (# 33 and # 38) offered no fresh tactical insight other than an account of attempted Sopwith evasion. Certainly, any RFC fighting aircraft whose defense was limited to evasion smacked of hopelessness – something was wrong.

A sense of the Sopwith 1½ Strutter problem was offered by RFC pilot Captain Balfour.[35] Carrying only 110 h.p., its performance was "vastly inferior to the Albatros in speed, climb and maneuverability." As for the updated gunnery aspects, they counted for little when measured against the deficient performance. Finally, when in a high-speed dive, "at above 160 mph, the wings were liable to come off."

Against such a monstrosity, Richthofen had little incentive to develop new fighting tactics – his old methods worked just fine. Oddly enough, this remained the case even when the opposing two-seater was a fine machine. None was better than the Bristol Fighter, equipped with a 200 h.p. Rolls-Royce. As with the Sopwith, the rear gunner had an effective turret for his Lewis and the pilot was given a bolted down Vickers. Able to climb to a fighting altitude of 10,000 feet in 11 minutes, as compared to the 1½ Strutter's 19 minutes, it offered a speed of 113 mph once there – some 10 mph more than the Sopwith.[36] In short, both a good performance and a solid platform for gunnery were offered by this rarest of wartime designs – one sound enough to survive the war and soldier on for many more years.

When a Bristol Fighter was encountered in March 1918, Richthofen opened with his usual long range shooting approach and was startled to see the gunner fire only straight upwards and then disappear from sight, presumably scrambling about for something on his cockpit floor. Offering no defensive fire, the aircraft was easily forced down. Only when about to land did the gunner emerge to offer a few defensive rounds. Of course, it was too late; and so, victory # 64 went to Richthofen.[37]

Bristol Fighter versus Fokker Triplane

The Triplane (upper right) opens fire in a shallow diving attack–a tactic frequently employed by Richthofen. Source: *The Aeroplane*, January 15, 1919, p.192.

There were encounters with yet other new breed two-seaters, including the RE8 and the Armstrong Whitworth. Yet, to the end, Richthofen remained satisfied with his old two-seater tactics – those developed in 1916 against inferior aircraft. Subsequent RFC aircraft modification was all very well, but the results did not offset the many disadvantages inherent in the RFC approach to two-seater combat.

Summing up, his quickest way to victory remained an unseen close approach, followed by execution with a few bullets. If the victim was too alert to permit this possibility, a long range fight against the gunner's single Lewis gun would do as well, though at the expense of many bullets. Here Richthofen was betting on the superiority of his bolted down guns with a relatively huge ammunition supply, as against the uncertainty of flexible gun aiming made worse by the painfully limited number of bullets contained within a Lewis supply drum. These gunnery factors, heavily favoring Richthofen, remained unchanging throughout the war.

Yet another factor that changed but little was the relative lack of experience displayed by many of his opponents. The British training system produced many pilots, but these low-time graduates usually lacked the expertise necessary for combat. Also produced were too many gunners unable to cope with simple gun jams. Inevitably these men and their machines became, if not Fokker Fodder, then Richthofen fodder.

Single-seater combat, with its promise of one against one offered a greater challenge to Richthofen – one where the numerous two-seater drawbacks were no longer a factor. Skill, speed and maneuverability were the deciding factors. Richthofen was ready.

6

Richthofen versus Scouts, 1916

Richthofen's introduction to combat had gone well, ending with the destruction of an opposing British two-seater. He had been fortunate in his background, consisting of much flight experience in equivalent German two-seaters. As a result, he knew what to expect of his opponent – the stately maneuvers and performance limits he encountered offered no surprise.

Scout combat was sensed as quite different. Knowing his own Albatros, he could grasp scout capabilities and regretfully, his own limitations. He found aerobatics difficult and gossip had it that aerobatic skills were crucial to success. It was certainly true that putting a scout control stick into the hands of Immelmann made for fancy aerobatics and that Immelmann had achieved stunning success. Cause and effect? Coincidence?

The world loves a romantic, swashbuckling hero. In a war made grim by poison gas and mud-filled trenches, it was natural that air duels featuring fancy maneuvers were treasured by the public. Here was war as it should be. Tales of aerobatic combat became the stuff of journals, including specialist aero journals. To pilots and especially beginning combat pilots, the issue was one of reality, i.e:, what portion of the aerobatic duel phenomenon was real, and what portion so much gutter journalism? To Richthofen, as a struggling early air fighter, a correct assessment was crucial.

The highly respected *Die Luftflotte* saw an important role for fancy aerobatics. In its discussion of air-fighting techniques, it offered the story of a clever looper, acting to simultaneously foil his attackers and win a dominant position, from which to destroy them.[1] Here was a complete reversal of roles, owed entirely to a loop. British aero journals offered similar loop-to-

Albatros D-II

Much used by Richthofen, it became his yardstick for measuring British fighter plane capabilities. Note superb upward vision. Source: *Flugsport*, May 1917, p.338

(translated from original) "The Tactics of Air Fighting"

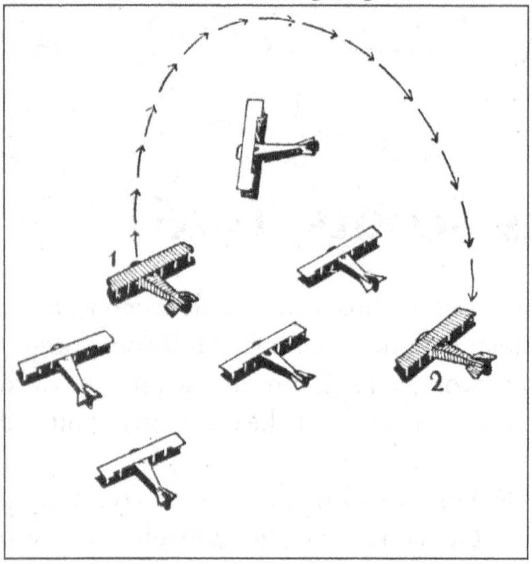

Outnumbered and under attack, clever pilot (1) performs a loop ending in new position (2). Once there, he's safe from enemy fire and well placed for launching his own attack. Source: *Die Luftflotte*, September 1918, p.194.

Alphonse Pegoud, Master of Stunt Flying

The greatest of pre-war aerobatic pilots, his skills were scorned by Richthofen as useless for air combat. Source: *AVIA* (Netherlands), June 1915, pp.159.

victory tales, some featuring precise details[2] of aircraft, time and place; impressive compilations smacking of the truth. To the press, the moral was clear: mastery of the aerobatic arts was the key to air combat success.

To Richthofen, this view was disturbing. Comparing himself to the famous French pre-war aerobatic specialist Alphonse Pegoud, he announced for open publication (Spring 1917): "I am not a Pegoud, and I do not wish to be a Pegoud … a flying man may be able to loop and do all the tricks imaginable and yet not succeed in shooting down a single enemy … the aggressive spirit is everything."[3]

Detailing his anti-aerobatic views in a confidential internal Air Service study, and singling out those very loops relished by the press, he wrote (also Spring 1917): "Looping the loop is worthless in air fighting. Each loop is a great mistake … a loop only offers a big advantage to the adversary."[4] More generally, he believed: "Many English airmen try to win advantages by flying tricks while engaged in fighting, but as a rule, it is just these reckless and useless stunts that lead them to their deaths."[5]

Clearly, Richthofen's views were strongly held. Certainly, there is no doubt as to his early 1917 position. Right or wrong, they reflected his 1916 experience combined with a mixture of personal bias and sound logic – the usual stew we prepare in order to arrive at a practical position in a too complex world.

For bias, there was his use of famed Pegoud to exemplify all-out aerobatic piloting. One of the earliest of aces (6 victories), French Air Service pilot Pegoud was shot dead by the rear gunner of a two-seater in August 1915. At the time, much was written about his career and the details[6] were certainly known to Richthofen. He reacted by treating the air combat death of Pegoud as proof of aerobatic ineffectiveness – no man could hope to be more proficient and yet, what good had it done him? Where was the gain?

The death of Pegoud was unrelated to aerobatics. Instead, he had been caught up in a shooting duel against a two-seater. The tactics employed were of the gun-versus-gun type sometimes used by Richthofen. However, the technical limitations of Pegoud's aircraft were much more severe. For example, Pegoud's fighter lacked an interrupter, instead requiring firing through its own propeller disk area – despite inevitable hits on the propeller. Finally, his luck was bad.

According to the *Berliner Tageblatt*,[7] victorious German pilot Walter Kandulski was initially attacked by Pegoud in the usual shoot-from-behind fashion. Return fire was offered by the two-seater's rear gun. However, after about 30 rounds, the rear gun jammed. The pilot then started a defensive circle, hoping to make Pegoud's shooting task more difficult. Well understanding the sudden lack of return fire, Pegoud closed in for the kill, only to find that the jam had been cleared by the frantic rear gunner. Pegoud himself, just yards away, had suddenly become an easy target. He was hit by a bullet to the head and killed.

Though certainly a brave man, it wasn't enough. The combination of bad technology, too close an approach, and terrible luck was too much and he lost out. Despite Richthofen's statement, aggressive spirit alone was not "everything". The right tools and tactics were essential, along with much luck.

A pro-aerobatic advocate might argue that Pegoud would have been wiser to employ his noted aerobatic skills to either confuse the two-seater gunner, or to occupy the two-seater's blind spot, rather than to approach closely in a shooting duel. In other words, the death of Pegoud could well be interpreted as a *vote for aerobatics*. Far from drawing that conclusion, Richthofen chose the opposite possibility instead.

As a part of his justification, Richthofen damned the loop. In truth, there were disturbing factors in looping. The loop sketched below, successfully shifting a fighter plane's role from that of a target to an aggressor, required an exquisite sense of control stick force application and timing, along with many hours of practice. Even then, a number of things could go wrong.

Loops – Good and Bad

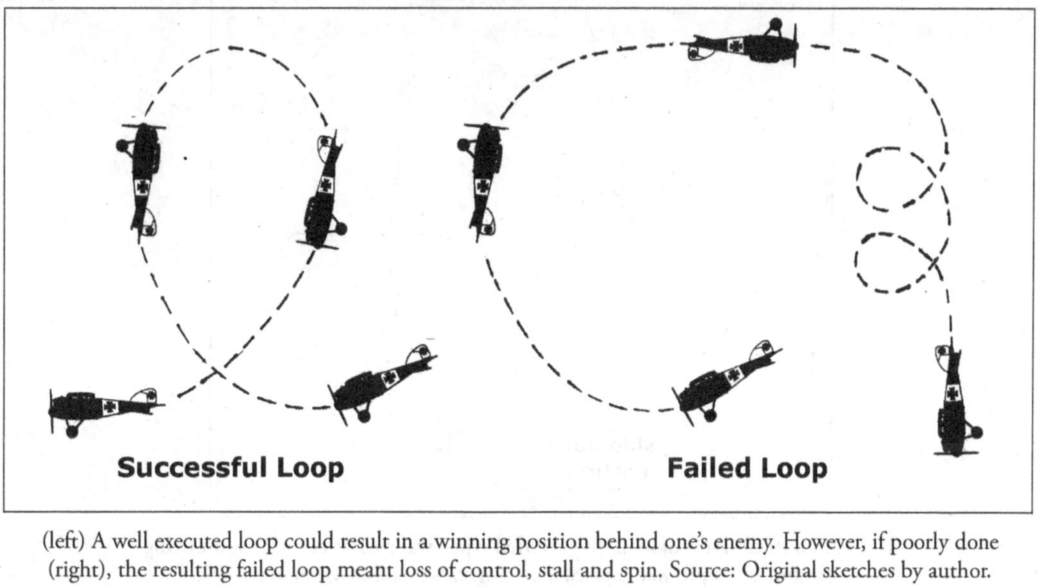

(left) A well executed loop could result in a winning position behind one's enemy. However, if poorly done (right), the resulting failed loop meant loss of control, stall and spin. Source: Original sketches by author.

For one, aircraft of the time were incapable of looping from the horizontal start shown, owing to a lack of engine power. Instead, it was necessary to first dive through a considerable change of altitude, building speed. Surrounded by attackers, it was likely that a hopeful looper would be shot down before he acquired enough speed to loop.

Looping was speed sensitive in other ways as well. Once into a loop with too little speed at hand, many aircraft had a tendency to "hang" at the top or upside down position. Breaking out of a failed loop usually involved loss of control, ending in a stall and spin. Should there be enough speed to complete the loop, there was still a question of the loop size and form, largely determined by the instantaneous speed of the wings meeting air in a slightly differently fashion each step of the way as the aircraft went around. Predicting the resulting loop format – ranging from a narrow, or up and down spike to a generous circle – was beyond the abilities of most pilots, even those who were highly experienced.

The loss of speed implicit in the looping maneuver was of itself a strong negative factor to Richthofen. He believed that a fast speed and high altitude were the most important virtues possessed by an aircraft moving towards combat. With superior speed and altitude, he could flee or attack as he chose. Without these, he was merely somebody else's target, with no say in the matter. Guided by this outlook, even the temporary loss of speed experienced on the up-going side of a loop seemed a threat.

As a final discouragement, with engine power output so heavily dependent upon altitude, knowledge gained from the practicing of loops at one altitude might well be useless should combat take place at a different height. In short, looping as a tactic had many genuine drawbacks.

To Richthofen, the single most important measure of tactic acceptability was reliability. To aid his planning, certainty was wanted. Anything smacking of loss of control was out. Looping,

Pegoud's Outside Loop

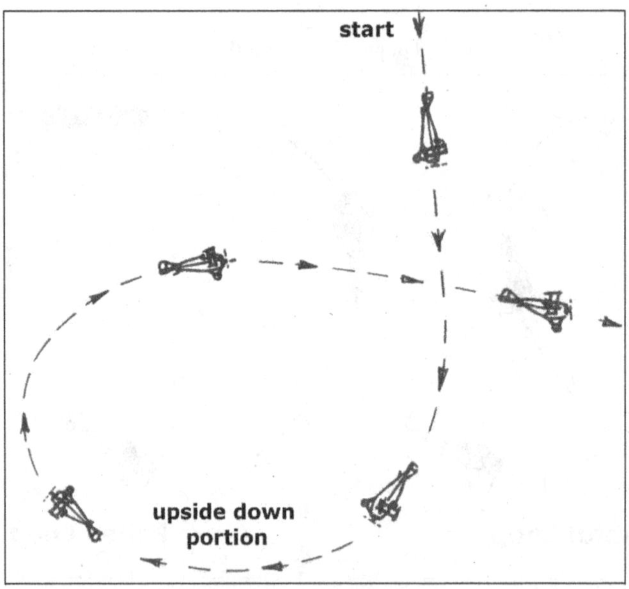

This most difficult form of loop–the inverted type– was part of Pegoud's stunt flying exhibitions in pre-war days. Source: *Flight*, September 27, 1913, p.1066.

with all its risks and possible nightmare conclusion – finding oneself stalled and upside down in a failed loop – was out of serious consideration.

Another form of loop – the outside loop – also widely associated with Pegoud was, if anything, assessed as worse. The resulting G loading on man and machine was severe and it was quite possible to sustain personal injury or aircraft damage, even in a well executed outside loop. In short, as Richthofen saw it, advocates were not only wrong, they were dangerous fools.

In addressing the aerobatics issue, he had moved a great distance from his original, open minded, beginner's stance. The change reflected his own skill, plus lack of certain skills, together with the application of much pointed logic. All was finally tested against two major influences: Boelcke's teachings, and those of his own combat experience.

Boelcke stood for simplicity and direct action. His 1916 dicta advocated no form of trickery. Instead, he offered only straightforward common sense. The result was a less than perfect fit to reality; in part, because so little was known of air combat at the time. A second limitation was the deliberate avoidance of many awkward aspects of combat. For example, it was all very well to advocate attack from the rear (see dicta # 5) but what of real life tactical situations where only frontal attack was possible? Was a frontal attack merely less than optimum, or truly wrong? If not a winning move, was it a losing move? On this sort of sticky issue, Boelcke had nothing to say. Unhappily, there were many such unmentioned matters.

Richthofen, an appreciative pupil of Boelcke, was determined to carry on his work. Loops were a poor fit to Boelcke's philosophy of straightforward attack. Furthermore, loops required some loss of eye contact with the enemy: a violation of dicta #4. In short, looping was suspect and unlikely to gain Richthofen's support, unless it demonstrated some saving merit. What of his own combat experience? True, combat against British two-seaters had produced no enthusiasm for aerobatics, but what about their livelier single-seaters? Wasn't looping of some use in keeping up with single-seater maneuvers?

October 1916 saw the initial three Richthofen victories over single-seaters – by chance, all BE12's. He was not impressed with their capabilities. His combat reports[8] offered nothing about maneuvers – aerobatics were never an issue. Instead, he noted the considerable altitude at which combat occurred – as much as 10,000 feet – a height suppressing engine power and therefore acting to curtail aerobatics. As in his two-seater combat, the number of rounds fired was in the high hundreds (350, 400, 500) – numbers suggesting not duels, or a struggle for superior position followed by an execution – but a remote and leisurely outpouring of bullets, offered in the belief that given enough time some would strike home.

In effect, he treated the BE12 single-seater as though it was one more sluggish two-seater. If anything, he found the BE12 to be an easier opponent than the usual two-seater, for there was no rear gunner to deal with. As for the anticipated single-seater high maneuverability, no such ability was apparent. Three combats at various altitudes convinced him that high altitude alone wasn't to blame – something else accounted for the BE12's lack of liveliness.

The British largely agreed. Read between the lines, the official British BE12 test pilot's judgement was damning: "This machine, if possible, is almost easier to fly and land as the BE2c … an excellent machine for night flying and Zeppelin chasing."[9]

What seems to be praise described a low maneuverability type of aircraft; an easy to fly machine far removed from the twisted, mean spirited, high maneuverability type. The BE12 was simply one more peaceful, highly stable aircraft. Landing slowly and without tricks, it was suited for night flying at a time when airstrip illumination was poor. Despite the lack of a

BE12 Fighter in close-up

A "booty" aircraft presents its side-mounted Vickers machine gun, unhappily located too far from the pilot's cockpit (extreme right). Source: *Luftfahrt*, March 1917, p.18.

serious aerobatic capability, it was capable of hounding Zeppelins, for those swollen monsters offered even less in the way of stunt flying ability. In short, BE12 maneuverability shortcomings prevented any comparison with the livelier set of contemporary single-seaters, such as the Nieuport Bébé. As a result, all-out aerobatics – loops included – were unnecessary in dealing with the BE12. Richthofen's assessment and tactics were exactly right.

What of friskier machines? What of British hopes for the DH2? Was it truly maneuverable or merely one more hapless fighting aircraft of the too stable, too stately persuasion? Employed to take on Richthofen's D-II, was it really capable of doing the job or was it just one more over-matched loser?

The DH2 had its good points. In some ways, it was superior to the Albatros D-II. One major virtue was a low gross weight, leading to a light wing loading, with each square foot of DH2 wing area carrying less weight than the D-II's: specifically, 27% less.[10] Given a lighter wing loading, the necessary flight speed required to generate sufficient lift was correspondingly less. The result was a lower minimum flight velocity for the DH2 as compared to the heavier D-II aircraft. The profit was real, for in a circling duel, the winning innermost circle was flown at the slowest speed possible. In short, the DH2's ability to fly at a lower speed met one of the key requirements for getting to the innermost circle.[11]

However, there was another crucial need for inner circle flight: great power. Flying slowly in a tight circle at the usual banked attitude produced much drag, which required extra offsetting power. Without enough power, a circling machine would lose altitude and become a tempting

Competing Fighters, 1916

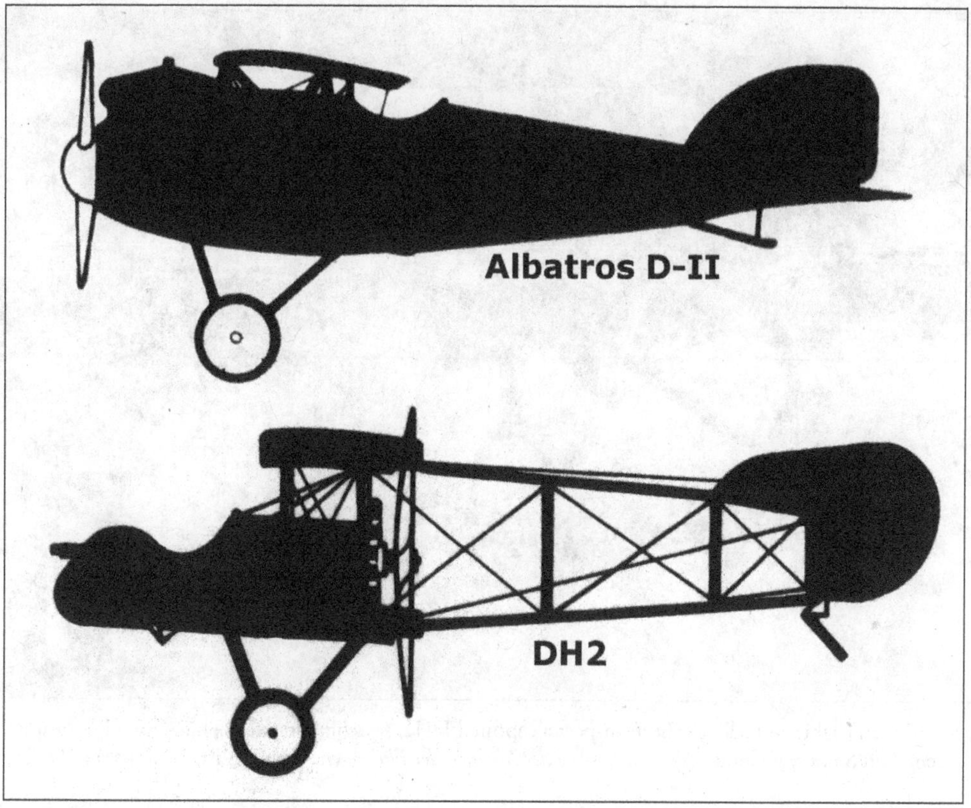

(top) The German Albatros was superior in terms of power and reliability. (bottom) De Havilland's machine offered a lower wing loading, leading to better maneuverability. Richthofen strongly preferred his Albatros. Source: Original sketches by author from 3-views in *L'Aérophile*, June 1917, p.203.

target for its more powerful opponent. Altitude could always be converted into speed, and so the more powerful machine's fully retained altitude permitted a diving attack upon a lower opponent. It was only necessary to leave the pursuit circle and dive on the enemy – a simple procedure.

In short, success in a circular duel depended on both one's wing loading and available power. Of these, the DH2 was superior in wing loading but inferior in power. It carried a French-designed Gnome Monosoupape rotary engine of 100 h.p. output – much lower than the D-II's 160 h.p. Mercedes – and offered much less reliability in the bargain.

Unfortunately, the low weight of the DH2 rotary – helpful in reducing wing loading – was obtained by accepting a dreadful engine capable of valve failure after a few hours of frontline flying. In contrast, the heavy Mercedes won a reputation for reliability; one known and respected even by the British.

Their profiles hint at the nature of the machines. We see a heavy, streamlined, powerful Albatros D-II tractor, as against a frilly, lightweight DH2 pusher. Neither was ideally suited for all-out aerobatics – the D-II was too heavy and the DH2 too limited by power constraints and diving limits.

Yet, both the D-II and the DH2 made for effective fighters. If unable to shine at stunt flying, each managed to be an able practitioner of pursuit circle dueling – always an important talent. The success of each type supported Richthofen's growing belief that aerobatics capability of

Checking the Enemy

Richthofen (right) and fellow officers inspect a captured DH2, searching for weak points useful in future combat. Source: Johannes Werner, *Boelcke der Mensch, der Flieger, etc.* (Leipzig: Koehler, 1932) p.188.

itself was unimportant. Too many other other factors shared the spotlight. There were forced choices to be made between a fast tractor as against a slow pusher offering better visibility; between a single Lewis gun without an obstructing propeller as against multiple Maxims and an interrupter; between the ability to evade through steep diving, as against survival despite serious injury, through no-hands stability. Indeed, the list of painful and uncertain choices was endless. In a world too full of choices, extreme maneuverability and stunt flying seemed merely one more option, and a largely profitless one at that.

One problem with Richthofen's early maneuverability assessment was a lack of personal stunt flying experience, either his own, or that performed by British enemies. However, in the special area of circular duels, Richthofen's experience was considerable, for his D-II met and fought against the DH2 type, producing victories starting in November, 1916.

To British DH2 pilots anxious to draw maximum power from their feeble engines, the altitude of the duel was critical, for Gnome output fell off badly at a high altitude; certainly more severely than did the competing Mercedes. As a result, the best tactic for the British was to engage on the deck; while for the Germans, it was best to fight only at upper altitudes. If combat started at a medium altitude, the natural tendency for all circular duels to drift downwards – the result of power inadequate to meet desperate pilot demands – produced tactical concerns of its own. At some low altitude, it was best for the D-II to quit, for the bottom 1000 feet belonged to the DH2.

On top of these basic tactics and worries came the special issue of one's own engine. All pilots sweated the number of flying hours between overhauls. Performance suffered as post overhaul hours accumulated. In the case of the Gnome, too many hours could well mean a dead engine – a final stoppage, delivered without warning.

Seeking victory #11 in November 1916, Richthofen engaged a DH2 at 10,000 feet.[12] Entering into a circular duel, he was surprised to find an opponent who was his equal in every respect. Many minutes later,[13] circling all the while and down to a low 1600 feet, it was time to think about ending the duel. Other tactical considerations weighed in: they were well behind German lines, with the prevailing wind towards German held territory, and despite an anticipated Gnome power surge at low altitude, the English pilot's circle showed no sign of improvement. To simply continue the same tight circling down to the ground meant surrender for the British pilot.

Major Lanoe G. Hawker's hopes for much improved engine performance and resulting victory at a lower altitude had failed – victim of one more lemon Gnome engine. Instead of winning the circling duel as he neared the ground, he found that he could barely hold his own position relative to Richthofen. A change of tactics was necessary. He broke from the circle and tried a diving exit towards the frontlines, about half a mile away.

Richthofen followed, satisfied to shoot too many rounds (his estimate: 900) at a remote and fleeing target, certain that some bullets would hit home. He was correct: though one of Richthofen's twin guns jammed, Hawker was shot dead.

Learning afterwards that his opponent had been a famous ace, known for aerobatics in the Immelmann style, Richthofen employed Hawker's death as further support for his ever-stronger anti-aerobatics stance. After all, what had Hawker achieved with his special skills? True, given an aircraft with an inferior engine, he had been able to match Albatros turning ability – an effort requiring great aerobatic skill on Hawker's part. But to what end? Avoiding lemon engines mattered, not aerobatics.

Richthofen's next victory (# 12, December 1916)[14] was also gained through a circular duel. In this match a less able pilot – again flying a DH2 – lasted for only a short fight at about 9000 feet. Next came (# 13, December 1916)[15] a lengthy replay of the Hawker circular duel struggle, also against a DH2 as opponent, but with a different ending. Losing patience, Richthofen crossed the circle's diameter to open fire a plane length away – defying his own concerns over collision – and succeeded instantly.

With all his 1916 experience pointing in one direction, his assurance concerning the worthlessness of all-out aerobatics was complete. To Richthofen, what counted was the right aircraft – fast and powerful – together with a set of no-nonsense tactics. If the British foolishly pushed the fancier aerobatic skills as crucial, too bad for them.

Of course, some elementary stunts and maneuvers were necessary to change position or altitude. At times a full knowledge of maneuvers was required in order to pursue enemies – especially those fools convinced that some tricky maneuver was a sure path to victory. For these practical reasons, Richthofen studied and practiced the more popular maneuvers. Truly profitable was the sideslip.

In its simplest form one flew with a great deal of yaw, produced by rudder offset, automatically losing altitude while continuing to move in the same basic direction. In effect, one was flying slightly sideways, with the resulting high drag causing a drop in altitude. To end the process, the rudder was simply returned to neutral. Every pilot made occasional use of the notion in landing: if coming in too high, a bit of slip corrected matters by cutting altitude. In combat, full-scale sideslip made judgement of one's flight direction difficult for an enemy,

Advanced Side-slip

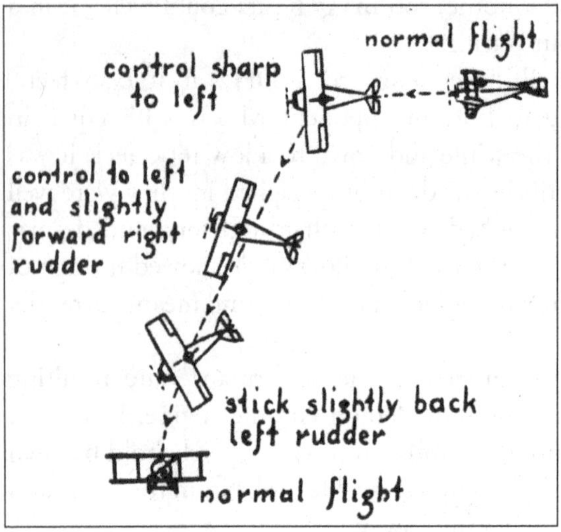

A useful maneuver offering a difficult target and a quick loss of altitude. Source: *Aerial Age Weekly*, November 4, 1918, p.422.

Spin

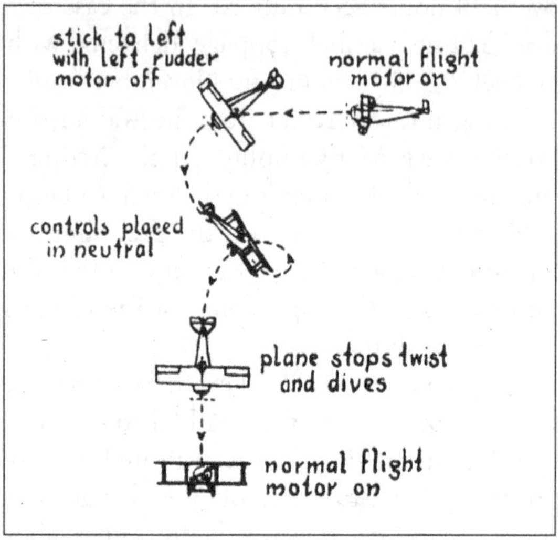

If real, a spin meant a major problem on board; if faked, a trap for those willing to follow. Tricksters delighted in this one. Source: *Aerial Age Weekly*, November 4, 1918, p.422.

for the resulting aircraft flight path trajectory was at some uncertain angle with the fuselage centerline. As a result, shooting allowance became a matter of guesswork.

The French version shown was ambitious, simultaneously cutting altitude and changing direction to permit as much as a 90° angular shift of flight path. To a pursuing enemy unfamiliar with the maneuver, confusion was likely and accurate shooting impossible. However, with enough practice all became predictable – and so offered little gain. Richthofen's response was to work at becoming a knowledgeable, practiced pursuer; one impossible to fool.

A spin was a more effective way of evasion through loss of altitude, for the spin's wild spiraling descent offered recovery and gunnery problems to those enemies daring to follow. The likelihood of unwanted spin was real enough to all pilots, with stalled wings first, plus some yaw, leading the way. Even cautiously flown aircraft were vulnerable, sometimes inducing spin as a result of a failed maneuver or a broken flying surface. No aircraft type was exempt: even the docile BE2, if pushed beyond its limits, would spin readily.[16]

Despite the grim atmosphere surrounding spin, spin in combat was frequently employed as a deception, fooling attackers by pretending serious or even fatal injury. Faked spins were especially useful as a ploy for those on the receiving end of heavy attack, with the spin convincing the attacker that he had succeeded in hitting hard. Should the attacker follow his fast descending victim, he might be caught out by an instantaneous spin recovery at a much lower altitude: fake spins were frequently used as traps.

Real or fake? Never an easy call, the spin's sense of impending calamity attracted users who saw profit in the wild gyrations. One such was Richthofen's younger brother and sometimes fellow combat flier, Lothar. Fiercely competitive and well aware of Manfred's disdain for trickery, Lothar practiced a form of one-upmanship by deliberately using the faked spin in Manfred's presence.[17] Introduced whenever the immediate opposition seemed too skillful, his faked spin was usually followed downwards by an opponent sensing victory and seeking a confirming crash. Instead, upon nearing the ground Lothar would suddenly use his speed and power bonus to get above the surprised enemy; and once there, to blast him.

Manfred was unmoved by Lothar's success with faked spins. A spin was of itself a worrisome thing, offering an iffy recovery path that was never certain. Another serious drawback was the inability to see one's opponent steadily, if at all, while spinning. As spinning tactics broke important rules, they were suspect at best.

His brother's very use was an additional negative vote. Tricks were all very well for Lothar, who lacked the right hunting instincts and therefore twisted air combat into a strange, hardly recognizable game. In Manfred's considered view, "Lothar was a butcher, not a sportsman."[18]

Some slight chance did exist for combat pilots to fight a noble war; a war rather like a series of duels, where one might respect a fallen enemy. To Manfred, this chance was worth pursuing, for otherwise all was mindless destruction of the poison gas or monster cannon type. Trickery could not lead to the desired result. To generate respect, fair play was necessary. As guidance concerning acceptable, if sly practice, best were those hunting rules found honorable over the centuries. For example, there was hunting's "flushing a covey", used to excite game birds into flight. In this ploy, shots were fired without aiming, simply to urge the birds to take wing.

His own version of this tactic consisted of opening fire much too early at an out of range enemy; spooking the previously unwary opponent into a fearful retreat, seeking his side of the lines and safety. This form of straight line exit was exactly suited for an attack by Richthofen's higher performance machine; with the straight line aspect making accurate shooting easy. Soon caught up, his enemy would be readily destroyed. True, a trick of sorts was involved, but it was of the approved hunting type. His contempt was directed at the other kind: aerobatic trickery. Here, practitioners flew striking but pointless maneuvers aimed at deception instead of attending to business: that of attack or defense.

Not all maneuvers made for trickery. A quick turn about was essential for all combat fliers. Both the Immelman turn and the similar French *renversement* successfully changed flight direction. To French ultras, the Immelmann turn was simply a warmed over copy of their own

Renversement

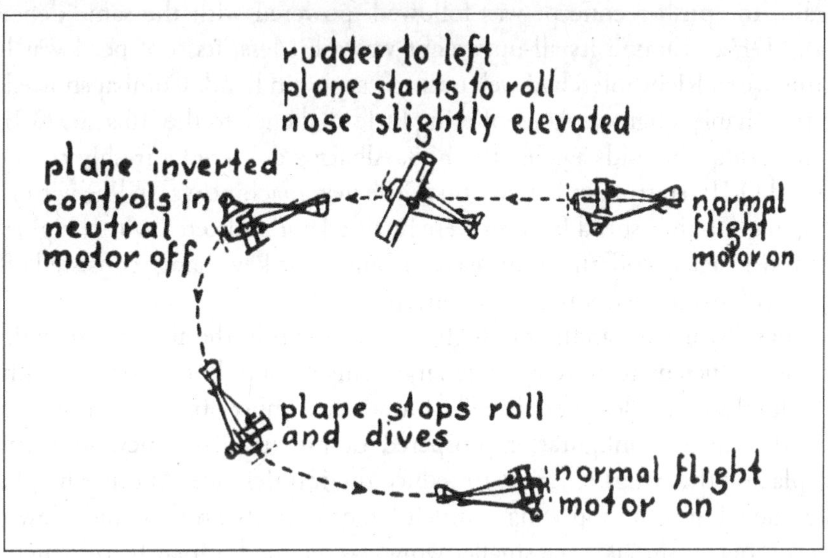

The standard pre-war means of quickly reversing flight direction. Source: *Aerial Age Weekly*, November 4, 1918, p.422.

Last of the Pusher Fighters –FE8

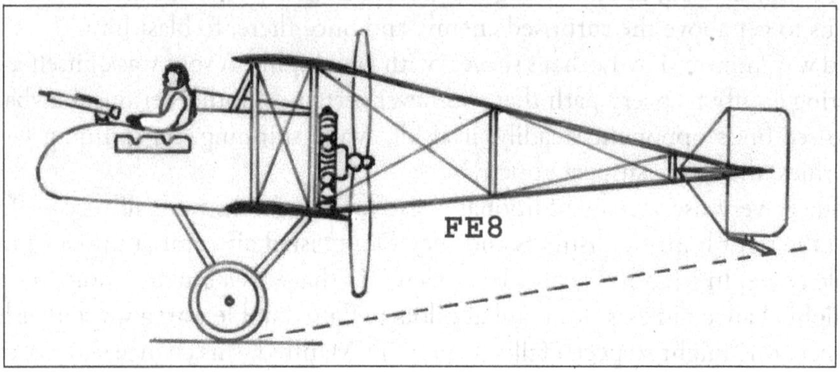

One more mediocre aircraft, low in performance and cursed with an unreliable engine, this RFC scout came and went in 1916-1917. Source: *Flugsport*, July 1917, p.430.

pre-war *renversement*. Of the two, the *renversement* usually resulted in a greater altitude loss. In making a choice, pilots reasoned that superior altitude was essential for most forms of attack, and so for the most part favored the Immelmann. However, those trained in pre-war days sometimes continued with the more familiar *renversement*.

To Richthofen, the Immelmann was superior because attack logic favored it. Yet he found it necessary to master the *renversement*, for he might find himself in pursuit of one of its practitioners. Indeed, far from fading away, the *renversement* was attractive to hopeful tricksters because it lent itself to a faked spin. We suspect that the pressure to acquire unwanted aerobatic expertise – largely because some enemy pilots thought well of tricky maneuvers – increased his resentment of both tricksters and aerobatics.

Better than trickery was the right aircraft – a fast one capable of a high climbing rate – but the British seemed incapable of changing their ways. Late in 1916, with the woes of the DH2 known, came the FE8 of similar appearance, presumably offering a revised, up to date fighter capability.

Once again, the pusher concept was followed, powered with the same deficient engine burdening the DH2. Though its all-up weight was a bit less, its top speed was less than 95 mph[19] at a time when Richthofen had well over 105 mph[20] in hand. Combat showed the FE8 to be but one more hapless fighter plane, offering little challenge to the Albatros D-II.

Further increasing the odds against the FE8, Albatros delivered a freshly re- designed and much improved D-III, starting in January 1917. The new machine was in line with Richthofen's wishes: the twin gun, high-speed features were retained and bolstered with a higher climb rate, all placed within a package offering improved visibility. The key change consisted of new wings, largely "borrowed" from Nieuport design concepts.

Biplane wings disturb one another in flight. Each wing roils the air through which the other passes. It is more efficient to have a single large wing to supply the necessary lift. However, Great War fighter aircraft designers usually found this impossible for reasons of stress and strain, and so the biplane configuration prospered, despite its inefficiency. Some gain could be achieved by placing the wings far apart to reduce the interference. Another helpful approach was to make one wing – the top wing – much larger than its brother, and draw the bulk of the lift from this bigger surface. The smaller wing was retained primarily for structural reasons, its low value of generated lift minimizing the roiling of the air though which the large wing moved. Such was the D-III.

Though its reduced total wing area meant less drag, there was a price involved – wing loading increased, making tight circling that much more difficult. Other design factors were pushed, seeking a compensating gain. Rounded wing tips were introduced, as were "trapezoidal" ailerons. Finally the engine output was boosted.

When all was done, the greater efficiency produced a profit – less drag at any speed. How to best use the profit? There were two possibilities: faster speed or a higher climb rate. We would expect a compromise: some modest improvement in each. Not so. As the old D-II was much faster than opposing British machines, its speed was ruled sufficient and retained rather than improved in the D-III. Instead, the profit was poured into climb by carving the propeller blade angles a bit differently. At low altitude levels,[21] the D-III climb rate was upped by 25% as compared to the D-II. Eliminated was the only area of DH2 performance superiority – low altitude climb rate. Compared using the yardstick of performance, both the DH2 and its brother aircraft the FE8 were decidedly inferior to the D-III.

Revising the Albatros

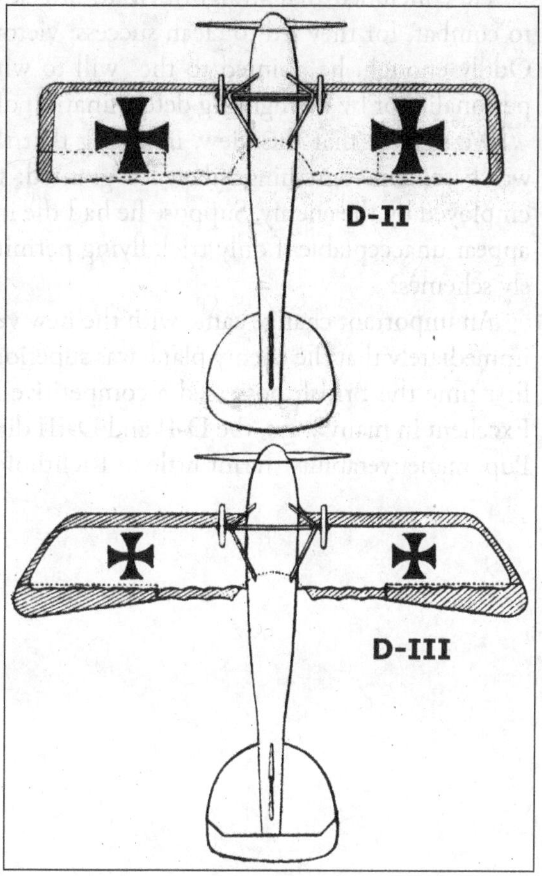

The updated D-III of 1917 was given less wing area, but used it more efficiently. After adding more power, the result was a much higher climb rate. Source: *L'Aérophile*, June 1917, pp.203-204.:

There were D-III problems: early wing failures when diving steeply, required a lengthy de-bugging process. Once corrected, the D-III represented a striking improvement over the D-II. Despite a large supply of competing German fighter aircraft, it would serve as a first line machine for many months in 1917 – as able as any.

To a considerable extent, Richthofen's anti-aerobatic stance was made possible by the performance superiority of his D-II and D-III machines as compared to those of his British opponents. With a lead in speed, climb and dive, he could dictate whether and when combat would occur. Against his enemy's sluggish fighters, simple tactics prevailed; he learned that many victories came from pursuing frightened pilots at a safe distance, simply filling the sky with bullets. Given a machine as capable at circling as any possessed by the enemy, he could win circular duels without concern for stunts. If matters grew unpleasant, he could leave at any time without employing tricks of the faked spin type. Instead, he could exit simply by diving away at high-speed. No enemy was capable of following.

He concluded that straightforward attack or retreat were the only reasonable approaches to combat, for they led to clean success; victory without the sleazier aspects of aerial trickery. Oddly enough, he pointed to the "will to win" as all-important. "The thing is done by the personality or by the fighting determination of the airman."[22]

We suspect that this view, implying that the individual counted more than the machine, was based on something taken for granted: the superiority of his fighter airplane to those employed by the enemy. Suppose he had the inferior machine? What then? Would trick flying appear unacceptable if only trick flying permitted him to survive? What price his rejection of sly schemes?

An important change came with the new year. In a fight occurring on January 1917 he "saw immediately that the enemy plane was superior to ours."[23] It was the new Sopwith Pup. For the first time the British possessed a competitive fighter, and a highly maneuverable one at that. Excellent in many ways, the D-II and D-III did not excel in maneuverability aspects. Until the Pup, maneuverability meant little to Richthofen. What of the future?

7

Maneuverability Triumphs, 1917

Beyond noting his first sighting of a Sopwith Pup, Richthofen paid it little attention for it came at a time (January 1917) crowded with important professional achievements. In recognition of his 16 victories, he received the *Pour le Mérite* award ('the Blue Max'), Prussia's highest military award. Simultaneously, another form of award came with his appointment as commander of *Jagdstaffel* 11 [i.e., Pursuit Squadron 11; abbreviated: *Jasta*].

Of the two awards, he preferred the medal,[1] for it was that rarest of gifts – one without drawbacks. In contrast, the command position was laden with problems. It would take time and public relations pressure before he was able to describe this task as "delightful."[2]

One of his many command concerns was the assembling of a logical approach to the issue of maneuvers and maneuverability – an issue highlighted by the Pup. Before the Pup, Richthofen could afford to dismiss aerobatics and trick flying, opting instead for speed as a fighter's most important property,[3] and straightforward attack from behind as the best tactic. Given the reality of the Pup, he was forced to consider a fresh enemy approach – one that combined good speed, a high climb rate and *superb maneuverability.* How was this to be treated? What should be done in the way of preparation?

A fighting aircraft possessing speed and climb capabilities roughly matching that of its enemy could well force the resulting action, pushing some preferred form of combat upon its

Performance: British Fighting Aircraft 1914–1917

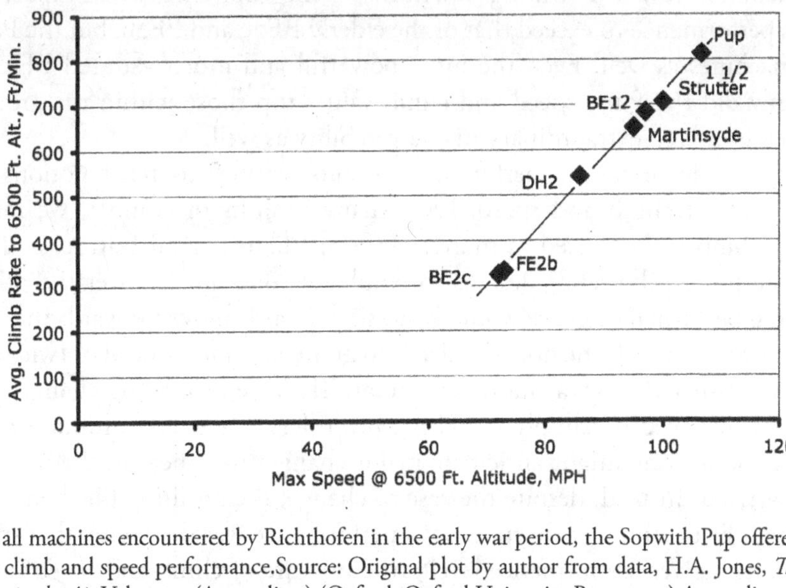

Of all machines encountered by Richthofen in the early war period, the Sopwith Pup offered the best climb and speed performance.Source: Original plot by author from data, H.A. Jones, *The War in the Air* Volume 7 (Appendices) (Oxford: Oxford University Press, 1937) Appendix 27.

Performance: British Fighting Aircraft 1914–1917
Trend Lines Only

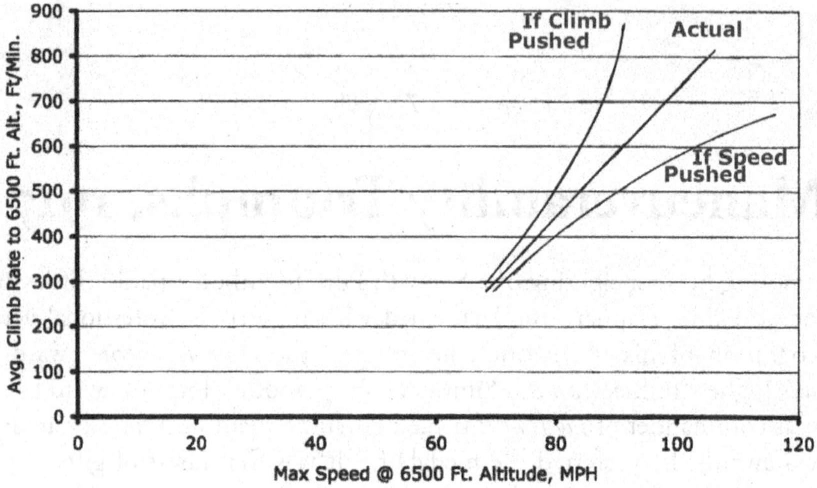

Aircraft performance could be altered to emphasize either climb or speed. The actual straight line performance output over the years suggests satisfaction with the blend.
Source: Original plot by author, based on previous performance sketch.

opponent – such as the aerobatic duel. Under these conditions maneuverability couldn't be ignored. Might not combat take on an entirely different perspective?

In 1916, the British had no such machine, and the question was entirely academic. Boelcke's truisms proved sufficient to deal with the resulting straightforward form of combat. Well and good, but what of the Pup and 1917? As a first hurdle, just how good was the Pup? Did it offer enough performance to qualify as a serious contender?

Accepting speed and climb rate as key performance criteria, a plot of official values[4] for early British war machines shows the striking superiority of the Pup. One would expect almost any 1917 machine's performance to exceed that of the elderly BE2c and FE2b, but the Pup bettered more recent machines as well. Even the more powerful and much vaunted BE12 was easily bested. Not only did the Pup's speed and climb values top those within the group but as a bonus, the aircraft offered extraordinary maneuverability as well.

The straight line form of the performance results testifies to fixed notions about the relative importance of climb and speed. Over many months of combat, we might expect either speed or climb to be sensed as more significant than its rival feature, and as a result, newer and more powerful aircraft designs to emphasize one quality over the other. In this case the resulting performance curve would bend slightly as it moved towards the right, either drooping downwards towards the horizontal axis to grant a bit more speed or twisting upwards to reflect the belief that climb was more important. The ease of making changes in the field – much could be achieved by simply switching propellers – acted to promote performance modification. In short, one might anticipate major changes to appear in the output curve as newer aircraft arrived. Instead, despite the ease of change, the resulting line bends neither up or down. Though British hunger for more *total* performance was desperate, that special blend of factors defining a given performance level – the mixture of climb and speed – was viewed as just right.

Whether its design represented an optimum combination of speed and climb or not, there was no doubt about German respect for the Pup. Details from captured aircraft were assembled by *Idflieg* (Air Service Intelligence) and published as instructional aids for interested buffs and technical workers.

Of course, German praise had limits. Speed was still king and as pointed out by *Leutnant* Werner Voss[5] the Pup was slower than the standard Albatros fighter, though superior in climb and "handling", i.e., maneuverability. Lacking in speed, the Pup could not quite force an Albatros to fight on its own terms – the German fighter could always speed away if the odds seemed bad. Given this limitation, what did maneuverability offer, i.e., maneuverability combined with a lower top speed?

Consider a simple case: maneuverability in defense; not the complexities of the circular duel, but defense against a straightforward, classic attack from above and behind. The cardinal rule of defense against this possibility was simple: "never let the enemy machine get behind you."[6] As usual with sound advice, the sticky part was in the implementation – in this case, preventing an enemy from occupying a superior attack position. Given enough combat

A German Appreciation

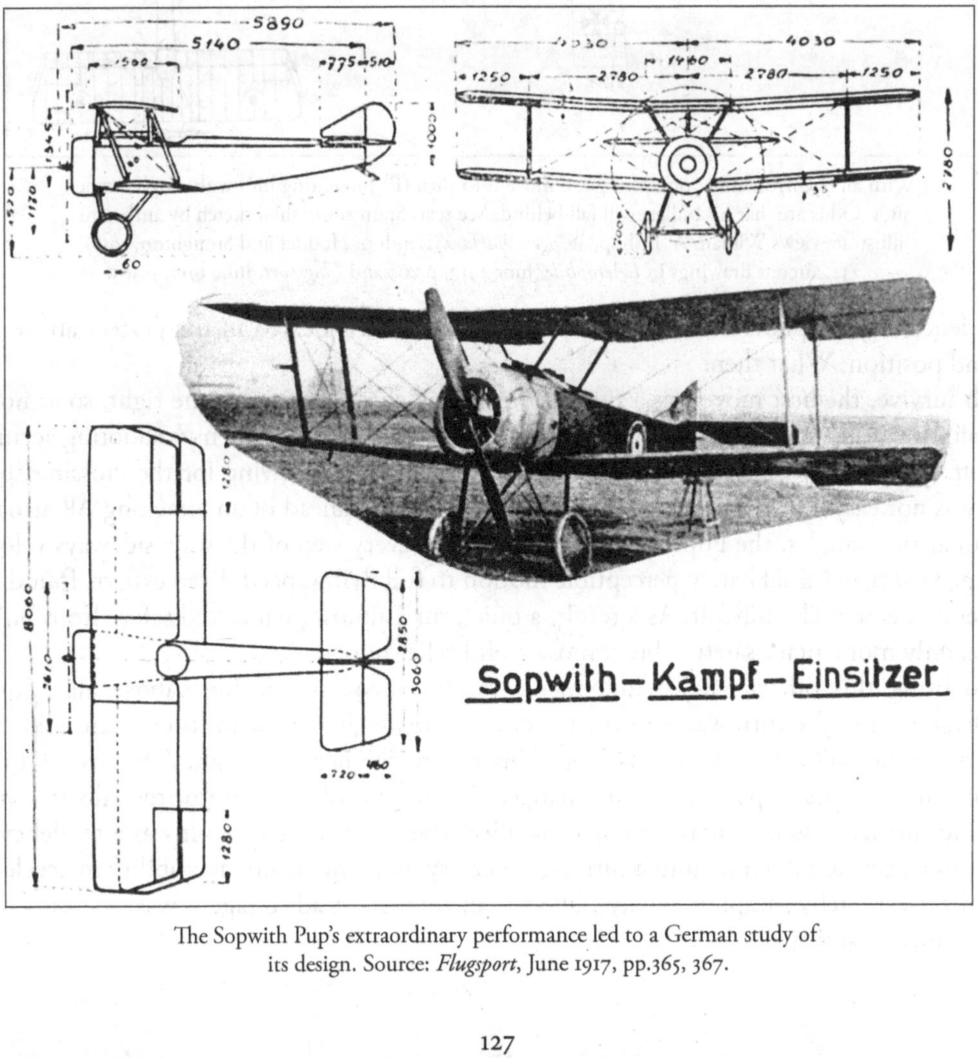

The Sopwith Pup's extraordinary performance led to a German study of its design. Source: *Flugsport*, June 1917, pp.365, 367.

The Right Angle Defense (top view)

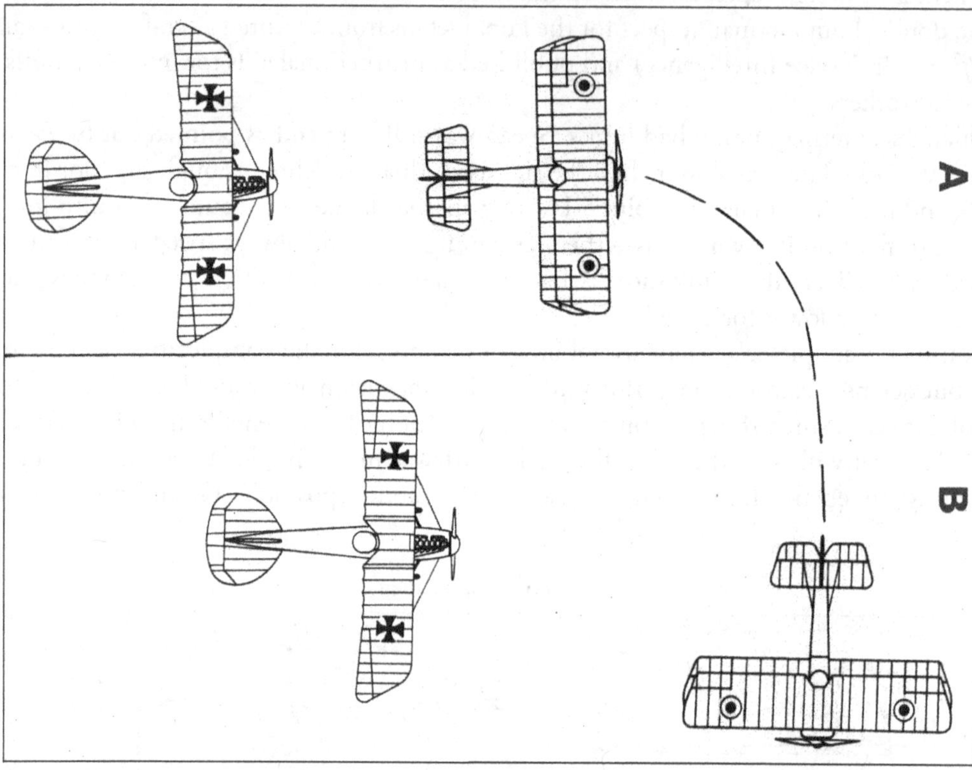

With an enemy behind you (A), a good move is to turn (B) presenting him with a right angle shot. Odds are that his bullets will fall behind. See text. Source: Original sketch by author to illustrate views William A. Bishop, *Winged Warfare* (London: Hodder and Stoughton, 1918) p.232, aircraft drawings in *L'Aérophile*, June 1917, p.203 and *Flugsport*, June 1917, p.365.

experience, fighter pilots inevitably encountered an enemy located in the perfect above and behind position. What then?

To survive, the best move was a turn; if possible, a climbing turn to the right, so as not to lose altitude. Once flying at an angle to incoming fire, the attacking enemy's shooting accuracy fell off, for gunnery precision depended upon knowing and allowing for the crossing speed. This was not easy, for in changing position from that dead ahead of an attacking Albatros, to a path at right angles, the Pup's crossing speed varied every step of the way: sideways velocity changed from an initial barely perceptible motion to full flying speed. Even experts found this judgement extremely difficult. As a result, a quick turn almost guaranteed safety from bullets – true, only momentary safety – but a most useful relief nonetheless.

To bring this off, the key requirement was for speed in turning. Above all, a quick acceleration into the turn was wanted. Here, the lightweight Pup with its concentrated mass (rotary engine, pilot, gun, fuel) was much superior to the heavier weight Albatros. Not only did its greater mass impede any swift change, but the spread out form of the Albatros mass acted to further slow its initial turning capability. The usual combat result was a tendency for Albatros bullets to fall far behind a turning adversary. In sum, an aircraft's ability to accelerate into a turn, thereby escaping enemy bullets – an important advantage – was one associated with maneuverability.

Head-On Combat

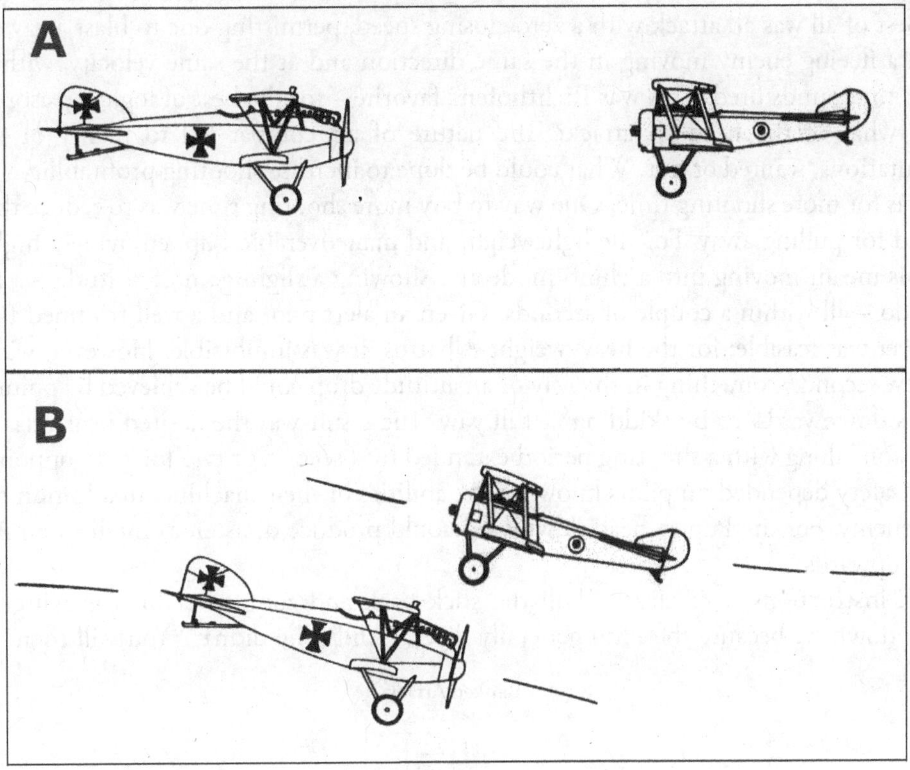

Was seldom used (A) owing to too short a shooting period and the possibility of collision. Pup maneuverability helped make head-on attack practical (B) by offering a longer time for shooting while decreasing the probability of collision. Source: Original sketches by author from description *Fighting Instruction Data* TNA file # AIR 1/1625/204/89/8 and aircraft drawings in *Flugsport*, June 1917 and *L'Aérophile*, June 1917, p.203.

Other special combat cases led to the same pro-maneuverability, pro-Pup conclusion. For example, there was head-on attack, in which opposing aircraft fly and shoot directly at one another. Here the attack form itself included two strong inherent drawbacks: a lack of time available for shooting and the danger of collision. Consider aircraft maneuverability as a factor in making this type of attack feasible.

In head-on attack, aircraft closing speed equaled the sum of both machine's velocities. At the usual high scout speeds, the intervening space was quickly traversed. If we assume a velocity of 100 mph for each airplane, every passing second reduced the distance between machines by roughly 100 yards.[7] If we imagine the pilots opening fire at 400 yards range, only four seconds of shooting was possible before collision. Four seconds was very little. With a machine gun cyclic rate of 10 rounds fired per second, and discounting cooling breaks, the total of rounds fired per gun amounted to less than 40. Assigning two guns to the fighter plane, the firing of less than 80 rounds was possible. As compared to Richthofen's usual expenditure of some hundreds of rounds to bring down an enemy, 80 bullets were few indeed – and this number does not take into account the necessity for an early cease fire so as to pull away; a matter of sacrificing shooting time to prevent collision. Taking gun cooling and time for evasion into account, a 20 round grand total was likely.

The calculation above was easy to perform and fully supported real life experience. We suspect that Boelcke ignored this form of attack because the numbers were so unprofitable. An attack featuring a low closing speed was obviously a better tactic from the gunnery point of view. Best of all was an attack with a zero closing speed, permitting one to blast away, directly behind a fleeing enemy moving in the same direction and at the same velocity, without any limit to the rounds fired. This was Richthofen's favorite – for the best of logical reasons.

But what of the head-on attack? The nature of air combat led to plenty of head-on confrontations, wanted or not. What could be done to increase shooting profitability? The key need was for more shooting time. One way to buy more shooting time was to reduce that time required for pulling away. For the lightweight and maneuverable Pup, enjoying a high climb rate, this meant moving into a climb mode and showing a slight gain of altitude – a few feet would do – all within a couple of seconds. Given an alert pilot and a well trimmed Pup, this maneuver was feasible; for the heavyweight Albatros, it was impossible. However, within the same few seconds, something in the way of an altitude drop could be achieved by pointing the Albatros downwards, or by skidding at full yaw. The result was the desired near miss instead of collision, along with a shooting period extended by a second or two for each opponent. Of course, safety depended on pilots knowing the abilities of their machine, in addition to those of the enemy. For the Pup to head downward could produce disaster, as might if an Albatros headed upwards.

RFC instructions were clear:[8] "Pull the stick back and zoom over his top wing … pull up, not down … because the Hun generally dives." And if he didn't? "You will then only hit

Banked Attack

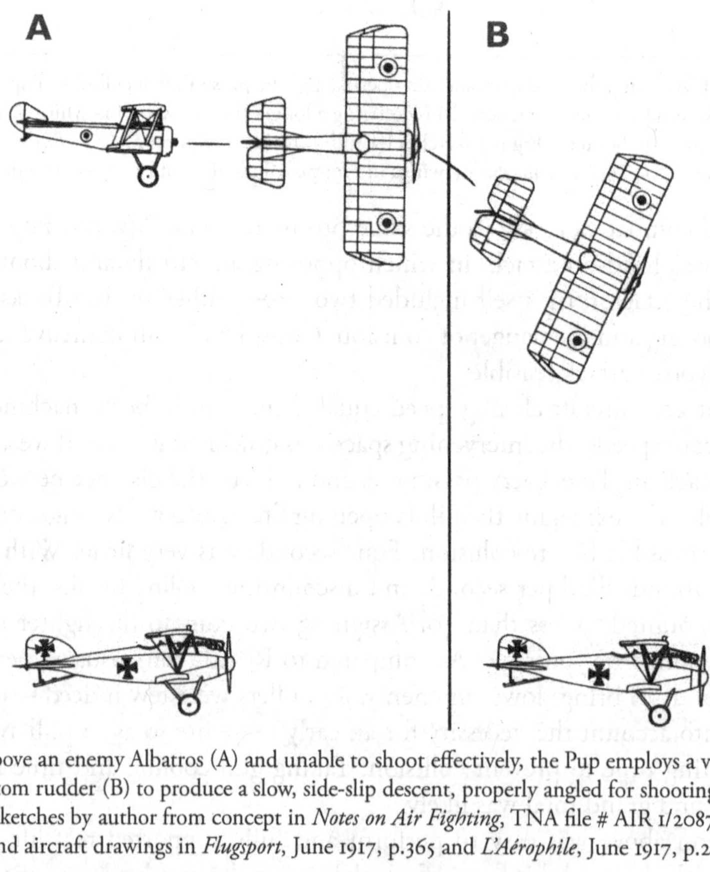

Directly above an enemy Albatros (A) and unable to shoot effectively, the Pup employs a vertical bank and bottom rudder (B) to produce a slow, side-slip descent, properly angled for shooting. Source: Original sketches by author from concept in *Notes on Air Fighting*, TNA file # AIR 1/2087/ 207/7/38 and aircraft drawings in *Flugsport*, June 1917, p.365 and *L'Aérophile*, June 1917, p.203.

him with your undercarriage (i.e., landing gear)." Perhaps, but perhaps not; head-on collision remained a real possibility. Yet, so desperate were the needs and hopes of combat that even these frightening instructions seemed promising. The ability to fire off another ten to twenty rounds was highly significant. In this manner, while far from a complete solution, the Pup with its quick mobility and longer shooting time made head-on tactics more profitable, helping to move a neglected technique into the mainstream.

Consider another, and quite different tactical problem: that of sitting directly above an opponent, several hundred feet higher, and moving in the same direction at the same speed. Achieved was that desired zero closing speed, but it was of the wrong sort – at different altitudes – and so, worthless. Most single-seater scout aircraft were equipped to shoot only along their axis; i.e., in the direction of flight. This had the advantage of simplifying the setting of gun sights, for the aiming of guns in close combat could be achieved to a considerable extent by aiming the entire airplane. However, there was a disadvantage to this process: it was impossible to shoot at any enemy plane flying along a parallel path.

Given parallel flight paths, the standard solution was for the uppermost aircraft, let's say a Pup, to dive, directing its bullets just ahead of the unaware Albatros shown. The difficulty consisted of limited shooting time, for the diving Pup gained unwanted speed and overtook his adversary. After a few seconds, collision became a menacing possibility, forcing the Pup to break off contact – likely before a decisive number of shots could be fired.

Pup maneuverability led to another, and better solution.[9] Instead of a diving attack, a combination of vertical bank and bottom rudder could be employed to produce a slow, angled, stalled descent that helped keep the Pup's sights on the enemy. The main gain was an increase in shooting time duration. As a second advantage, the slowly descending Pup was unlikely to overtake its target, ruling out collision. True, the shooting time difference was small, but to a fighting pilot the opportunity to get off ten more rounds could be life saving.

There was a third advantage. The resulting Pup aircraft attitude – in effect a vertical sideslip owing to much bank and yaw – was just right for entering a spin. Should the Pup attack fail, or encounter a furious Albatros brother pilot seeking revenge, it might be wise to do a couple of spin turns and then scoot for home. Official advice was mixed on this point. British flight school advice pointed to the short spin as " ... a good way of getting away from a fight you do not wish to carry on."[10] However, another official source offered doubts:"This is one way of getting an enemy off one's tail ... [but] It is not recommended as one loses such a lot of height ... "[11] We suspect that those rich in altitude and hungry for safety were willing to make the trade. For those pilots, Pup maneuverability made quick spins easy and profitable.

Another offensive move made practical through maneuverability was attack from beneath. Here an initial attitude suggesting head-on attack was frequently converted into a very different form: one of bullets from below.

Shooting from down under had two major advantages as compared to a head-on strike. First, the enemy scout plane had no way of replying effectively – his guns were pointed elsewhere. Secondly, the enemy pilot lost his usual personal protection, gained from employing the engine as a barrier. Exposed to incoming fire, it was possible to hit him directly, ending the battle quickly.

To bring this about, RFC instructions were attractively simple: "Dive your machine till you can see the enemy over the top plane. Then pull out and shoot him at an angle from underneath."[12]

Attack from Underneath

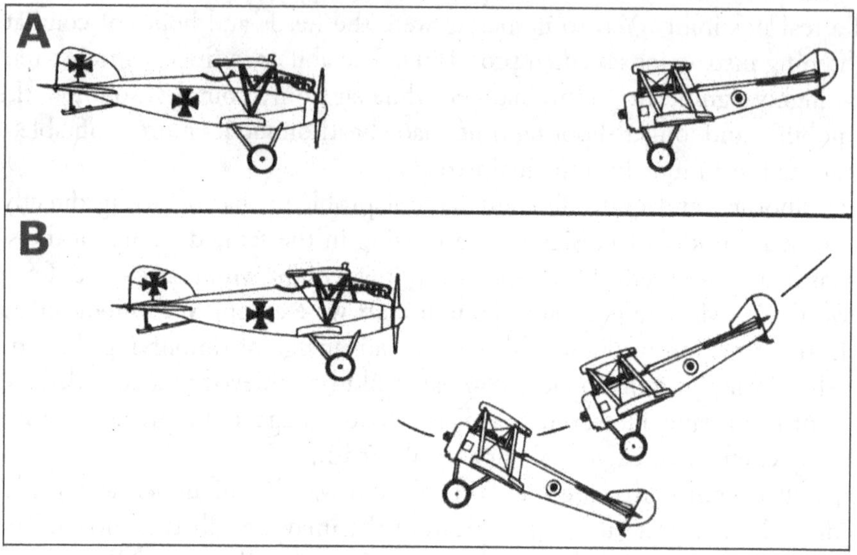

Facing an Albatros head-on at long range (A), a Pup's best move was to dive and zoom (B), aiming at the vulnerable underside. Source: Original sketch by author from concept *Notes on Air Fighting*, TNA file # AIR 1/ 2087/207/7/38 and aircraft drawings in *Flugsport*, June 1917, p.365 and *L'Aérophile*, June 1917, p.203.

Preventing a Second Act

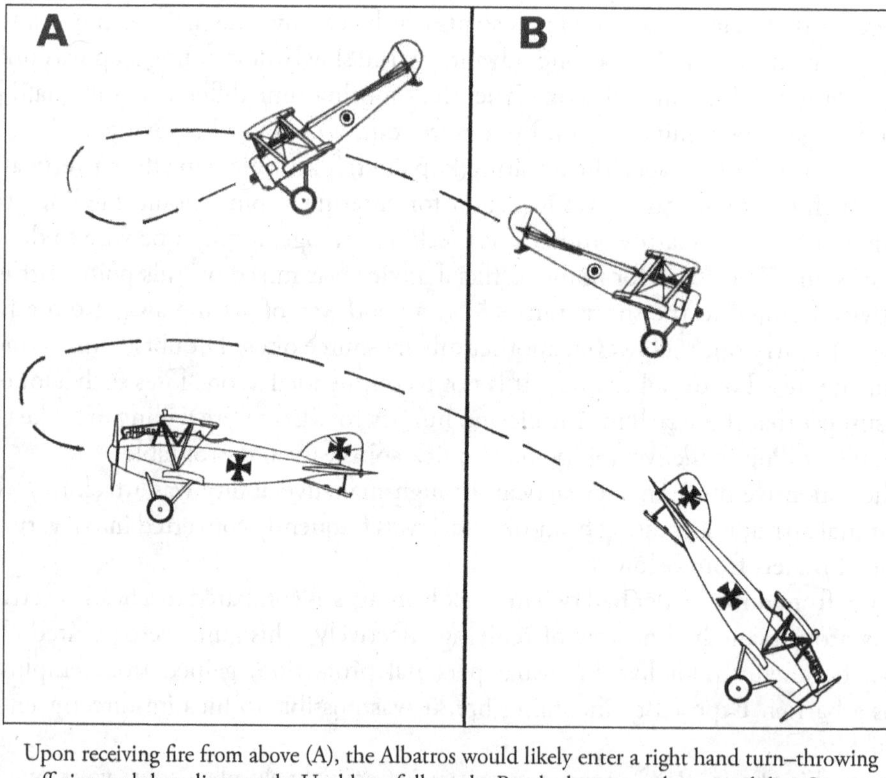

Upon receiving fire from above (A), the Albatros would likely enter a right hand turn–throwing off aim–and then dive steeply. Unable to follow, the Pup had no second act possibility. Source: Original sketch by author from concept in *Aerial Fighting 1917*, TNA file # AIR 1/920/204/5/885 and aircraft drawings in *Flugsport*, June 1917, p.365 and *L'Aérophile*, June 1917, p.203.

Left out was the well-known Albatros tendency to dive when sensing trouble. In this case, the Pup would likely lose the advantages of attack from below, and instead encounter an enemy head-on; one prepared to give as well as receive bullets. This drawback aside, an underneath attack could be effective, especially so against an unwary opponent. As for the Pup, its extra maneuverability offered more time in which to engage and then break away, after firing a respectable number of rounds.

Pup agility had its limits. Certainly the diving ability of the Albatros was beyond anything it might offer in the way of competition. As a result, "second act" strike opportunities for the Pup were frequently curtailed. For example, consider a conventional attack, with the Pup as the aggressor.

The Albatros's initial choice, between diving steeply or turning to the right, would most likely favor the turn.[13] Doing so quickly added to the Pup's aiming problems, and the Albatros pilot gained a chance to check the sky for friends and enemies, all without loss of precious altitude. Once into the turn, and after making his survey, he was likely to enter a near-vertical dive – one the Pup couldn't follow. Altitude loss was always painful, but the Albatros dive led to one important gain: the Pup was deprived of a second act. Should the Pup persist, its Albatros antagonist – alarmed, and in possession of a considerable speed advantage by virtue of the dive – could enter into a profitable zoom attack from below. A wise Pup pilot would not persist. Once into its exiting dive, the Albatros was likely free from further immediate attack.

A Second Act Tactic

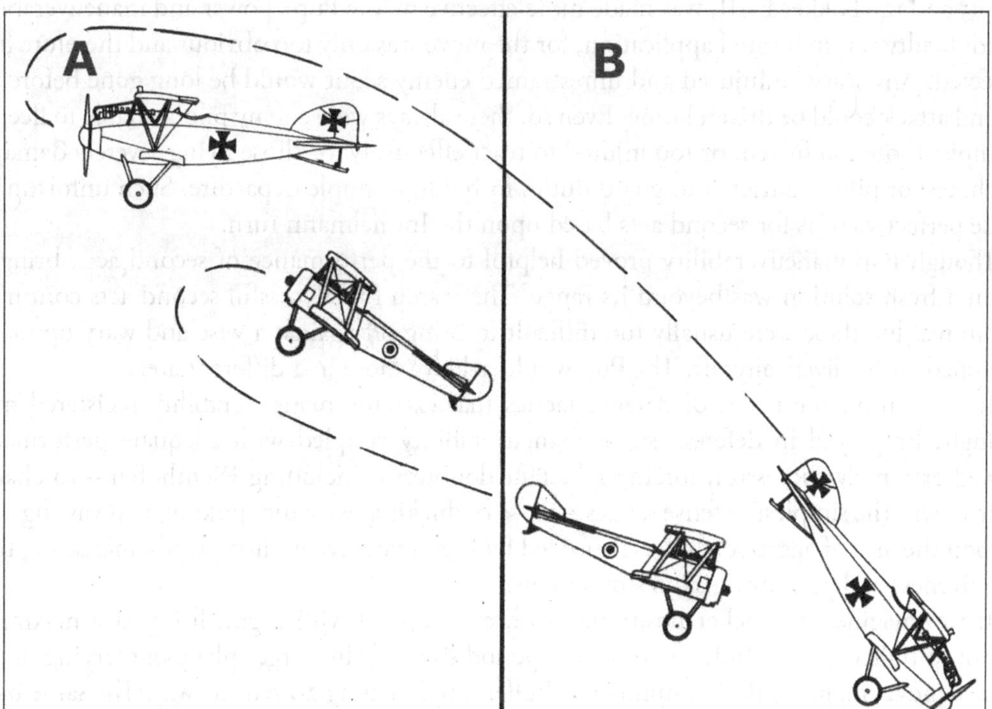

After attacking from underneath (A), Pup breaks off action and (B) heads down to intercept escaping enemy. Source: Original sketch by author from concept in *Aerial Fighting 1917*, TNA file # AIR 1/920/204/5/885 and aircraft drawings in *Flugsport*, June 1917, p.365 and *L'Aérophile*, June 1917, p.203.

To fill the need, suitable tactics permitting or promoting a second act were pursued. Consider one such officially certified RFC plan, starting with a Pup initiating an ordinary "single-seater method of attack, from below."[14]

Expecting the routine turn-and-dive response of his Albatros target, the recommended countermove for the Pup was *not to follow* its foe into the usual right hand climbing circle. Instead, the Pup was to dive towards the expected Albatros exit trajectory. If the Pup pilot proved fortunate in his prediction and timing, the Albatros would come hurtling by, permitting a second attack.

The drawback was one of uncertainty concerning the enemy's future path. Just as predicted, somewhere along its evasive turn, the Albatros would likely peel off and dive. Though the dive itself was a good bet, the compass heading of the dive was far from certain, and any estimate by the Pup pilot so much guess work. With only a limited ability to shift heading at the last moment, the Pup was unlikely to intercept with the necessary degree of precise shooting. In short, a Pup following this tactic would find success unlikely.

In rebuttal, it might be argued that all tactical plans are built around an assumed enemy response, and that no such prediction can ever be certain. True, but we suspect that this particular tactic leaned too heavily on predictive ability, and so had more to do with hope than reality – proof that the need for a second act was a powerful motivating force.

More realistic second act plots did exist. For example, after completing a conventional "above and behind" type of shooting attack, a zoom plus Immelmann turn could be used to prepare for a second act – one of simple repetition. This well known procedure, dating back to 1915 and the Fokker E-III, was made more effective by the Pup's power and maneuverability. The difficulty was in limited application, for the move was only too obvious and therefore fully expected. Any wary, uninjured and unrestrained enemy scout would be long gone before the second attack could be driven home. Even so, there always were enemy pilots unable to flee; for example, those too frozen, or too injured to react effectively; or those flying severely damaged machines; or pilots restricted to guard duties forbidding simple departure. Such unfortunates made perfect victims for second acts based upon the Immelmann turn.

Though Pup maneuverability proved helpful to the performance of second acts, bringing about a fresh solution was beyond its range. The search for successful second acts continued, but in real life these were usually too difficult to bring off against a wise and wary opponent equipped with a lively aircraft. The Pup would achieve more in a different area.

It was within the realm of defense tactics that extreme maneuverability registered most strongly. Employed in defense, super maneuverability coupled with adequate performance proved extremely successful, forcing reluctant doubters – including Richthofen – to change their views. The simplest defense tactics – those of ducking, weaving, jinking, and yawing so as to spoil the aim of aggressors – were speeded by high maneuverability, greatly increasing their effectiveness and preventing aggressor success.

If we imagine an attacker positioned to fire, equipped with a gun firing at a maximum rate of 10 bullets per second, a two second period spent by his target plane in carrying out an evasive move might result in a number of bullets approaching 20 sent its way. The same burst, fired at a livelier aircraft able to carry out its evasive maneuver in half the time, would receive only half of the bullets before moving out of harm's way. i.e., only the first half of those fired would have a chance of hitting. As an additional advantage, this initial batch of bullets usually lacked tracer or visible damage guidance, for the correction of aim depended upon visual feedback gained from the rounds fired. Lacking aiming correction, such early rounds were likely to be less accurate than later ones. In sum, not only were the number of rounds capable of being directed at the target aircraft reduced by greater maneuverability, but even this lower number consisted of rounds lacking in aiming correction, and so were less likely to hit their target.

Maneuverability's profits involved more than a lessening of properly aimed incoming rounds. In certain cases, a fast maneuver could take a defending aircraft completely out of the line of fire, ending the attack. As an example, consider the use of a full roll to wash out a prime "above and behind" attack.

Given a Pup about to come under diving attack from the well placed enemy machine shown, RFC advice for its pilot was to execute a full roll in the conventional fashion, with stick full back and over to one side, employing full rudder on the same side. During and after rolling, the machine would continue in the same direction. However, the extra drag and loss of lift experienced in the maneuver would cause both an altitude drop and a relative decrease of distance traveled. As a result, the enemy Albatros was out of position for effective shooting, being both too high, and too near in the horizontal sense. The latter was viewed as especially important. Relative to the Pup, the Albatros had been forcibly repositioned to an "overshot" condition, with its attack effectiveness eliminated, and all done by a quick maneuver.

In short, for scout machines flying defensively, extreme maneuverability plus a wary, skilled pilot meant a much smaller chance of being killed. To pilots desperate to survive, the necessary path was clear: all other things being equal, go with more aircraft maneuverability. Even if other things were not equal – for example, if a bit of speed had to be sacrificed in the name of maneuverability – there was still much to be said for superior maneuverability.

Escape by Rolling

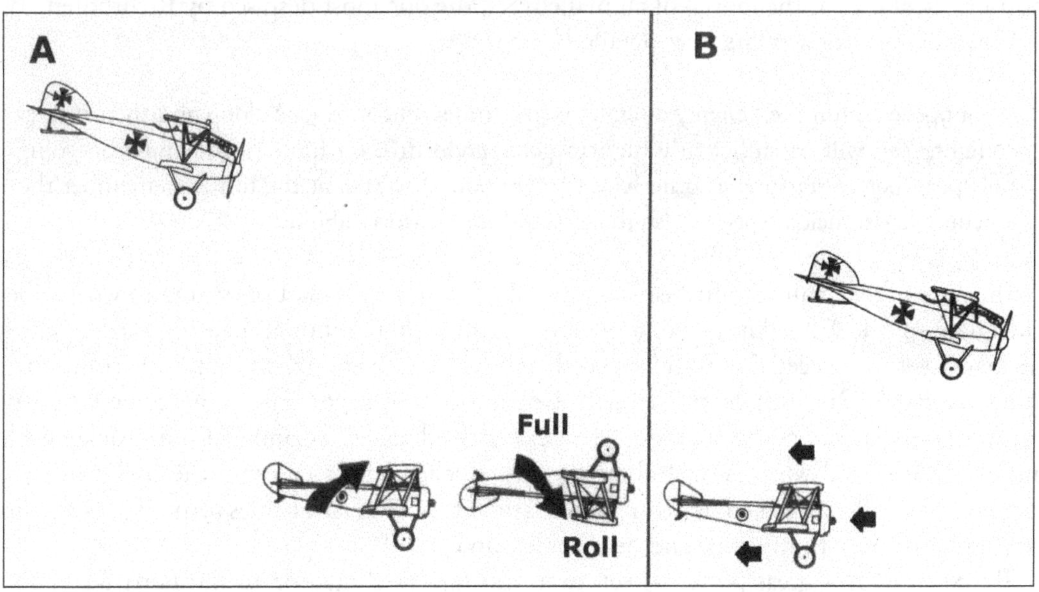

To defend against an attacking Albatros (A), the Pup employs a full roll and (B) continues in the same direction. The maneuver reduces the horizontal distance from the attacker sufficiently to prevent accurate shooting. Source: Original sketch by author from concept in *Notes on Aerial Fighting*, TNA file # AIR 1/2087/7/38 and aircraft drawings in *Flugsport*, June 1917, p.365 and *L'Aérophile*, June 1917, p.203.

Backwards Loop

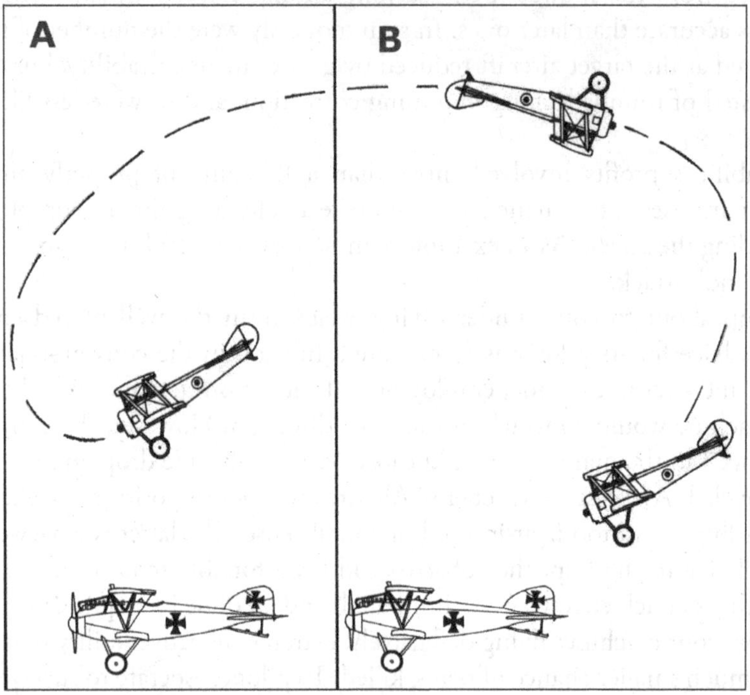

To attack an aircraft directly below (A), a backwards loop (B) could be used to place the aggressor right behind his target. Source: Original sketch by author from concept in *Fighting Instruction Data*, TNA file # AIR 1/1625/204/89/8 and aircraft drawings in *Flugsport*, June 1917, p.365 and *L'Aérophile*, June 1917, p.203.

Moving energetically to experiment with its new capability, the RFC managed to find a most practical use for the loop – of all maneuvers, the one most despised by Richthofen. Instructions to new pilots were detailed:

> Suppose a Hun [i.e., enemy aircraft] is just under you … do a ¾ loop and then rudder straight. You will be sufficiently high to get a good dive on him … you must be going full speed before starting, as otherwise you are bound to stall at the top … remember the machine has sufficient speed … so there is nothing to worry about.[16]

The note of determined optimism suggests that there was at least one thing to worry about – adequate speed. With Pup power a bit low for the task at hand, all had to be just right for the maneuver to succeed. Yet it did succeed, and frequently enough at that, to become a trick flying standard. One year later, the arrival of newer, more powerful scout aircraft resulted in routine use of the backwards loop. For example, there was Captain Eddie Rickenbacker and his SPAD XIII, who successfully wiped an attacker off his tail with the backwards loop maneuver, and then followed up with a most satisfactory reversal-of-roles form of act two: "one short burst from both my guns and he tumbled down … "[17]

The SPAD XIII's great power – well over 200 h.p. as compared to the Pup's 80 or 100 – led to a machine offering not only superb maneuverability, but offered additional speed and climb advantages as well. Those pilots attracted to maneuverability but hesitant to go with the Pup's barely sufficient power found the packaging of extra speed and climb along with maneuverability to be a complete answer. Ever since, fighter design has pushed all three virtues as critical.

Despite Richthofen's initial skepticism, evidence before his own eyes convinced him of maneuverability's ability to improve survival odds. Trick flying could pay off – and handsomely at that. This bitter truth was forced upon him in April 1917 when the Pup's successor, in the form of a single Sopwith Triplane, frisked about over German held turf despite attacks from the full complement of his own *Jasta* 11's pilots and machines.[18] The achievement was extraordinary: a single scout had easily fended off a squadron of experienced fighters. This time, Richthofen did more than make a note.

Always able to change his mind when logic so insisted, he studied the case for maneuverability as offered by the Sopwith Triplane, and decided that it deserved support. Given time, maneuverability might change the game. He became an active triplane supporter. Using his new found prestige, he pressured the German Air Service to study and even copy the Sopwith Triplane. He helped push the notion that air flow about three wings was wonderfully effective, with supremacy proven by the Sopwith's performance and maneuverability. The belief was mistaken. In reality, triplane wing configurations are inefficient.[19]

Nature taxes every wing tip heavily. Carrying six wing tips, every triplane aircraft pays a steep price in the form of lowered flight efficiency. Added on is another type of loss, that owing to mutual interference by wings in close proximity, for unfortunately, each wing roils the air through which its brother wings pass. The single wing monoplane is best – there are no brother wings – biplanes less so, and three wings pay a considerable interference price. Taking all losses into account, triplanes tend to offer high drag. This inherent tendency can't be eliminated, no matter how clever the designer.

There are offsetting triplane advantages. A most thorough 1916 British aerodynamic wind tunnel investigation[20] pointed to the use of stagger, i.e., a fore and aft displacement of the upper wings relative to the lower, as a means of offsetting the interference loss. However, to achieve a significant benefit, much stagger was required. In the case of the Sopwith design, one side effect of the great stagger employed was curtailment of the pilot's vision, with cutouts of the middle wing necessary to permit adequate sight. As for the aerodynamic benefit, it was paid only at extremely low speeds, at or near stall, by making flight more viable. The classic circular duel was such an occasion and survival itself could conceivably be influenced by the presence of large stagger. However, when at typical combat speeds, there was no benefit, and top speed itself was lessened by the triplane wing drag, with or without stagger.

For a triplane to be competitive against the usual monoplane or biplane design, it was necessary that something extra be thrown in as compensation. In the case of the Sopwith design, an engine change from the Pup's 100 h.p. Monosoupape, initially to 110 h.p. and then to a more powerful 130 h.p. Clerget, more than compensated for the Sopwith Triplane's reduced wing efficiency. The resulting climb was striking, and its speed (116 mph)[21] exceeded the maximum velocity of the Albatros D-III (108 mph).[22] Finally, through careful weight control, much of the Pup maneuverability was retained. All in all, the machine was impressive – despite the disadvantages of the three-wing arrangement.

Richthofen's push for a triplane, beginning in April 1917, encountered little enthusiasm within the German aerodynamic establishment. Researchers were aware of the negative British

Idflieg **Studies a Triplane**

A downed Sopwith Triplane drew much attention from German Intelligence. Note large forward wing stagger. As for the missing insignia patches, they likely graced the victorious officer's mess. Source: *Flugsport*, August 1917, p.517.

triplane experimental findings and had strong additional reasons, based on sound theory, to doubt triplane effectiveness. The conflict grew until management was forced to resolve the issue: wanted was a means to placate both Richthofen and the aerodynamicists. Here was a perfect opening for that much-maligned designer, Anthony Fokker.

Despite the great success of his E-III, succeeding months had seen Fokker become something of a liability, cursed by a string of unsuccessful follow-on designs, poor workmanship at his factory, and his inability to keep up with the increasingly mathematical nature of design work As a last straw, a false scandal[23] arose concerning his Dutch (neutral) citizenship involving a loony, imaginary plot featuring an escape to Britain, where rumor had it, he would be well paid to reveal German military secrets.

Though his reputation suffered, he continued to hold the respect of most pilots for reasons of great flying skill and open-handed support. Former exhibition and stunt flyer Fokker knew the flying game from the inside. To fellow pilots he was that rarest of men: a full-scale manufacturer, still in his twenties, young enough and sufficiently at odds with the establishment to understand their problems. Added to this agreeable background was a rare generosity suggesting something else, for Fokker was always ready to offer a trial flight in his latest machine at the Schwerin factory, or better yet, a hotel room in jammed Berlin – at no charge. Moving beyond "hospitality suite" largess, Fokker has been accused[24] of bribery; of openly buying the support of his most important customers: not official purchasing agents, but fighter pilots.

As the rumors grew, the atmosphere surrounding Fokker became difficult. To have one's design hopes assigned to Fokker for implementation was not a good sign. Any Fokker linkup implied low expectations from top Air Service management.

An undaunted Tony Fokker, given the go-ahead to proceed with a triplane, turned the design process over to Reinhold Platz, a holdover from the days of trial and error, whose background was that of a welder. Though his knowledge of advanced theory was weak, few could match his intuitive feeling for practical design; a creative sense that approached genius. Once satisfied that a triplane was under way, Richthofen stepped back to concentrate upon combat as before, flying standard service biplane fighters. To Fokker, this was for the best, for "Richthofen knew little or nothing about the technical details of airplanes."[25] Perhaps, but as the British would learn, Richthofen knew a great deal about what could be done with airplanes – especially fighter aircraft.

Returning to a form of combat that was basically unchanged, Richthofen continued to blast the standard opposition British observation, fighters and light bombers: BE2c, FE2b, RE8, etc. To defeat such opponents, great maneuverability wasn't required. Certainly his 1917 victories owed little to the presence (starting in September) of the Fokker Triplane. As for the relatively maneuverable Sopwith Triplane, so impressive to Richthofen, they were few in

Richthofen Victories per month: April 1917–April 1918

1917:			1918:	
	April	20	Jan.	0
	May	0	Feb.	0
	June	4	March	11
	July	2	April	6
	Aug.	1		
	Sept.	2		
	Oct.	0		
	Nov.	1		
	Dec.	1		

From "Bloody April" 1917 until his death one year later, monthly victory numbers depended on infantry thrusts, leave and weather. He used the Fokker Triplane almost exclusively starting in September 1917. Source: Author's list from data in *L'Aérophile*, April 1918, p.110.

number and rarely encountered. Only one combat victory over a Sopwith Triplane has been assigned to Richthofen (victory # 52 on April 29, 1917)[26] and even that sole conquest was clouded by evidence suggesting that the defeated machine was really a Nieuport biplane.[27]

British disappointment in triplanes is suggested by the total of only 150 Sopwith Triplanes manufactured, curtailing its combat life to a short period – seven months[28] of 1917 – in which some 40 of the type were claimed as downed in combat.[29] Grounds for disappointment certainly existed. The Sopwith Triplane was handicapped, not only by the inherently modest top speed demonstrated by all three-winged aircraft, but by the effects of excess stability as well, preventing the machine from making full use of its maneuverability potential. In reality, there was but one extraordinary feature: a high rate of climb. To the British, Sopwith's sibling biplane – the Sopwith Camel – was a better fighting machine. Not only did its two wings yield a superior speed for a given amount of power, but it enjoyed maneuverability advantages as well; those derived from instability. These took the form of quick movements, wanted or not, and so were frequently dangerous. To pilots, the tradeoff was acceptable, for speed plus maneuverability spelled victory, and even that sick maneuverability owed to instability was better than the slow, safe, graceful maneuvers granted by the Sopwith Triplane. Inevitably, the Sopwith Triplane was phased out in favor of the Camel.

Unlike the Sopwith firm, the Fokker/Platz team was in no position to shrug off the three-wing concept as less than optimal, and so not worth pursuing. While a correct judgement, such reasoning pre-supposed a free choice between a biplane or triplane. Fokker had no such choice available. Wanted by the German Air Service was a world beating triplane fighter, and his only alternative was to continue building trainers on sub-contract, a venture he detested. He sensed the triplane challenge as a chance to regain world respect as an inventor and innovator. He pushed hard, using every skill and bit of trickery he possessed.

First, it was necessary to beat the competition: either match or excel those Sopwith traits that had excited Richthofen. There were two positive features: climb and maneuverability.

Climb was mostly a matter of weight, wing area and engine size. To save weight, streamlining was abandoned. All lines were simple and straight. As for the drag penalty – so be it – triplanes were innately slow anyway. Next, the resulting machine was made as small as possible, effectively scaling up the modest engine power while simultaneously reducing weight. As for the welded fuselage plus wooden wing construction, though intrinsically sound, they were demanding; perfectly adequate if carefully done but only marginally safe, with little spare strength left over. Executed by unskilled wartime labor, and guided by slipshod quality control measures, this optimistic design process could lead straight to wing failures. Its dangers unheeded, the work went on.

Those thin wings used by Sopwith, low in drag, were dropped in favor of high drag, thick wings. The one virtue of thick wings was the greater thickness itself – permitting use of deeper and more efficient spars to carry wing loads. With the light spars made possible by fat wing sections, overall wing weight was reduced – a significant step in achieving a low weight machine. It was even possible to eliminate all the usual bracing cables (lift wires) along with their requirement for endless adjustment. As for the additional drag entailed by fat wings – it was accepted with a shrug.

So critical was weight that range and flight duration were deliberately cut to reduce fuel weight. Proud of this questionable expedient, an unrepentant post-war Tony Fokker argued

Triplane Wings Compared

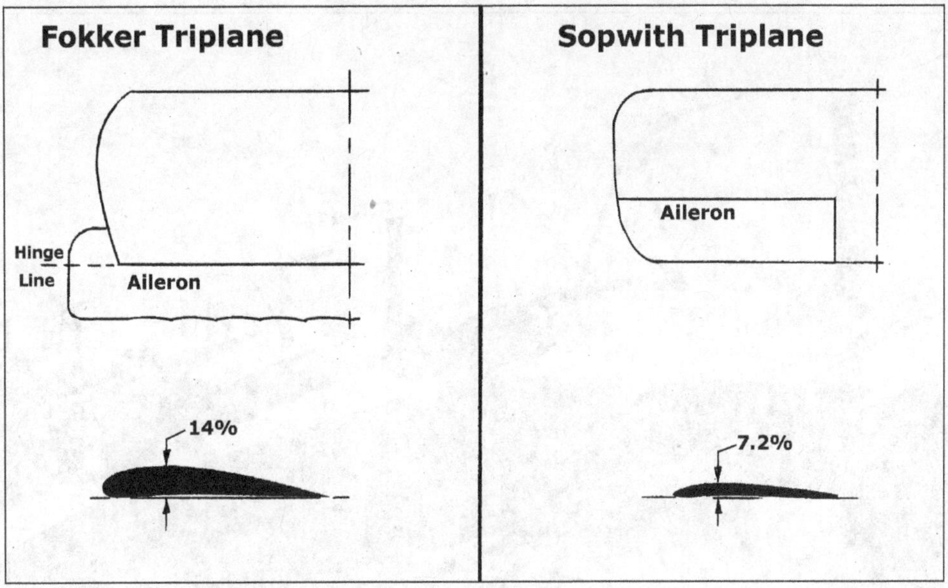

Rejecting Sopwith's design, Fokker employed a thick wing carrying deep spars, together with balanced ailerons. He hoped for a lightweight result offering fast banking. Source: Original sketches by author, redrawn from *Flugsport*, March 1918, p.104 and *Flight*, May 30, 1918, p.586.

Fokker Triplane 3-View

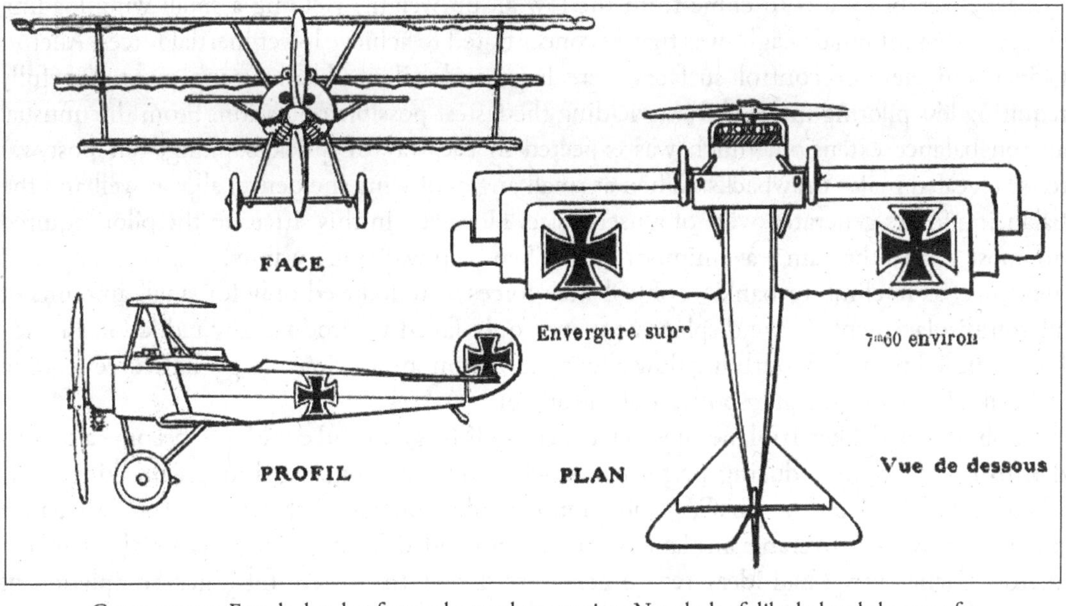

Contemporary French sketches featured a rare bottom view. Note lack of dihedral and absence of a fixed fin. Maneuverability was wanted–not stable flight. Source: *L'Aérophile*, March 1918, p.65.

Preparing for Flight

Unmoved by his satisfied mechanic (extreme right), a pilot readies his Dr.I by checking off the pre-flight list. Source: *Flugsport*, July 1918, p.344.

that Allied airmen had acted unwisely by not "outwaiting the Triplane, which carried less petrol, and then with their greater speed, running them down."[29]

Maneuverability was to come from the low all-up weight, yielding a small wing loading, and even that minimal weight was tightly concentrated to achieve lower inertial forces. Aileron, rudder and elevator control surfaces were large and balanced, an arrangement hopefully requiring less piloting input and yet yielding the fastest possible operation. From the unusual aileron balance extension, much was expected in the way of quick banking, but post-war tests[31] revealed major drawbacks. When at small angles of wing incidence, all was well and the balancing forces generated were of a useful size. However, in this situation the pilot required no boost and so the gain was unimportant. When help was really wanted – at large angles of incidence, as in climb or bank – control stick forces were reduced only for small amounts of aileron displacement. Large displacements not only failed to produce any reduction in stick force, but led to stalled, burbling flow about the aileron, producing a large drag force tending to break off the overhanging portion of the aileron.

In short, the Fokker Triplane aileron balance did little good and could well become a serious detriment, either by reducing performance when maneuvering, or through breaking apart when heavily loaded. The NACA evaluation carefully concluded that use of such a balance "on any highly maneuverable airplane is not recommended."[32] In practical terms, the Triplane aileron balance was a bad idea. Yet, so great was the wartime drive for quick completion of the Triplane that the balanced aileron continued in place without question. Indeed, design momentum was so great that the notion continued beyond the Triplane. Despite growing evidence that the aileron balance was a poor idea, it was also employed on the succeeding Fokker D.VII biplane.

In the midst of the headlong rush for an acceptable Triplane, Richthofen suffered a major reverse of his own. Flying an Albatros, he was shot down on July 6, 1917, suffering a severe scalp wound, hit by a bullet to the head. Though key details of the engagement remain uncertain,[33] he was most likely hit by the gunner of an FE2 in an otherwise routine fight. The wound produced momentary blindness and paralysis, resulting in a crash landing. Hospitalization followed. Yet he was back in action one month later, downing his next victim (victory # 58) on August 16.

The life-threatening nature of Richthofen's wound has produced speculation concerning his subsequent state of mind. Evaluation is difficult. Every fighter pilot was under great stress. Headaches, too much alcohol, and violent temper tantrums were standard reactions. In Richthofen's case, no clear sign of unusual fear, depression or poor judgement was apparent to his peers. Were it otherwise, the standard military solution would have been employed: long leave and transfer to a desk. That he continued to lead men in combat was a sign of acceptable mental and physical health, as measured by the standards of his time.

In the meantime, after many changes the emerging Triplane was submitted for preliminary stress and performance testing in mid-August 1917. The prototype's carefully constructed wings passed with a high safety factor – if properly built, the wing structure was more than strong enough.[34] By late August the Triplane was officially approved and in service.

An early recipient was *Leutnant* Werner Voss, commander of *Jasta* 10. A believer in aerobatics, he was pleased with the light, frisky and fast climbing Triplane. Here at last was a German machine sufficiently maneuverable to put the case for aerobatic combat to the test. Starting on August 30, 1917, he succeeded in downing 21 enemy aircraft by September 23 – an awesome achievement. He was then brought down in a fight against at least five SE5a machines; a fight he could have avoided had he not full confidence – too much confidence – in his Triplane. Even if not equal in ability to five of the top British aircraft, the Triplane was very good indeed.

Richthofen's experience backed that of Voss. In early September, victories 60 and 61came with the aid of the new Triplane. Furthermore, he was impressed with the September exploits of his friend Voss. All seemed fine. However, with the delivery of the next batch of machines in October, the Fokker curse returned. In separate incidents, *Leutnants* Heinrich Gontermann and Herbert Pastor were killed when engaged in moderate stunting over their home fields. Wing failure was the cause in each case. Richthofen, a witness to the Pastor death, called for a close inspection of all the new Triplanes. The results were disturbing: the wings displayed shoddy workmanship everywhere, and factory inspection was obviously non-existent. Especially poor were wing rib and aileron construction techniques.

Richthofen was at a great divide. The Triplane was clearly a highly mixed blessing, presenting many problems. Good men were dead owing to its irresponsibly defective construction, and the correction of its manufacturing flaws would take many months. The war wouldn't wait. In the meantime, he was forced to continue use of the Albatros series of fighters; well built, if unexciting machines that had served him well, but smacked of the past.

We don't know his thoughts, but he must have considered certain possibilities. Surely it occurred to him to drop the Triplane, or Dr. I (official designation), as coming from a too deeply troubled Fokker manufacturing source. Instead, he could simply continue with the Albatros series, or perhaps choose another sound biplane, manufactured by a proven source.

In making his decision, one important item was the matter of engine superiority. In contrast with the superb in-line Mercedes engine of the Albatros, the Dr. I's rotary Oberursel engine, like most rotaries, was less certain in operation and subject to seizure. True, the rotary engine was light, and this quality led to a highly maneuverable machine with a superb rate of climb, but what of its relatively low power output? How could the Dr. I dominate combat if enemy aircraft could readily outspeed it?

As for Voss and his series of victories employing the Dr. I – yes, the facts were impressive – however, Voss had a feeling for trick flying that bordered on genius. Even the British thought so.[35] What of the typical pilot with his limited skills? How would the demanding Triplane serve him? For that matter, what of Richthofen? Though endless practice had improved his flying skill, he would never match Voss in ability. Would he really profit by switching from his customary "above and behind" attack pattern to the "catch as catch can" format of the maneuverability advocates?

Then, what of the politics of combat and its influence on tactics? The Army had steadily pressed for the right personal attitude, rather than gadgetry, as the key to victory. Infantry officer and fellow *Pour le Mérite* holder *Leutnant* Ernst Junger reflected this view: "Security rests on the fresh and unwearied courage of its defenders, not on the strung-out … approaches or the depth of its fire trenches."[36]

Richthofen's corresponding statement was a good fit: "The decisive factor does not lie in trick flying but solely in the personal ability and energy of the aviator."[37]

To the Army these were useful expressions of the right attitude. So long as the typical soldier lived and fought in muddy holes, to suggest some form of sophisticated trench building or flying machine as necessary for survival could produce unrest. To Air Service General Ernest von Hoeppner, Richthofen's contribution was one of " … steadfast purpose … fine modesty, frank and knightly bearing … "[38] Nothing was said about campaigning for a special breed of extremely maneuverable Triplanes as the way to win.

Finally, if he changed tactics and pushed hard for maneuverability, what of his *The Red Air Fighter* book, just published and carrying only his previous views condemning trick flying? True, they were only words, but to sophisticated readers, switching course by 180 degrees would make him look like a fool. Was this to be borne?

Yes, it was. What mattered was winning in the future, not the past. Maneuverability plus climb and speed was the way to win and nothing else mattered. Had he not cheerfully abandoned the horse cavalry, despite years of training, when it proved unequal to a machine gun war? Just so the decent and carefully constructed Albatros series must go. Of the big three performance requirements, it offered only speed, and speed alone wouldn't do.

Fokker and the Triplane it would be, despite Fokker's questionable production capability. With the Dr. I there was a chance against the just emerging Sopwith Camel. Without it, there was none. As for the Triplane concept itself, the main drawback was one of low speed. Here Fokker had some interesting ideas about a new, highly maneuverable biplane. If given a Mercedes engine, fat airfoils and the design genius of Platz, perhaps something rivaling the Triplane could be prepared in a faster biplane format. It must be tried.

Maneuverability had triumphed, despite Richthofen's strong initial doubts. As for suitable tactics there were, not Boelcke's many rules, but only one: catch as catch can.

8

Formations and Combat

The planning of Boelcke's pursuit squadrons led to questions concerning the size of each unit; i.e., the number of fighters to be employed per squadron. Experience showed that most successful air combat ventures were limited to two aircraft: a single fighting airplane against a single enemy machine. Did this tendency reflect some deep truth about all air combat? Could additional machines be useful in ongoing combat, or were they best employed in waiting their turn to accost yet other enemies? More to the point, could squadron members fight together effectively as a group, or were entire squadrons to be deliberately broken apart into multiple single fighters in order to engage enemies? Did joint fire, offering a large number of bullets, serve to assure hits? Certainly the seeming advantages of joint fire in downing enemies seemed attractive; advantages gained while providing mutual protection for one's fellow squadron members. However, were these virtues real?

The drive for an effective joint effort sought a means of launching more bullets at an enemy within those few seconds when aligned on target. As a basic gunnery tactic, the firing of only a few bullets at a time had long been employed by the world's air services. Much testing had shown the concept useful, not only for gun cooling purposes, but to avoid the serious wastage of bullets owing to mistaken judgements of enemy airspeed, orientation and range. Additional flaws were those arising from the machine gun's lack of precision, for each cartridge had a slightly different bullet weight and powder content, and each gun bore diameter varied a bit from the ideal. With so many uncertain factors controlling the outcome of each bullet fired, it was best to fire a handful of bullets, or a "burst", and then check their average trajectory as a guide to the truth of aim. Corrections were made through visual feedback obtained from tracers or bullet strikes.

By firing and correcting enough bursts, one hoped to place a few bullets on target. While this process worked, it could take many hundreds of rounds to achieve a single victory. Each burst was to be short, achieved by pressing the trigger just long enough – one second or less – to fire a standard group of five to ten rounds.

Twin machine guns helped by increasing the intensity of fire. Logic suggested that directing the fire of several attacking aircraft towards a single target machine would help even more. However, experience showed that joint attacks tended to fail owing to difficult and even overwhelming problems of communication.[1] Success in directing a known but complex attack plan at a time before radio was unlikely. Subtle, last moment alteration of such a plan was usually hopeless. It was a time when only flares, lights, and agreed upon maneuvers – such as violent tail shaking – were the basic means of communication between aircraft. Crude messages of the "go" or "no go" type could be passed quickly and were useful. However, variations on a standard plan made necessary by joint attack could not. In Boelcke's time, the issue of joint attack lacked a practical solution.

Boelcke Memorial

Killed in a collision with his wingman, Boelcke left the issue of formation size and management unresolved. Source: *Flugsport*, November 1916, unpaginated addendum.

Even so, the apparent virtues of formations in combat drew much effort and experimentation. Especially attractive were the hoped-for protective advantages. Perhaps formations could be so arranged that incoming attackers were encountered by friendly fighters placed at the best vantage points. For that matter, where was the formation's single best defensive position? Much speculation had it as high and to the rear. Was this really the case?

Resolution of the many formation uncertainties came slowly. So sluggish was progress that large formations seemed a curse to many throughout the war, for they often led to confrontations resulting in much uncertain 'milling about', rather than true combat. Given each aircraft's high-speed and close proximity, combat by formations frequently led to collisions and death. For one, there was the strange death of innovator Boelcke.

Always willing to experiment, October 1916 saw Boelcke flying in a formation of 5 to 7 highly experienced fighter pilots, designated a "swarm". These were loosely grouped about himself and his wingman, serving as leaders. On October 28, eyewitness Richthofen, one of the formation members, saw Boelcke tackling an RFC fighter with apparent success when suddenly there was a brief, light contact between one of the wings of Boelcke's fighter plane (an Albatros D-II) and that of his wingman Lieutenant Ernest Boehme. So slight was the impact that in Richthofen's words: "What happened was not a collision"[2] Despite the minimal contact, both machines crashed. Boehme survived; Boelcke did not.

Accidents and disappointments in battle notwithstanding, the formation concept continued to draw interest. More than firing a greater number of bullets within a given time was involved. Here was a way of introducing raw beginners to combat, by placing them at the center of a formation and instructing them to avoid combat. Instead, they were simply to follow the leader at all times. Given a few such flights, the beginner developed a sense of combat, and did so at low risk. There was even a useful shock effect resulting from a large formation's mass.

Boelcke's Swarm

A loose group of roughly half a dozen Albatros fighters was typical of his 1916 approach. Source: *Flugsport*, June 1917, p.373.

Formation of Two Aircraft in Defense

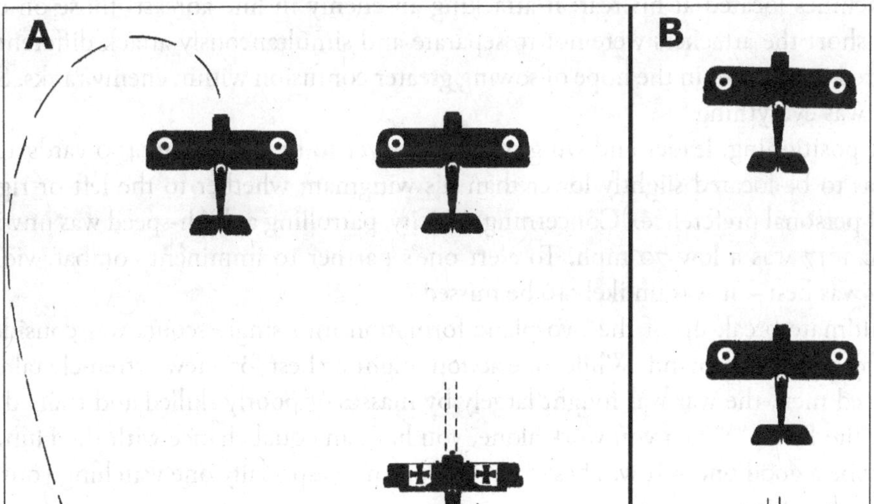

When attacked, a side by side arrangement (A) permitted the free machine to circle about and hit back, whereas a fore and aft setup (B) placed the free machine too far ahead to be effective. Source: Original sketch by author.

Should it contain enough aircraft, the sight alone could cause small enemy formations to break off their observation duties and flee, pleasing friendly troops below – at little cost.

Though the struggle to perfect the handling of formations continued throughout the war, for the most part success came only with smaller groups. Of these, the two-machine formation was the earliest resolved. Consider the best defensive arrangement for a team consisting of leader and wingman. How should they be placed? Side-by-side or fore-and-aft?

After much combat testing, the RFC chose the side-by-side arrangement (A) as clearly superior.[3] When under attack, a side-by-side arrangement permitted the free or unburdened machine to side-slip or circle around, reaching for and then hitting back at the aggressor. Fore-and-aft pattern (B) put the lead machine too far ahead of potential aggressors. Given action to his rear, the lead pilot might not become aware of the attack until too late. Even when finally aware, circling about would take longer owing to the greater distance to be covered.

The two-plane formation was well regarded throughout the war by both sides, not only for defensive purposes, but for its offensive abilities as well, starting even before[4] the 1915 introduction of the Fokker E-III. In 1917 the RFC continued to rate it as best, concluding that with "the same two always working together … they form the strongest offensive in the air."[5] So superior was the performance of a leader plus wingman combination to other formations, that breakup of a standard six-machine flight into three fighting pairs, upon entering combat, was viewed as wise and proper. Similarly formations of four planes, though encouraged to patrol together, were to break into pairs should combat loom.

With experience, certain measures were found to increase the effectiveness of the two aircraft formation. If the enemy was moving in a column format, it was best to attack only those machines located at his rear; if attacking an enemy in line abreast, those on one flank only.[6] In short the attackers were not to separate and simultaneously attack different parts of the targeted formation, in the hope of sowing greater confusion within enemy ranks. Solidarity in attack was everything.

As for positioning, leader and wingman were never to be more than 400 yards apart. The leader was to be located slightly lower than his wingman; whether to the left or right was a matter of personal preference.[7] Concerning velocity, patrolling at high-speed was unwise. Most useful for 1917 was a low 70 mph. To alert one's partner to imminent combat, violent side-swinging was best – it was unlikely to be missed.

The ultimate break-up of the two-plane formation into single scouts was considered and rejected by higher command. While lone action might be best for a few extremely talented and experienced men, the war was fought largely by masses of poorly skilled and trained men. As noted by the RFC: "When you work alone, you have an equal chance with the Hun, and the Hun may be a good one."[8] It was best to have a partner; especially one watching your tail, just as you watched his.

Though successful, the limited scale of the two-plane formation pushed the development of the three-plane triangular or V-type formation. While not as widely used, the V had many supporters. In attack, it offered the concentrated fire of three machines. In defense, each aircraft was supported by at least one other machine; the leader by two. As for drawbacks, its maneuvering traits were certainly inferior to those of a two-plane formation, and its potential for collision much greater. Consider its operation in detail.

The Triangular or V Formation

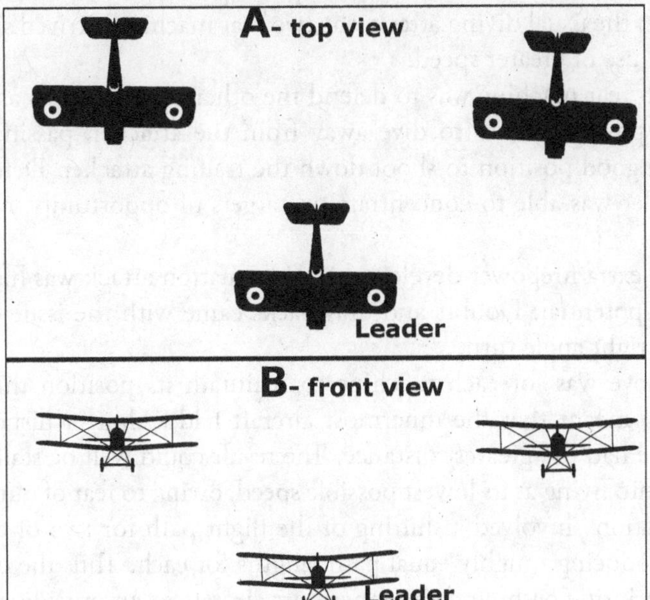

Working together, three aircraft offered more firepower and a better defense as compared to two. Source: Original sketch by author.

V Formation Turn

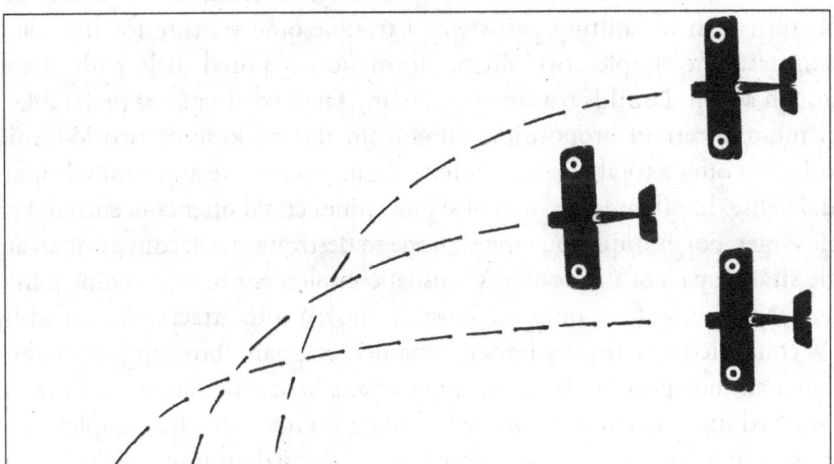

The crossing paths necessary in a turn greatly increased the possibility of collision. Source: TNA file # AIR 1/1625/204/89/8 redrawn.

The V leader was located in front with a supporting machine on each side,[9] placed above and behind him. In the usual diving attack, the two rear machines arrived simultaneously with the leader through use of greater speed.

In defense, each rear machine was to defend the other by turning so as to trail the enemy attacker. Another possibility was to dive away from the attacker, passing under the leader, who was then in a good position to shoot down the trailing attacker. Defended by both rear machines, the leader was able to concentrate on targets of opportunity, rather than his own safety.

In practice, the extra firepower developed in V formation attack was highly valued, as was its greater defense potential. Doubts and drawbacks came with the issue of maneuverability. Consider a simple right angle turn.

The obvious move was for each machine to maintain its position throughout the turn. However, doing so meant that the innermost aircraft had a shorter distance to fly and the outermost machine had the greatest distance. The result could well be stall for the innermost machine, pushed into flying at its lowest possible speed, owing to fear of outrunning its friends.

The official solution[10] involved a shifting of the flight path for two of the three machines, a plan aimed at producing roughly equal path lengths for each. Thus the outermost machine was to swing to an inside path, and the innermost aircraft to an outside path, with only the leader continuing his old, on-center track. The profit in equal path length was one of the same velocity for all, eliminating the necessity for drastic slowing with its risk of stalling.

However, a new problem was introduced: that of collision by airplanes deliberately crossing the flight paths of others. While a safe enough maneuver in the hands of expert pilots, the V-formation turn with its shifting paths was a troublesome venture for the war's usual raw pilots. In contrast, the simpler two-aircraft formation required little path alteration when moving through a turn. For this reason alone, many saw two aircraft as preferable.

An even more uncertain proposition came from the stacking of two V-formations, one above the other, to offer a total of six machines. Again there were apparent advantages in both offense and defense. In offense, the total of six machines could offer concentrated fire against a large, simple target. For example, one might hope to destroy a truck convoy or an ammo dump with a single strafing pass of the double V's usual complement of 12 machine guns. In a more typical case, against aerial foes, only the lower V moved into attack, controlled by its leader. The upper V, controlled by a deputy leader, remained on guard, hovering above the action and using its higher altitude position to intercept attackers bent on striking the lower V.

Reality showed the concept to be flawed, dealing poorly with the complexities of combat. Let us suppose that a large incoming enemy group attacked an upper V, at a time when the lower V formation was already involved in another, separate down-going attack. Should the lower V abandon its own attack and return and aid the upper V? Ideally, fast signaling would handle the necessary change of plans, but as noted, the signaling of revised plans couldn't possibly keep up with the speed of events. Instead, the usual result of German attack, by RFC admission,[11] was the breakup of both V groups, and transformation of the battle into "a series of single combats." Though not fatal, this action amounted to throwing away the supposed advantages of formations at precisely the time of need.

Interested in the stacked V concept, the British attempted a number of variations. In one modification, two additional single machines were added to the basic group of six, flying above all the others. Given a battle opportunity, the lower V dived to attack as before. After waiting

The Stacked V Formation

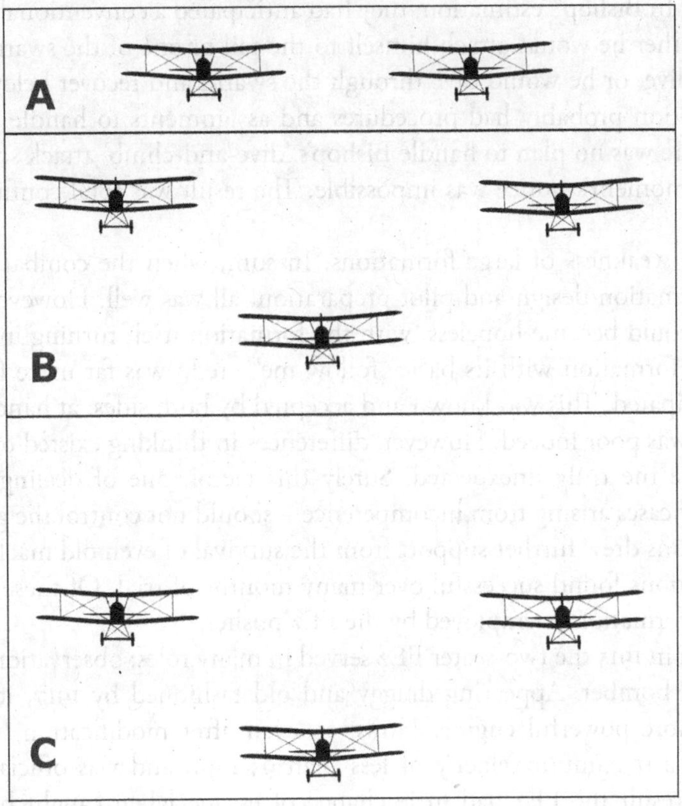

Of the eight machines shown, the top two (A) were assigned to dispatch stragglers; the middle three (B) to provide cover, and the lowest three (C) to serve as offensive fighters. Source: Original sketch by author.

a bit for the scene to clear, the two top single machines dived to bring down stragglers. As in the original plan, the upper V remained above the combat scene, offering cover throughout the battle.

Despite its seeming logic, this highly structured plan was even more poorly equipped to accept the inevitable changes forced by reality. What if the enemy "stragglers" dove away at speeds the British could not match? Wasn't it wiser to use the extra two single machines in the initial attack? Given trials, and the lack of positive results produced by this special stacked formation arrangement, the RFC glumly concluded that all combat, whether employing formation grouping or not, was for the most part a one-versus-one experience.[12] In short, it was unwise to expect too much from formations – especially this one.

A sense of the harmful rigidity and lack of communication within formations was offered by William A. Bishop.[13] In April 1917, flying in his favorite Nieuport scout without a wingman, he spotted five scarlet painted Albatros scouts working together in a loose swarm. These were likely one of Richthofen's groups. Reaching a superior altitude unnoticed, he dove at them, his gun firing most of the way down. Just prior to reaching the Albatros level, he pulled his machine up and zoomed straight upwards. He then looped and dove again, repeating the "performance several times."

His enemies were trained fighting pilots flying well-regarded fighting machines, and yet there was no useful response. Instead, the "formation broke up and scattered." Why this strange reaction? In Bishop's estimation, they had anticipated a conventional attack taking one of two forms. Either he would attach himself to the tail of one of the swarm machines upon completing his dive, or he would dive through the swarm and recover below. He did neither. While the formation probably had procedures and assignments to handle either anticipated contingency, there was no plan to handle Bishop's 'dive-and-climb' attack scheme. To prepare new plans on a moment's notice was impossible. The result was total confusion, followed by breakup.

Such was the weakness of large formations. In sum, when the combat action happened to match the formation design and pilot preparation, all was well. However, if there was no match, matters could became hopeless, with the formation itself turning into a liability. Any small two-plane formation with its basic "follow me" credo was far more flexible in dealing with the unanticipated. This was known and accepted by both sides: at handling surprise, the large formation was poor indeed. However, differences in thinking existed over the likelihood of having to face the truly unexpected. Surely this factor, one of dealing with unforeseen events – in many cases arising from incompetence – should not control the game? Enthusiasts for large formations drew further support from the survival of even old machines through use of certain formations found successful over many months of trial. Of these, the best was the circular defense formation as employed by the FE2 pusher.

From its birth in 1915 the two-seater FE2 served in many roles: observation, artillery spotter, fighter and light bomber. Appearing draggy and old fashioned by 1917, it was updated by substituting a more powerful engine. However, even after modification, the revised FE2d machine offered a maximum velocity of less than 93 mph and was officially classified as a non-diver. As a result the FE2 had little chance of escape when caught by enemy fighters.

Close-up of a Captured FE2b

A pusher, it flew to the reader's left. The gunner, located at the very front, could shoot forward readily. By clamping his gun to the top of pole (A), he could also shoot to the rear, within that zone above the top wing. The pilot, immediately ahead of the engine, could also shoot forward but was blind to the rear. Source: *Flugsport*, June 1917, p.385.

FE2 Defensive Formation

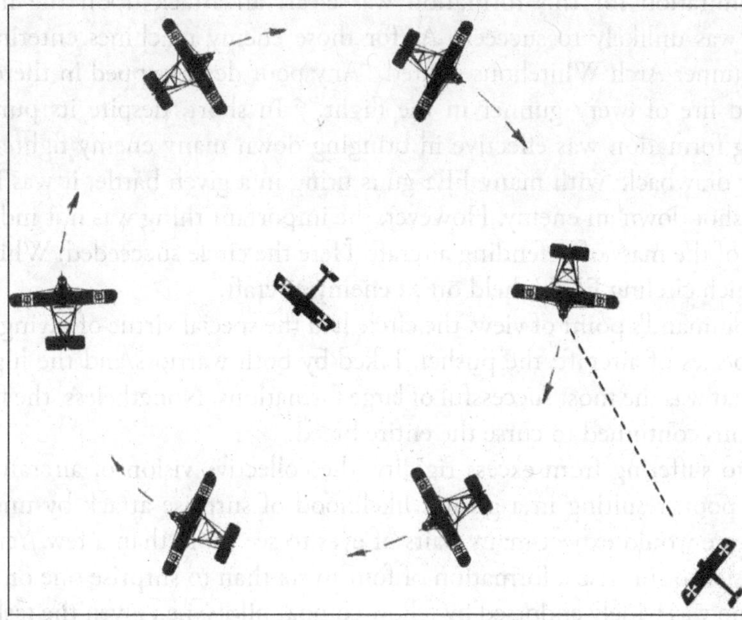

Moving in a circle, the FE2's offered one at a time, consecutive gunfire against attackers (lower right). Enemies within the circle drew simultaneous gunfire from every FE2. Source: Original sketch by author.

Though the gunner/observer was able to shoot forward at almost any angle, and rearwards at an upwards angle through use of a special pole, he was unable to direct fire downwards to the rear. A general lack of rearward vision made matters worse, for the pilot was placed immediately in front of the FE2's enormous rear-mounted engine, his seat so positioned as to prevent any sight of enemies approaching from behind.

Flying within a formation format helped FE2 defense. In July 1916 the format usually employed was yet another variation of the basic V; achieved by adding two more single aircraft, positioned well above and five lengths behind the V.[14] The extra, loose machines were to first signal danger and then pounce on incoming attackers, especially those seeking the FE2 blind spot, behind and below.

Though common sense of "stay together – hold height – stay on a loose course – keep changing altitude"[15] guided the FE2 formation of five, and also that of the stacked V's six machines, their ability to withstand enemy attack remained limited. The FE2 was too old and too slow. Sound defense required special additional steps.

Of these, the best move was the formation of an endless circle. When attacked, the leader would turn and the other machines would follow, generating a huge rotating circle containing the group's five or six machines.[16] Their direction of fire was to the front, where vision was good and both gunner and pilot could shoot easily. The usual result of attacking the circle was the receipt of countless bullets from consecutive machines, delivered as they swept by. On the issue of effectiveness, Canadian Colonel Hartney, FE2d pilot and ace concluded,[17] "To attack such a circling formation was sure death." As he saw it, the usual German counter-move was to abandon broad offensive moves and turn to smaller game; i.e., to "lay back and await a straggler with engine or other troubles and jump him."

Hartney's admiration for this formation was clear: an attack upon the members of a defensive circle was unlikely to succeed. As for those enemy machines entering the circle's interior, FE2b gunner Arch Whitehouse noted, "Any poor devil trapped in there came under the concentrated fire of every gunner in the flight."[18] In short, despite its purely defensive role, the circling formation was effective in bringing down many enemy fighters. There was a curious minor drawback: with many FE2 guns firing in a given battle, it was impossible to determine who shot down an enemy. However, the important thing was not individual credit but the survival of the mass of defending aircraft. Here the circle succeeded: Whitehouse lists[19] one battle in which circling FE2b's held off 23 enemy aircraft.

From high command's point of view, the circle had the special virtue of saving and utilizing an outmoded species of aircraft: the pusher. Liked by both warriors and the high command, the circular format was the most successful of large formations. Nonetheless, the flaws inherent in large formations continued to curse the entire breed.

In addition to suffering from excess rigidity, the collective vision of aircraft within large formations was poor, resulting in a greater likelihood of surprise attack by unseen enemies. This seems odd: we would expect many pairs of eyes to see more than a few. Yet, as noted by Bishop, "It is easier to surprise a formation of four to six than to surprise one or two."[20]

His conclusion was widely endorsed by fellow combat pilots; i.e., given the task of detecting enemies, more heads were inferior to fewer heads. There were two causes. The first was a tendency to place too much faith in those serving as lookouts; the second, a fear of collision.

The typical lookout responded to his assigned duty by believing that with so many men sharing his responsibility, overkill resulted. In short, many eyes were being wasted. In reaction, some men decided to concentrate on a more evident danger: collision and the signaling necessary to avoid collision. As a result, the always difficult search for enemies was slighted, along with its painful peering into the sun and the endless bodily repositioning necessary for maximum vision.

Fokker Triplane Lineup

Rejecting camouflage, many German pilots relied on startling colors and insignias to confuse the enemy. Source: *La Guerre Aérienne*, October 17, 1918, p.790.

In contrast, the small two-plane formation had a limited number of observers; in turn, lookout responsibility was clear and couldn't be dodged. Furthermore, collision was a relatively unlikely problem, not requiring the attention level demanded by large formations. These factors favored superior sighting characteristics by small over large formations. As to which was the most important factor, British test pilot Major Oliver Stewart pointed to the basic irresponsibility of all men, "On keeping a good lookout, two heads are worse than one."[21]

The milling about form of combat had another, very different vision problem: an excess of visual input. Men found it difficult to handle the countless split second appearances or disappearances of what might be friends or enemies, sightings conducted a few yards short of collision and requiring life threatening shooting decisions.

After experimenting initially with a bright covering color – usually red for Richthofen's *Jasta*s – as a form of "come and get me" challenge, German pilots moved to increase the color dosage, painting their machines with wild colors and complex personal insignia. The results tended to over-saturate enemy eyes with information. Given the inevitable visual confusion and extreme tension of those seconds spent milling about, any wild or excessive sight added to the uncertainty, requiring an extra split-second of thought to confirm reality. To some German pilots, this delay suggested greater personal safety.

Whatever the large formation's vision problems, one other concern proved groundless: their machines were not more likely to be downed by anti-aircraft fire than individual aircraft or those within small formations. Here too, one is surprised. Surely large formations were more easily seen than small. Furthermore, a large formation's numerous targets implied that near misses might accidentally hit another aircraft – one not even targeted.

RFC experience proved otherwise. True, it was important to employ the usual defensive[22] precautions against anti-aircraft guns, including a stepped upwards layout (one echeloned in height), along with a continuously changing altitude and endless course variations, such that any straight line flight segment was of short duration. High altitude itself was another important defensive step, with 12,000 feet or more regarded as reasonably safe, in part because it lacked low altitude's (3000 feet or less) exposure to small arms fire, and in part because many seconds were required for a shell to arrive, permitting successful dodging. With these steps taken, the accuracy of German anti-aircraft was unaffected by formation existence or size.

In addition, flying within a tight formation did not increase one's risk. Even extreme close-up flight was without penalty, i.e., "under 100 yards is not too close."[23] The reason had to do with the difficulties of anti-aircraft range assessment when monitoring a number of similar targets, each located at a different altitude and flying along changing paths. The very number of machines contained within a large formation meant "that large errors are made."[24]

The risk itself posed by anti-aircraft was real. Some 1520 aircraft were believed to have been shot down by German cannons and small arms weapons during the war.[25] However, the risk was not increased by the type of formation format: lone aircraft or full formations shared the same 'per aircraft' risk of being brought down.

In sum, from the British point of view, big formations were a useful answer to the problem of fielding fighting aircraft in sizable numbers over German-held territory, and doing so without paying an extra anti-aircraft penalty, However, despite this support, the major drawback of most large formations remained: a lack of combat effectiveness leading to break-up into small, two-man groups upon engagement. At times, not even this could be achieved and transformation into single aircraft followed, with each machine milling about, seeking opponents while desperately avoiding collision.

Bishop has pointed to the milling about type of combat as "generally indecisive",[26] usually resulting in one of the pair of opponents tiring and quitting the scene. The level of pandemonium was too great, and grew steadily greater. Unless one's bullet was fired "within the space of a minute"[27] an enemy machine was unlikely to be brought down.

Especially damaging was the self-destructive tendency produced by the combination of a large formation's rigidity, taken together with milling about confusion. It was possible to profit from this tendency and Lt.Colonel L.W.B. Rees received the Victoria Cross for doing so, combining great bravery with much cunning in single-handedly routing a 10 aircraft bombing formation.

Flying the generally disliked De Havilland 2 pusher fighter in July 1916, Rees came to accept its virtues of tight circling ability and maneuverability, despite drawbacks including a painfully low maximum speed and lack of diving ability.[28] Though the DH2's fighting pluses were limited to those of superior agility, together with a pusher's straightforward means of frontal shooting, it was a better fighting machine than his prior Vickers Gunbus. If not equal to the latest Albatros, the DH2 was capable of offering it considerable competition.

Lt. Col. L.W.B. Rees, RFC.

Rees received the Victoria Cross for routing a large bombing formation, fighting single-handed in a DH2. He is shown perched on a Sopwith artillery spotter. Source: *Air Service Journal*, July 12, 1918, p.18.

Alone and on patrol, he spotted a group of bombers at a distance, well behind the British lines. Assuming them to be British, he moved to join up. Once close, and with their identity clear at last, he made the decision that would result in fame – he attacked.[29]

His target LVG bomber responded by dropping out of formation and circling about, seeking to offer its gunner a clear shot at Rees, i.e., one safely away from the surrounding mass of aircraft. However, this amounted to playing to Rees's strength, for his was a much more maneuverable machine, and the act of quitting the formation meant that he would face only one rear gunner instead of the formation's ten. After flying a few circuits to position himself properly, Rees began to score hits and the bomber dived for home.

Rees returned to the formation, picked another bomber as a target and attacked again. This time two nearby machines came to their companion's aid and moved to challenge Rees. They dove past him, guns blazing, but missed. In the meantime Rees's target, steadily absorbing hits, dived out of action, apparently out of control. His defenders, realizing that it was too late to save their friend, simply departed the scene. In total, some four machines had been either put out of action or forced to flee from the scene of battle.

Next tackling a sub-group of three remaining machines, Rees may have overreached himself. Unable to watch all three enemies as they maneuvered separately, he was hit by a round from a machine he did not see. Though painful, the resulting leg wound didn't prevent further battle. He continued until all the bombers had fled.

Clearly, Rees was an unusually brave man. That said, there was something terribly wrong with the performance of the large formation he encountered. Their confusion, upon attack, was striking. Clearly, there was no settled procedure to handle even the modest menace that he represented. Their actions made it plain that German bomber protection was to come from separate fighter squadrons, and not from the bombers themselves. While a reasonable concept, there was no alternate emergency plan, other than for individual machines to offer fighting support to those attacked, if so inclined, or to flee. This wouldn't do. Yet, so great was the confusion surrounding large formations that the Rees battle registered, not as a strange failure in German planning, but as a portrait of remarkable bravery. In reality, it had something of both.

Such was the range of available formation experience encountered by Richthofen in late 1916. With Boelcke dead, he became leader of the Boelcke Squadron. Proving his skills superior through the downing of renowned Major Hawker in November, the following months saw many line patrols led by Richthofen, yielding ever more experience and victories. Overall, he had a total of 16 victories by January 1917, a score placing him in the top position among German aces. In February he shot down FE2 expert Colonel Hartney, some of whose views we have offered above. The fight was a classic, involving two FE2's in a two-aircraft formation against Richthofen as a lone attacker.

Hartney and his wingman, initially hit by Richthofen's swarm of six machines, were able to form a defensive circle and bring down two. Repulsed, the other attackers moved on. Richthofen arrived late, long after his swarm departed, likely hoping to down the two apparent stragglers. He first dove on the wingman and shot his propeller to bits. As for the circle, he countered it by joining up. Frustrated by Richthofen's unreachable position, Hartney reasoned that more altitude was the solution, for with extra altitude he could manage a diving attack upon Richthofen. Still in the tight circle, at a near stalling incidence, Hartney zoomed upwards – only to fully stall. With his controls soft and flabby,[30] he could not achieve the precise alignment necessary for accurate shooting. Hartney's gunner fired anyway, despite the odds, hoping to hit Richthofen's machine somewhere, anywhere. However, his bullets passed well over Richthofen's head. Hartney attempted to regain control for still another attack, but his time had run out. Richthofen had initiated his own attack, firing bullets that sawed off one of the FE2 propeller blades. Next,[31] the "left part of his wings came off." Richthofen ceased fire, certain that Hartney must crash. Instead, helped by a powerful wind Hartney was able to cross the lines, despite his wrecked machine, and glide to a safe landing on the British side.

More than the usual confusion surrounded this battle. Richthofen was left without physical evidence of victory, i.e., no bodies or machine, and so misidentified Hartney's machine as a BE type. Hartney's escaping aircraft, in truth hard hit and all but destroyed, might have been playing dead, and Richthofen was fortunate to receive credit for victory # 21. Of course, Hartney and his gunner were even luckier: both were alive and able to soldier on.

The battle offers a sense of Richthofen's early approach to small formations, one derived from Boelcke. Testing indicated that the maximum number of formation aircraft capable of being controlled by one man came to roughly six. At times he would accept many more machines as necessary, but his favorite total remained in the neighborhood of six, or about half of a full squadron typically containing 11 to 13 pilots.[32] The finding of six or so pilots to be optimal for control by one man was universal; for example, Americans seeking to avoid "the inefficiency of extremely large and unwieldy formations" settled upon "three to seven airplanes as a fighting unit."[33]

Each of Richthofen's fliers was to have a partner looking after his tail, but this assignment was not rigid, for guarding the other fellow's tail was not the purpose of combat. No man was entitled to a full time bodyguard, including himself. If separation was required to make the best of battle opportunities, so be it.

The flexibility he sought included the right to leave the swarm whenever he desired in order to nail enemy stragglers. Here was a way to gain victories at a low risk, for the act of straggling suggested either an inexperienced enemy, or one already half defeated as the result of prior battle. Those enemies flying obviously defective aircraft were to be shown no mercy: either they were to land immediately or be shot to pieces. As most of his fighting took place on the German side of the lines, landing meant surrender. To permit them to escape, as in the Hartney instance, meant facing them again on another day. Perhaps they would be more fortunate the second time around and it would be Richthofen's turn to lose. No, this was unacceptable. Better to shoot the stragglers down at the first encounter, when the odds were very much against them. As for those British fliers who complained of poor sportsmanship, i.e., the shooting down of stragglers as "Richthofen's racket"[34], his position was clear: air combat was not a sport.

His preference for a modestly sized swarm notwithstanding, Richthofen was forced to face the issue of large British bombing formations, each containing a mixture of bombers and protective fighters, at times reaching a 30-machine total. It was obvious that his favorite five to seven machine swarm was too small for effective opposition. A greater number of defenders was all very well, but how were they to function – to be guided?

Putting his thoughts together for the high command, some two days after the Hartney encounter, he pictured large fighter formations as very different from the loosely connected fliers making up swarms. Instead, they were to consist of groups set in rigid close order; each pilot without the right to alter position and instead, holding a fixed speed and altitude at all times. As straight line flight eased the enemy's interception plans and led to anti-aircraft problems, the large formation was to follow a curved path, a path defined by the leader from his position beneath the formation, where he continually maneuvered to achieve optimum vision. Full responsibility for prevention of surprise attack was placed upon the leader: "If he cannot see to that, he is no good as a leader."[35]

Any advance in thinking beyond Boelcke's outlook was slight. There was no concern over the detailed tactics or tricks of mass combat. All effort went into the safe arrival of a large formation at a combat site. Once there, combat of the one-against-one machine type, with every aircraft tackling the nearest enemy – milling about type combat – was to follow, for at the time he didn't believe in joint efforts or complex attack schemes. In his words: "If one airman has tackled his enemy the others can not assist. They can only look on and protect his back."[36]

What counted were the technical properties of the aircraft: speed, altitude, maneuverability, wing strength, plus "the personality or the fighting determination of the airman."[37] These values were borrowed from the necessary qualities for successful single combat. Richthofen simply applied the same standards to formations. Real life experience would shortly show the limitations of this approach.

For example, in July 1917, *Jasta* 6 formally concluded that for large formations, "combat activity is mostly without result because … friend and foe get so entangled with each other that generally only short, ineffectual combats are possible."[38] It had become clear that successful formation combat demanded skills other than shooting at the nearest enemy. Detailed knowledge of the weak spots and likely maneuvers of enemy aircraft likely to be encountered would be most helpful. Especially wanted was a supply of useful tricks and schemes for dealing with the superior aspects of enemy aircraft. Given the right knowledge, perhaps even such highly regarded tactics as the FE2 defensive circle could be overcome.

Ace *Leutnant* Werner Voss of *Jasta* 10 agreed and supplied a sample of exactly that information required: how to go about downing an FE2.[39] If limited in time, he saw attack from the front as best, owing to the FE2's lack of frontal protection. In a split-second attack typical of large formation confrontation, he would keep below the FE2 at all times, and execute a firing pass from front to rear. As the attacker's speed was opposite to that of the target FE2, the two would diverge rapidly. Though unsaid, given the large number of fighting aircraft in the area, each offering combat or blocking one's path, or both, a second round of combat against the FE2 was unlikely. It was best to press for a single pass and then move on.

In a very different post-war RAF review, the best attack plan for Germans fighting the FE2, given time and possessing "the power of maneuver" was "to reach a position beneath and behind the [FE2] tail at close range."[40] Doing so exploited the aircraft's well-known blind spot to the lower rear.

Here were two good formulas; Voss's for handling a frontal confrontation typical of both milling about and circular formation fights, plus the RAF plan for winning an extended one-against-one struggle. Their very different scenarios made clear the need for knowledge of the right tactics, those suited for the occasion. Success required a good deal more than Richthofen's short list of virtues: the right attitude and a competitive machine.

Leutnant Werner Voss

Fourth ranking German ace (48 victories), Voss was a believer in aerobatics as a fighting tool, a view initially scorned by his friend and competitor Richthofen. Source: *Flugsport*, April 1917, p.244.

Responding to the need, details of successful tactics and tricks were compiled by *Jasta* leaders, some by Richthofen himself. Despite his earlier anti-trickery views, Richthofen was capable of great change, doing so to accommodate himself to the day's reality. For example, his stated belief that of all aircraft virtues, speed was the single most important[41] was dropped in 1917. The game had changed; other traits mattered more and he had openly campaigned for the manufacture of the Fokker Triplane: a nimble but slow machine.

This change in fighter design priorities reflected 1917's German fighter role: that of defense. It was the offensive-minded British who needed speed, with which to attack or retreat. German fighter pilots, whose basic task was to stay behind their lines and defend, found maneuverability to be more important. Covering the shift in thinking, Richthofen announced, with a wry aphorism: "It is better that one's customers come to one's shop than to have to look for one's customers abroad." [42]

As for trickery in combat, though initially seen by Manfred as both despicable and profitless when practiced by the British, his own brother's success in doing exactly that forced him to reconsider the issue. As noted, older brother Manfred had initially described newcomer Lothar as a "butcher"[43]; i.e., one lacking in the finer qualities. However, Lothar's results were startling. Starting in April 1917, some twenty victories were credited to Lothar within a four week period,[44] a striking performance by any standard.

Flying and fighting together, Manfred was struck by Lothar's use of a spinning nosedive to fake mortal wounds; a scheme he employed against any enemy pilot holding a superior position. To a nonplused Manfred, Lothar's resulting victory was " one of my brother's tricks."[45]

Trick or not, here was an important vote for the sly aspects of combat itself; tricks based on maneuverability.

Many similar votes were cast by his fellow commanders. *Leutnant* G.W. Groos of *Jasta* 11 noted[46] the British tendency to use dive and climb tactics, after positioning the sun at their backs. Full flights of six machines rarely dove together. Instead, "a few brave ones", perhaps half a flight or three machines, would attack and the rest would maintain cover. Once the initial diving attack was spent, the English would evade with "continuous tailspins and turns", sometimes employing a second attack in the form of a pass from below and in front. Groos concluded by complimenting the British on their "fine" pursuit machines – a backhanded way of complaining about the Albatros's lack of maneuverability.

British stress upon maneuverability as a key tool for successful formation combat, plus the pressure exerted by the many maneuverability-based victories of Voss and his own brother Lothar, all helped push Manfred towards change. Taken together with the views of important *Jasta* commanders, the result was clear: maneuverability was the new top aircraft virtue; the new 'speed'. It must be found and manufactured.

As noted in connection with Scout tactics, he had previously rejected extreme aerobatics of the Alphonse Pegoud [47] type. His new approach stressed the machine rather than the man, hopefully enabling most any pilot to become a Pegoud. With the aid of the Fokker Triplane, many did so – including himself. Here was a machine with the ability to hang in the air at extreme angles of incidence and shoot upwards. Equipped with Fokker's fat wings, one could ignore the supposed advantages of superior altitude and attack from below.[48]

Fokker Triplane Details

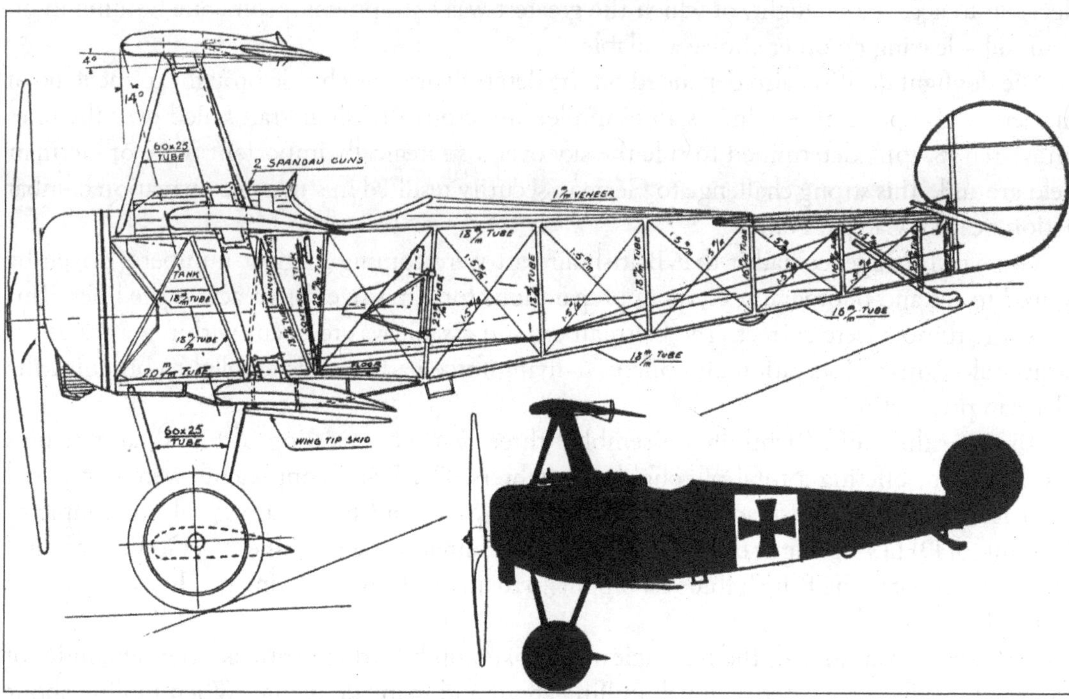

Striking maneuverability was achieved by combining lightweight steel tubing construction with Fokker's own fat wings. Source: *Aeronautics* (UK), May 22, 1918, p.436.

If some tactics changed with time and development, many did not. The hope of bringing order to formation combat, of eliminating the wild confusion and milling about associated with the fighting of large groups was rarely achieved. Similarly, the dogfight itself, converting an individual pilot plus machine into a fighting force, showed great staying power despite much criticism. From the official point of view, dogfighting required too much skill, with aerobatics and flight training playing too large a role. Instead, they pressed for joint group action as better suited for 1917, a time of little training and few skills. Their reasoning was solid. Successfully employing those thousands who could barely fly might conceivably win a war; whereas schooling those few gifted pilots capable of winning a dogfight would not.

Corrective plans existed for the necessary shift of tactics, supposedly eliminating dogfights and making for large formation success, but their results were unimpressive. Most failed by attributing too much power to an asset; for example, altitude, leading to the official British late-war view: "With the advantage of height, superior numbers may be attacked with impunity, as the fight can be broken off at will."[49]

At times, yes, by converting an initial height advantage into speed, a small formation could flee readily. However at other times, when caught up in a wild melee, there was no easy exit. In this case, the official accompanying advice: "do not fight it out … re-climb to repeat the attack"[50] was a poor fit to a grim reality. Similarly, criticizing the dogfight as unworthy, in the belief that "only bad leadership leads to a dogfight" was an attempt to banish an awkward truth through denial.

Richthofen knew better. To fight and win a dogfight was every fighter pilot's basic task. True, there were more efficient, less deadly ways of conducting a war, but planning to evade deadly dogfights simply through use of special tactics was unrealistic. Many factors entered into the decision to accept a dogfight, of which the greatest was entrapment – someone homing in on your tail – leaving no other choice available.

The dogfight decision also depended on the determination each side brought to the issue of mastery over a piece of terrain. As an example, numerous British aircraft sailed over the lines on March 18, 1918, determined to rule the sky over a strategically important piece of German-held ground. This strong challenge to German security resulted in a massive formation combat action near Le Cateau, France.

German Intelligence had it that British aircraft were coming in great numbers, driven by a need to see and photograph German preparations for a massive thrust across the lines. This time, the rumors were correct. The German ground assault was to occur within a week and a large-scale British observation and offensive flying force had been assembled to pinpoint the German preparations.

To drive them off, Richthofen assembled three *Staffels*, consisting of his usual # 11 plus # 6 and # 10, offering a total of roughly 30 fighters. His British opponents were composed of at least two fighting squadrons, containing ten SE5's and nine Camels, plus a couple of handfuls of DH4's serving as bombers and photo reconnaissance machines.[51] A German ground observer estimated the British force as: "about 30 to 40 machines … flying neatly within a large rectangle."[52]

Once battle was joined, the rectangle was broken up by a diving attack. The remainder of the half hour fight consisted of much milling about and many dogfights. When milling about, the best of single-handed tactics; i.e., positioning oneself on an enemy's tail and staying there, failed completely, for attempting to do so attracted a protective wingman determined to sit on the aggressor's tail. Even shooting off the necessary rounds of aimed fire at a target was most unwise, for accurate shooting required a fixed trajectory all too likely to draw murderous incoming fire. Instead, all was snap-shooting and dodging.

The resulting British losses at Le Cateau, totaling 8 or 9 machines including 5 Camels, as against 3 officially admitted "unsuccessful air combats"[53] (i.e., losses) by the Germans, demonstrated the unpredictability of large scale air combat operations. Despite good men and machines, use of a large formation format made it only too easy to suffer losses greater than those of the enemy.

As given by Captain Alan Botts,[54] the worst feature of large scale tactics was the need to switch from the offensive to the defensive and back again within split seconds, all while being swept up into a huge swirling mass of men and machines. An ability to make lightning decisions, backed with snap shooting, was everything.

Targets consisted of the nearest enemy machine without concern for size, type, trajectory or likelihood of hitting. It was enough to fire at any enemy aircraft crossing one's sights, despite the discouraging lack of success. The difficulty was well known. To highly experienced ace pilot Wing Commander Ira Jones, it was almost impossible to bring down targets with snap-shooting – even those that looked easy.[55]

Though the wasted efforts of most large formation combat was obvious to both sides, it continued nonetheless, driven by necessity. Large formations did have one crucial virtue: they offered domination of the sky over a limited area, through sheer mass of aircraft. Once in place over an ongoing ground battle, a large formation could well prevent enemy access or observation, both important for land war victory. As the proper counter move, an equally large formation seemed right and so the stage was set for a massive battle, effective or not.

For local control of the air to have importance, it was necessary that the war take on the form of intense battle over a limited area – the more intense, the better. A Verdun-type confrontation was well suited to the needs and traits of large offensive formations, whereas a mobile, shifting battle of tanks or cavalry was not. Given June 1918's static front, there was routine use by the German Air Service of offensive formations consisting of twenty plus aircraft, as noted by American ace Captain Eddie Rickenbacker.[56] However, by the summer of 1918, an open German retreat led to smaller formations and Rickenbacker reported a fight with a group of seven Fokker D.VII machines as typical for the period.

By October 1918, smaller formations completely dominated aerial activity. Hartney described [57] these as containing six machines, each roughly 200 yards apart, and moving forwards in a large circular path. More ground was covered, if more slowly, with the hope of preventing surprise attack. At times several such groups were working in a given area and in principal were to cooperate. However, the considerable distance and lack of communication between groups made such cooperation unlikely. In any event, the notion was well-liked and both sides came to use the same idea almost exclusively, until the war ended.

Formation fighting, large or small, had profound difficulties. SE5a pilot Captain Duncan Grinnel-Milne neatly summed up the many disappointments he had personally experienced. Fighting over the German-held Le Cateau terrain in a standard three-machine V formation, he had hopes for the employment of dive and zoom tactics. However, he learned that a far more likely event was the sudden sight of incoming enemy tracers, followed by "hard rudder and no bank: side slip!..every man for himself."[58]

Altitude versus Aircraft Task

Task	Altitude
Infantry Support	500 Ft.
Artillery Spotters	5,000 Ft.
Long Range Observation	6,000 Ft.
Fighters	15,000 Ft.

Planning for the interception of enemy formations was made difficult by uncertainty as to altitude. Much depended on the task. The official 1917 British standards shown offered a helpful, if crude guide. Source: *Aerial Service Journal*, November 8, 1917, p. 565.

Despite the indecisive performance of formations, both large and small, in terms of victories gained and lost, the process of interception itself continued to have great value. The ground war had its own demands, and goals. To the infantry, shooting down opposing aircraft was all very well, but there were more important goals. With the help of interception, bombing might be curtailed, infantry strafing stopped, artillery spotting halted, and long-range observation prevented. With so much at stake, the problems of interception drew attention, with much thought centered on weather and altitude. The role of weather in interception success was obvious; that of altitude less so.

The right altitude granted superior height to the intercepting fighter, enough for a diving attack. Wanted was approximately 1000 feet of extra altitude in hand, as compared to the enemy. As for the enemy's altitude, much depended on his assignment, with those fighter units aimed at challenging enemy fighters placed highest, and infantry support squadrons lowest. See chart above.

Other factors influencing operational altitude included anti-aircraft gunnery, with its tendency to force aircraft altitude upwards as a means of evasion, and oxygen deprivation, reducing the efficiency of both men and machines as higher altitudes were reached. With oxygen masks in a primitive state, concern for pilot health led to an understandable desire to fly at lower altitudes. Engines were also strongly influenced by operational altitude. In the pre-supercharger days of 1917-1918, engines reaching 20,000 feet developed only half the power realized at ground level.[59]

Individual bias – upwards for anti-aircraft safety; downwards for pilot health and engine performance – meant that pilot judgement ruled. Those who had experienced the painful effects of extreme cold and oxygen deprivation would likely push for lower altitude missions, just as those who had barely survived being bounced by higher altitude enemies favored an upward move. The net effect was to increase the spread of likely altitudes where enemies might be found, adding to the uncertainty of interception.

A final difficulty burdened pursuit operations. Though desperately needed, radio transmission equipment was too heavy for the usual lightweight fighter aircraft. British experiments with lights and flares had produced a modest success, and made communication possible, though limited to only a few key words. A commanding 'yes' or 'go ahead' signal took the form of a red light or flare; a basic 'no' or 'washout' was signaled with green. To announce a personal washout, the troubled flyer used a white color.[60] While these were useful, the inability to communicate more complex concepts continued as a serious handicap in the handling of large formations.

Late in 1918, the unresolved problems of large formation tactics, plus those of interception failure, led to a fresh approach. Drawn from bitter experience, this final re-structuring of formations produced good results.

As a starter, there was the well-known truth that smaller formations were more easily controlled than large. A group leader could expect to control six or seven machines. To simply add more was impressive, but ineffective. Well then, let formations be of a modest size. Furthermore, sending out many modest formations, each at a different altitude and at a somewhat different time, meant a better chance of interception, as compared to a large single formation, necessarily limited to a single altitude and a single time. In short, the large formation concept was set aside in favor of the small.

For both the British and Germans, the four to seven man pursuit group prevailed. Formation makeup and tactics varied according to the wishes of the group commander. The resulting variety itself proved useful. As an example of the new reasoning, asymmetrical formations became popular. Here, the neat balance so strongly embedded in military thinking,

Asymmetrical Formations

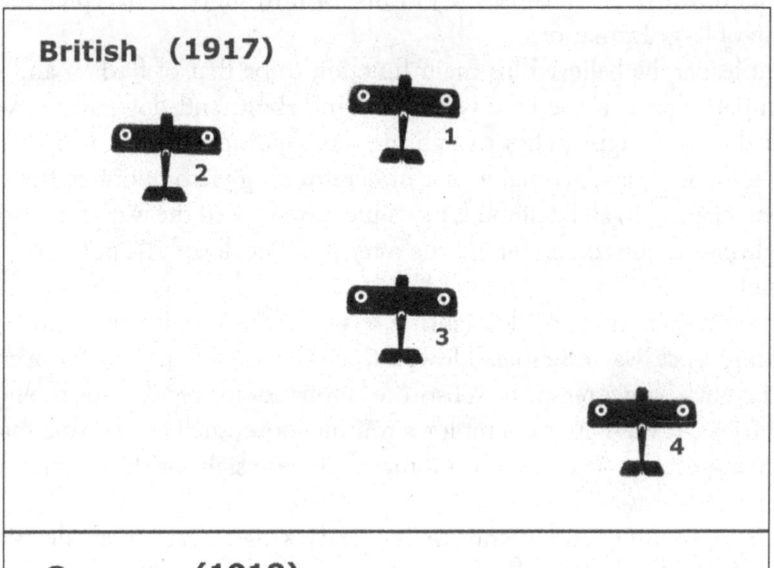

Unbalanced formations permitted disabled machines to exit more readily. Aircraft #1 was the leader's, flying lowest to be easily seen by all. Other machines were stacked up accordingly. Source: (top) *Air Service Journal*, July 12, 1917, p.93; (bottom) German document, serial # 200, Aug. 1918, TNA file # AIR 1/1189/204/5.2595.

from parades to flyovers, was abandoned in favor of a deliberate, and provocative unbalance. Perplexing the enemy was a good thing. Were those few aircraft to be seen mere decoys, set out as bait? Were the missing machines close by, ready to pounce?

To Colonel Rees, a lack of symmetry offered a practical advantage as well: once properly stacked in height, "any disabled machine can turn out of the formation without interfering with the others."[61] For example, consider an aircraft hit by anti-aircraft fire and suddenly unable to turn left. Given asymmetry, a pilot need not fear the presence of a friendly machine to his right, blocking his exit from the formation, for there was no pilot to his right. In short, each aircraft, unblocked and free of its old mirror image twin, was able to drop out of the formation whenever necessary. This was a valuable plus: if attacked, one could join a dogfight without restraint.

Richthofen's view of formation size changed with the times. Starting with Boelcke's swarm of roughly 6 machines, he moved on to simultaneously lead four *Staffels*, offering a combined potential of approximately 45 fighters. As their commander, he accepted and promoted the large formation. Certainly his leadership of three *Staffel*s at Le Cateau was successful, with nine British machines downed in exchange for 3 of his own. In short, he accepted and was at ease with the notion of large formations.

As a combat leader, he believed his main function to be that of finding and engaging the enemy. The initial impact, to be followed by milling about and dogfighting, were accepted as natural. Of these two approaches to fighting, dogfighting was much to be preferred, for skill and determination played a major role in determining victory, unlike the milling about dependent upon chance. In all likelihood, he would have viewed the war's final British decision against dogfighting as mistaken, for to the very end, he favored one-on-one dogfighting wherever possible.

As for the aerobatics aspect of dogfighting, every man must be taught the fundamental moves, for competence was essential. However, aerobatics was not to be overdone. To be avoided especially was any attempt to substitute aerobatics for combat, or to engage in tricks for the sake of tricks. It was better to employ a routine move, such as shooting many hundreds of rounds from a great distance, than to momentarily lose sight of the enemy by performing astonishing aerobatic feats.

His death in April 1918 came before the general swing toward a smaller size formation. However, there is reason to believe that he would have approved such a move as more favorable for individual fighter pilots. In Richthofen's view, a proper war was to be a contest between gifted, trained warriors. As he well knew, once formations grew beyond a small size the individual's importance diminished, with each pilot changing roles from that of warrior to that of a cog.

His last day reflected this view, one strongly favoring small formations. It started as an ordinary day with no pressure to perform duties other than those of a standard patrol. With four *Staffel*s under his command, he flew with only # 11. Their machines, less than a dozen Fokker Triplanes, were divided into two groups, of which he headed one, numbering five aircraft. Expertise within his group was mixed. It contained a beginner – a remote cousin – and also Richthofen's occasional wingman, ace *Leutnant* H.J. Wolff.

Richthofen's decisions on that day displayed his bias: where formations were concerned, smaller was better, and so he opted for the fewest fighters possible. Even the apparent total of five machines was deceptive, for one was flown by a beginner. Instead of adding useful force, beginners required protection. Perhaps only three fighters were truly available for combat purposes. Of these, part-time wingman Wolff could be relied upon to permit Richthofen to dogfight as he wished. To fight alone was a rare treat for a Richthofen increasingly burdened with administrative problems. He eagerly accepted the chance.

The events of that day remain unclear. As previously detailed, he died alone, without a friendly witness able to see his end. The *Jagdgeschwader* War Journal report filed to cover the day's activities stated only that "according to irreproachable testimony, he landed smoothly in the area of Hill 102 … while in pursuit of an Englishman."[62] The vagueness and lack of detail suggest an observer too remote to be useful. Australian eyewitness reports have been hopelessly contradictory and subsequent investigation has changed little. His death points to one disadvantage of the small formation: the lack of eyes to report back on the sights and events of the day.

In sum, the positive features of fighter formations included the ability to fire more bullets at a given target within a split second, domination over a limited sector through sheer numbers, placement of machines at superior defensive positions, and the managing of an endless circle form of defense. Small, two or three aircraft formations proved especially effective. The feared increase of formation losses to anti-aircraft gunnery did not occur.

Formation drawbacks included a greatly increased possibility of collision, the ineffectiveness of most large aircraft groups owing to confusion and lack of communication in combat, the breakup of formation conflicts into single combats, a weakness in spotting enemies and a final British turn against the dogfight itself.

Richthofen's initial proposal for a German version of the large formation pictured a rigidly structured form. With experience he developed the necessary flexibility, including an acceptance of tricks and aerobatic importance. He then proved his ability with a major victory over a comparable large British group at Le Cateau. Personally preferring the role of a one-on-one dogfighter, his last moves favored the small formation over the large.

9

Tactics and The Right Kind

In the endless search for more victories, tactics were never permitted to become rigid. As aircraft and guns improved, offering more in the way of performance or maneuverability, combat techniques shifted accordingly. The endless changes required a certain free-floating outlook for acceptance and survival. Pilot personality mattered. Determination was necessary; however, rigidity could be fatal.

In turn, pilot temperament exerted considerable influence on tactics. Their usual short life span led to great respect for those few men who managed to survive beyond the usual several months of frontline duty. However, even admirers sensed some of the techniques employed by the best fighter pilots as odd. Did their very oddness mask genius? Was pilot survival a matter of the proper genes, assuring superior intelligence and faster reactions; or had some men quietly mastered superior tactics of their own; tactics better suited to combat than those of the enemy? Finally, was the achievement of a great many victories in aerial combat itself a matter of skill or luck?

Each Air Service struggled with these questions. As background, each strained to keep its pilot supply pipeline full, a severe burden at best, but when facing the huge demands of 1917, an impossible task. The practical result was to speed training along by offering tyro pilots the least instruction possible. In April 1917, by official admission, British pilots were "going overseas with an average of 17 ½ hours instruction in the air."[1] These were men who could barely fly, much less fight. In the view of General Frederick Sykes,[2] many such poorly trained beginners "fell easy prey to experts like Richthofen."

In similar fashion, starting in the autumn of 1917 German pilot trainees were no longer drawn from those who had previously served as observers or gunners. Instead, recruits with no prior war experience of any kind were trained and sent into combat directly,[3] a shift assuring a greater immediate supply, plus larger losses soon to come – losses owed to ignorance.

For those who survived, there came the inevitable question: how was it done?

Was it mostly a matter of background? The right parents?

At the highest military levels, the European class system dominated the search for personnel, pressing a belief that the best men came from birth within the right family: one of ancient, land owning nobility, with a long military tradition. As a prime example, there was Captain Baron von Richthofen, solidly maintaining his role as first among Pursuit Wing leaders. To General von Hoeppner, one of Manfred's key qualities was "a knightly bearing."[4] Unsaid, but implied, was the respect due to a warrior descendent of Prussian warriors, fighting along side his younger brother, Lothar.

Here was a gifted pair reflecting every quality capable of delighting recruiting officers, for they were military school graduates with a strong hunting background, expert horsemen, active rather than reflective, well spoken and physically sturdy – in short, the best sort of professional

The Richthofen Brothers

Many believed aces such as *Oberleutnant* Lothar (left) and *Rittmeister* Manfred (right) owed much to their ancestors and upper class background.Source: (left) *Luftfahrt*, June 1917, p.15; (right) *Deutsche Luftfahrter Zeitung*, April 1917, p.12.

soldiers, obviously slated for command. So clearly were these "the right kind" as to raise doubts about all other backgrounds and abilities.

Confusion came with the second highest German scorer, *Leutnant* Ernst Udet (62 victories). His father[5] was a plumbing expert, specializing in installation of the newly popular coal-fired hot water bathtubs. Though an honorable task, its lack of nobility was all too evident. Furthermore, his father despised Ernst for failing in those qualities considered manly. Instead of sports, or better yet, hunting as a hobby, young Ernst was content to build and fly model airplanes, or to draw, for his ambition was to become an artist – an ambition bitterly opposed by his father.

To some extent, Ernst was pushed into a passive role by his small size. He never reached the 5 feet 3 inch height (160 cm.) officially required to become a German airman.[6] His physique was correspondingly slight. Inadequate at conventional sports, he sat out school play periods, his time spent in drawing.

With the war, and quick rejection as a volunteer soldier, came flying lessons paid by his father, pleased to see Ernst do something other than draw. Once a licensed pilot, the Air Service proved unable to resist the bargain that he represented – that of a volunteer pilot trained at someone else's expense – and so, height be damned, Udet was in. Assigned to a quiet sector, he acquired the necessary skills on his own; learning the shooting and aerobatic arts necessary to survive while slowly accumulating victories.

Of command capabilities, he had none. Instead, he was a "lost generation" character, determined to make life a non-stop party, with each partygoer a personal friend and every short woman within reach considerably more than a friend. His wish to become an artist matured into a caricaturist's wicked skill. After the war, he survived and even thrived as a

Oberleutnant Ernst Udet

Totally unlike Manfred in either background or personality, playboy Udet became the second-ranking German ace by war's end. Source: *Flugsport*, July 1918, p.331

Udet on Udet

A gifted cartoonist, Udet made fun of those prominent in the aeronautical world, starting with himself. Source: Ernst Udet, *Hals und Beinbruch* (Berlin: Wilhelm Kolf, 1928) p.104 (left) and p.79 (right). Cartoon captions have been translated and updated by author.

light aircraft manufacturer, but slowly wearied of a life spent as an alcoholic (Champagne) womanizer. Coming off the highs was difficult and there were periods of black depression. Nonetheless, a splendid reputation as an exhibition pilot and designer brought him a position as a top ranking Luftwaffe General, concerned primarily with warplane design. However, working directly under the thumb of a thoroughly hated Hermann Goering was one burden too many. In a final fit of despair, Udet ended his life with a pistol shot[7] in late 1941. He was 45.

Surely few aces were more unlike the Richthofen brothers. Lacking in officer qualities, he was suited for few 1914-1918 roles other than the one he filled, that of a fighter pilot. Yet, like Manfred, he was undeniably one of the greatest of fighter pilots. His personal input was not of the revolutionary type. Instead, joining the Richthofen Squadron after his 19th victory, he made the best use of those tactical improvements already in place, following pioneering efforts by Boelcke or Manfred. These included emphasis upon combat itself, rather than the flying of patrols. In practice, this meant endless moving of the squadron to catch the tide of battle, plus five flights per day instead of the usual three. New fighter designs tended to come to his famous unit first, and he had the advantage of early introduction to the Fokker Triplane, followed by the later Fokker D.VII biplane.

His single greatest strength was that of flexibility – of not pushing any tactic to extremes. Aerobatics, always his strong suit even when flying the relatively immobile Albatros, was useful up to a point, as were gunnery skills. The trick was in recognizing the limit; of pressing hard when advantageous, and fleeing combat when not. His classic single-handed aerobatic struggle with French ace Guynemer[8] summed up Udet's ability: though he lost the encounter, he survived to fight another day. Given enough luck, skill and common sense, one could do well indeed.

What then of knightly qualities? Were those considerations of family background and athletic skill used in flying officer recruitment all wrong? Did a too short pilot hold some advantage over a similar opponent of standard height? Were there other aces of the too short or too tall variety? Were those men requiring eye-glasses really hopeless as fighter pilots?

To examine the effect of personal input on fighter pilot performance, it is useful to have a standard defining "superior", and we shall use the twenty victory level as a guide, limiting our choice of subjects, with some exceptions, to pilots achieving between 20 and 80 victories. Nations whose pilot scores were considered include Austria-Hungary, Belgium, France, Germany, Great Britain, Italy, Russia and the USA.

Those men chosen for detailed examination – roughly a dozen – reflect the limited sources of available personal data, drawn largely from articles or books written after the war by survivors and professional writers. Unfortunately, those who were shy or poorly educated tended to avoid this process. As for the dead, they were sometimes honored with highly distorted tales. Thus our sample may well be biased. Despite this inherent limitation, it can be said that every man considered below was a highly successful fighter pilot, serving in either the German, British, French or American Air Service.

The totals below reflect the difficulty of accumulating more than the usual run of several victories, a difficulty that increased with every victory gained. For example, some 94 men were able to reach the 20 to 29 victory level, but a grand total of only 4 men were able to reach the two highest categories, that of 70 to 80 and 80 to 90. Manfred and his kind were truly rare individuals.

Victory Totals: Top Aces

Victory Range	Achievers
20 to 29	-------- 94
30 to 39	-------- 37
40 to 49	-------- 19
50 to 59	-------- 6
60 to 69	-------- 2
70 to 79	-------- 3
80 to 89	-------- 1

The number of men achieving top aerial victory scores in the 1914-1918 war. Source: Assembled by author from data, Ezra Bowen, *Knights of the Air* (Alexandria, VA: Time-Life, 1980) Appendix p.196

Aside from Udet, what were these great achievers like? There was another short, slight, and most successful warrior: Captain Albert Ball (44 victories); height – 5 feet 6 inches. A very different sort, his personality was quite unlike that of Udet, for he was a dour loner. His fellow 60 Squadron member Lieutenant Stanley Vincent described Ball as "a quiet introspective little chap … living in a solitary state in a small hut with his violin … we called him 'The Lonely Testicle.'"[9]

Captain Albert Ball

Rejecting companions and crowds, Ball preferred to fight alone, despite the seeming advantages of wingmen and formations. Source: Frank A. Mumby, *The Great World War*, Volume 7 (London: Gresham, 1918) p.136

The Odds against Ball

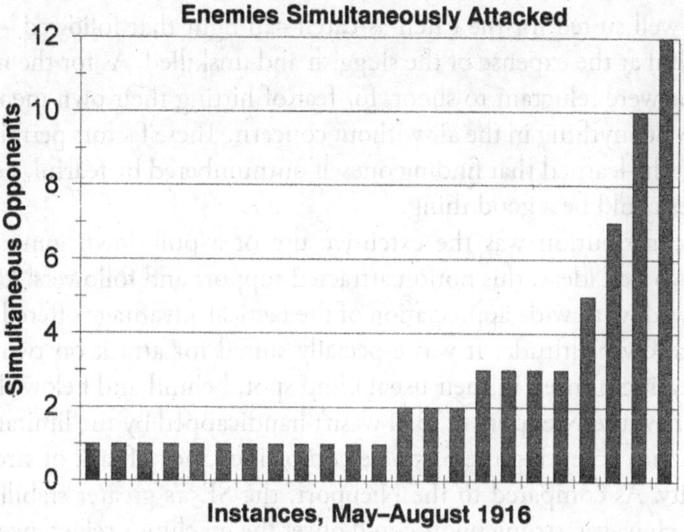

Loner Ball successfully tackled many opponents simultaneously, in numbers ranging from one to a dozen. His success raised the question: why formations? Source: Author-assembled chart from data in A.J.L. Scott, *Sixty Squadron, RAF* (London: Heinemann, 1920) p.16.

His withdrawn personality was confirmed by Lieutenant William Fry. "Not sociable … he would escape to his hut as soon as he could."[10]

Ball was markedly different from his own father, who moved socially upwards from the role of local plumber to become Mayor of Nottingham. Young Ball reacted by turning away from people and politics, instead busying himself with practical engineering of the DIY type. His ultimate peacetime ambition was to become an electrical engineer.[11]

Aside from his own impressive combat record, Ball made three distinct contributions to combat tactics. First, he preferred to fly and fight alone. His victory count alone stood as sufficient justification for a concept unpopular with high command, proving that a lone hand pilot, disdaining wingmen and formations alike, was capable of succeeding in a big way. His success suggested – as an awkward truth – that teamwork was largely pointless, for gifted individuals were the true rulers of the skies.

Secondly, the number of enemy aircraft he chose to engage simultaneously exceeded all norms, for Ball was willing to plunge into massive enemy formations. True, he did not employ this startling tactic frequently, and most of his fights were of a more conventional sort. See chart above.

Ball never rejected the prospect of dealing with only one enemy at a time and a dozen such one-on-one encounters were tabulated for the mid-1916 period shown. However, he was quite willing to accept unequal combat, should it present itself. Three fights against a pair of machines were recorded, as were four fights against a trio of opponents. Still larger numbers were tackled, and as many as a dozen enemy machines were fought simultaneously.

Schoolyard wisdom suggests that it's easier for five boys to gang up on one, than for one boy to gang up on five. Coming at a time when strategic thinkers saw overwhelming numbers as the path to victory, Ball's approach was truly unusual. Why did he persist? On his side were the well known problems of formations: fear of collision, inability to signal one's fellow pilots quickly, inability to handle novel situations and a tendency to fill formation slots with the newest, rawest pilots available. Bursting into the middle of an enemy formation, Ball's unstable Nieuport 17 was well suited for the catch-as-catch-can fight that followed – one that favored the lithe and skillful at the expense of the sluggish and unskilled. As for the many guns against him, enemy pilots were reluctant to shoot, for fear of hitting their own men, while loner Ball could shoot freely at anything in the air without concern. These factors permitted Ball to invert the odds. In short, he learned that finding oneself outnumbered by fearful, nervous enemies in sluggish machines could be a good thing.

A third Ball contribution was the extensive use of a pull-down gun to shoot upwards. Unlike the first two Ball ideas, this notion attracted support and followers. Use of this concept in the SE5a followed, with wide appreciation of the tactical advantage offered: that of attacking an enemy from a lower altitude. It was especially suited for attack on two-seaters, with the aggressor first locating himself in their usual blind spot, behind and below the tail.

So long as he flew the Nieuport 17, Ball wasn't handicapped by the limitations of his size or strength. Pushed into accepting the SE5a, he complained, not of lack of strength, but of lack of maneuverability. As compared to the Nieuport, the SE5a's greater stability meant inferior maneuverability. However, strong pilots could offset the machine's reluctance to change course by forcing the controls, through use of brute force.[12] Competing German pilots did exactly that throughout the lengthy series of Albatros fighters. Forced to do so, Ball complied reluctantly. There was something to be said for muscular pilots.

We know little of Ball's death. Whether he was downed by an enemy or a storm cloud remains unclear.[13] As with Richthofen, he paid the price of loners: going to his death with much uncertainty as to the means. Instead, there was acclaim from General Trenchard, and an admission by knowledgeable editor C.G. Grey that of all fighter pilot's deaths, that of Ball's "had a gravely depressing effect."[14] That so skilled and daring a fighter could not survive was disturbing. One needed more – what?

Major Edward "Mick" Mannock (61 to 73 victories) stood 6 feet tall and presented an impressive military figure. An Army brat, his father was a mean drunk who deserted his young family after slyly pocketing all available funds. In short, the man was a monster. In time, Mannock's openly expressed hatred for his father was converted into an anti-authority stance, favoring Anarchism.

To earn his bread, he dropped out of school at age 13 and became a manual worker, somehow managing to play ball (cricket, rugby) and study history while working a full-time schedule. Caught and interned in Turkey by the war, he was sent home (April 1915) where he enlisted, transferred to RFC flight training (late 1916) and achieved a back-handed appreciation from his instructor, "I always thought he was the type to do or die."[16] Nothing was said about skill.

Introduced to combat, he freely offered advice to old hands from the depths of his ignorance. Laughed at, and forced to face reality, he began schooling himself on the fine points of shooting and aerobatics. Success as a fighter pilot came slowly and respect even more slowly. He was too excitable[17] to fit the nerveless image viewed as properly heroic. When off duty, he joined drunken parties featuring indoor rugby with its pileups and injuries, to be followed by keening sessions where he wept for the dead.

In time, his success as a fighter pilot became obvious, though it was marked by excess. To wear a huge false beard while on patrol was Mannock's unique combination of rebellion along with dedication to duty. To machine gun an enemy aircraft already downed was pointless, yet it permitted him to express rage in an acceptable form. To fire warning shots at one of his own

Major Edward Mannock

Top ace Mannock was admired for his efforts to help beginners. Though subject to emotional spells suggesting nervous breakdowns, he fought on. Source: Ira Jones, *Tiger Squadron*, (London: White Lion, 1954) p.144.

Deflection Shooting: Mannock's Formula

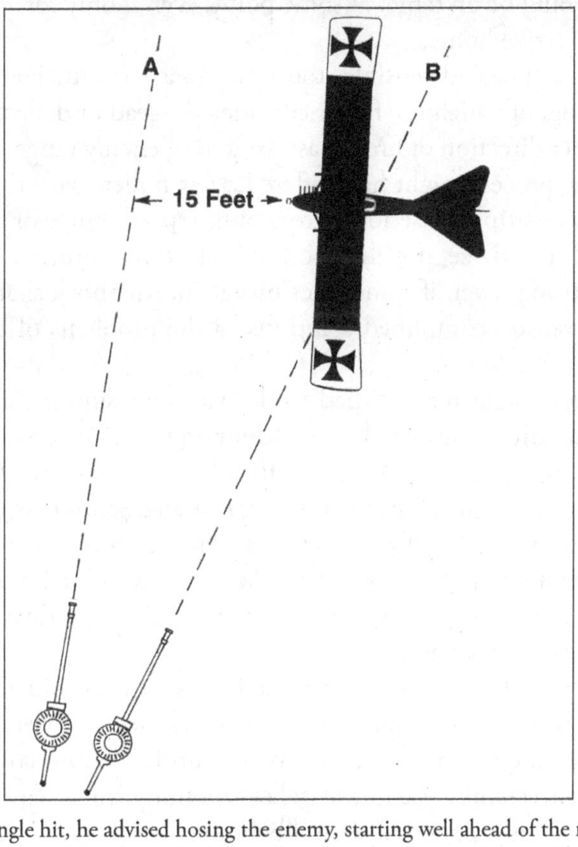

For a right angle hit, he advised hosing the enemy, starting well ahead of the nose (A) and moving rearwards to (B) before a final reversal, moving back to (A). Source: Sketch by author from data in Ira Jones, *Tiger Squadron* (London: W.H. Allen, 1954) p.102, 124

Squadron members sensed as cowardly was Mannock's own special solution to the problem of fear. No matter what his behavior, his Squadron members merely shrugged. Mannock seemed but a barely contained explosion.

Yet, there was a saving grace: he cared about, and actively helped beginners. At a time of withdrawn, loner aces, he put himself forward as a teacher, never losing sight of the tyro's agony. He taught not only with words, but with unforgettable deeds. The combination was most unusual.

Mannock possessed the gift of gab. His audience was thirsty for combat know-how. His particular strength was for simple solutions to complex questions; solutions that were neat and easily retained. Unfortunately, oversimplification was inevitable in such forced solutions, and omissions were common.

Consider the experience of Captain Ira Jones (40 victories). This short pilot (5 feet 5 inches) failed to score a single victory in his initial 16 combat encounters. For the most part, he saw and fired at enemy machines crossing his own trajectory; in other words, his targets moved at right angles to his bullets. He sought Mannock's advice. How does one hit a target moving at right angles to one's own path?

He was advised[18] to sight about 15 feet ahead of the enemy's engine before opening fire. Shooting steadily, he was then to shift the aiming point rearwards towards the pilot, before finally pushing the line of fire forward again. Mannock reasoned that by continuously shifting the stream of fire, it would be on target at some point, even if only for an instant, and so a few bullets were certain to strike home.

Though the concept appeared sensible, too much was left out. Four independent factors matter greatly in aiming, of which the factor considered – lead or deflection – is but one. Also entering into the proper direction of fire are assessment of enemy range, speed and attitude. At best Mannock's hosing process might have offered a few bullets with the right deflection, but was incapable of compensating for serious errors of the speed, range or attitude type.

When Jones tested the advice, it didn't work, much to his surprise. Yet his admiration for Mannock remained strong. Even if sometimes mistaken, Mannock shared his knowledge. To the truly desperate, even oversimplified solutions to the problems of combat seemed better than nothing.

One of Mannock's popular maxims had to do with choosing the altitude best suited for attacking an enemy machine: "Always above; seldom on the same level; never underneath."[19]

Again, a partial truth is apparent. A higher altitude did have merit. As one virtue, altitude could always be traded for speed. Thus, the top dog in a dogfight was assured a reserve of speed, if needed. Secondly, employment of a diving pass, starting from a superior altitude, had the special virtue of being safer than most aggressive tactical moves. If all went wrong, for example, should a suddenly jammed machine gun ruin one's chances, the dive could be extended as necessary; if need be, all the way home.

That said, Mannock's call for superior altitude ignored the considerable success gained by those attacking from below. For example, most of Ball's victories were obtained with a pull-down gun used against targets moving at a superior altitude. Even conventionally mounted, horizontal guns were successfully used by attackers zooming from below, after initially hiding in the target machine's blind spot – below and behind.

In short, "never underneath" managed to ignore many worthwhile, proven exceptions. Yet, Mannock's maxim was highly successful, for it offered a bit of easily recalled advice; a triumph of the pithy and memorable over the messiness of reality.

Mannock himself came to an uncertain end. He was likely brought down (July 1918) by anti-aircraft fire, as the result of breaking one of his own rules; that forbidding flight close to the ground, in pursuit of an "out of control" victim. The irony of his own death reminds us that despite flaws and omissions, each of his maxims contained more than a grain of tactical truth.

If neither Udet's 5 feet 2 inches height or Mannock's 6 feet were obstacles to a career as a fighter pilot, was there a limiting line to be drawn anywhere? Consider one of the tallest of British aces, Lieutenant Cecil Lewis, at 6 feet 4 inches.

Though his 8 victories were low as measured by our 20 and up standard, they were certainly significant. His solid background as both a fighter pilot (SE5a) and test pilot testify to practical piloting ability. Aside from his recruiting officer's plaintive: "I don't think you can get into a machine",[20] no real problem resulted from his excess height. As for the doubtful recruiter, he was converted by Lewis's description of his most proper upper class background; one strong on athletics. To either the RFC or the German Air Service, physique mattered somewhat, but other desirables – class and money – mattered more.

Lewis was another loner of the Ball type. He believed that one's personal outlook was crucial and sought "steely courage, drained of all emotion."[21] His later career as a scientific test pilot did call for a thoughtful approach and the same outlook may well have seen him through combat.

However, in the matter of combat, many types of outlook succeeded, so long as they were matched to the abilities, tools and tactics of the individual. Ball's contempt for the odds against him worked well – for Ball. Mannock's rules worked well – for Mannock. Others attempting to copy their success had little luck, for they lacked something in the way of skill or personality.

An especially striking difference in personality and approach was demonstrated by France's two leading aces. One national hero stood for open attack and stoicism, the other for cunning and forethought.

French Captain Georges Marie Ludovic Jules Guynemer[22] (53 victories) had the overlong name of those with a great many honored ancestors. His father graduated from the French equivalent of West Point and spent his life as a professional Army officer. However, from birth it was obvious that young Guynemer was not of the same stripe, for he was a sickly child without the good health and endurance necessary to achieve more than a minimal education. Though of average height, his slope-shouldered, broad-hipped body was not that of an athlete. Competitive sports were set aside and he turned to non-competitive exercise, such as roller-skating, for physical activity.

With the coming of war, and after repeated rejection by medical boards, he was finally accepted as an apprentice aircraft mechanic. Like Udet, he proceeded to make use of an open back door. Using family connections, he swung admission to an Army flying school and graduated, to become a two-seater (Morane) non-commissioned pilot. The downing of a snooping Aviatik launched his career as an aerial fighter. Demonstrating a strange fatalism, he attacked without concern for tactics or odds. The result was a mixture of victories and losses, for he drew many bullets, rarely finishing a fight without a few bullet holes on his machine.

Captain Georges M.L.J. Guynemer

(translated) "French Nieuport Biplane with machine gun fastened to top wing." Source: *Flugsport*, May 1916, p.267.

He appreciated the maneuverability of the Nieuport series, but moved on to enjoy the greater power of the SPAD.

The French public came to identify with him. Something about his frankly admitted defeats suggested honesty. Taken together with his frequent illnesses, rumored to stem from tuberculosis,[23] his resulting image differed from the usual Superman offering, to become that of Everyman, succeeding through sheer guts.

As for tactics, he stated[24] that there were but two useful for fighter attack. The first was his own or "mad" [dog] approach, whereas the competing method, used by most pilots, featured aerobatic maneuvering. In attack, his goal was to press for the classic position a bit behind and below the enemy machine, and once there, "cling to him like a leech … shooting in jerks [bursts]"[25]

Unfortunately, his approach was too direct and his goal only too obvious; the very lack of subtlety serving to greatly increase his risk. In his words: "Those who were rarely hit were better at maneuvering than myself … I never have recourse to aerobatics."[26] Here was another of the Ball school – to hell with cunning – just go for the enemy.

What about the drawbacks? These were obvious, for he was brought down seven times. Yet, he persisted. As he saw it, hunting must be done according to the temperament of the hunter, and his tactics, flawed or not, suited him perfectly. They were not to be changed.

He vanished in September 1917. When last seen, he was attacking a two-seater from above, challenging the rear gunner with a simplistic, you-or-me form of duel.[27] Though his tactics suited him, and led to an outstanding number of victories, the gods of war demanded more in the way of sophistication.

Captain René Fonck

No believer in luck, France's most successful fighter pilot bet his life on a striking ability to anticipate enemy maneuvers. Source: *La Guerre Aérienne*, January 1918, p.123.

Captain René Fonck (75 victories) wasn't surprised to learn of Guynemer's end. Questioned about rival Guynemer's tactics, Fonck said: "Guynemer fought differently. He faced fire regularly. This strategy is very dangerous. It places the pilot at the mercy of a jammed gun. I always utilize blind spots … "[28]

The criticism was fair. Guynemer's willingness to engage in open duels came with a built-in unhappy ending, for in the long run probability ruled: some day the enemy must win the duel.

Fonck's scenario was attuned to skill, not luck; his goal one of getting into an enemy's blind spot and staying there. He would outfly the enemy. We sense an innovator, a man who treasured logic above all. Yet the man himself, far from generating respect, was rated low by his fellow pilots. Here was one more complex, conflicted individual.

Called up at the war's start and assigned to the Engineers, Fonck found himself depressed by the endless labor of bridge building, relieved at times with calisthenics. He transferred out, training as a non-commissioned pilot. His license won, he served as a chauffeur to an officer/observer. Bored again, he sought the role of a fighter pilot. To test this possibility, he mounted a fixed machine gun aboard his twin-engined Caudron GIV; a gun that only he controlled. Though painfully slow and clumsy, Fonck's machine was a good match for older enemy reconnaissance machines. The lash-up's first victory (July 1916) sent his superiors a clear message of ambition. They responded wisely, transferring him to a single-seater Squadron flying SPAD VIIs. He was on his way.

Unlike Guynemer, he survived to see the war's end. As for victories, knowledgeable historians believe his true score to far exceed the official number.[29] Yet, despite his clear success,

Fonck ruled that victory alone wasn't enough. He insisted upon victory with the fewest possible number of rounds fired, and furthermore, victory without effective counterfire: no enemy bullet was to touch his aircraft. Should this last condition seem unrealistic, it has been reported[30] that "in several hundred combats he received only a single bullet in his fuselage." This alone was a striking achievement.

Despite his accomplishments, he was disliked by his fellow pilots. More than envy was involved. Unlike Mannock, he hid his gift, offering simplistic nonsense as the key to his success. As he told it, his basic secret was "the most complete disdain for danger."[31] Not so. If anything, his secret was one of carefully avoiding dangerous enemy bullets through brilliant flying.

Then there was his formula for combat effectiveness: "regular hours of sleep."[32] To his hard drinking, carousing comrades, Fonck seemed a bragging prig, playing the part of hero. When dislike threatened to undermine group effectiveness, he moved out of officer quarters to live alone in a separate building housing the Squadron restaurant. Nobody complained.

Early in WWII, after France's defeat, he was employed as an official within the air bureaucracy. Following the war, there were charges of collaboration with the Germans. This stigma, on top of the dislike shown by his 1914-1918 comrades, has made it difficult to place him fairly within the fighter pilot ranks. Though likely the single most successful of all Great War fighter pilots, he is seldom noted today. Lost to us forever is the means behind his uncanny ability to anticipate enemy maneuvers.

Whatever his quirks, Fonck represented forethought developed to a fine art. He was able to sense what his enemy would do next, and so place himself at the optimum position from which to open fire. This ability reflected an extraordinary skill.

Captain James B. McCudden (57 victories) was a British believer in forethought. In many ways equal to Fonck as a schemer, and likely superior as a stalker, he brought a level of patience to the task that was truly unusual. McCudden was another military brat, contending with a Sergeant-Major as a father and a formidable older brother as well. Brother William was the taller, livelier, and more athletic of the two. James was a small, shy lad " ... inclined to be tearful and moody."[33]

Inducted into the Army at age 15 to serve as a boy bugler, he proved a misfit. Interested in mechanics and motorcycles, he transferred to the RFC as an engine mechanic; swinging a berth as a non-commissioned gunner/observer, he was chosen for pilot training, worked as an instructor, and finally found success as a lone hand fighter pilot.

Enemy observation aircraft became his favorite target. His approach was that of a patient bird watcher, analyzing bits of knowledge and constructing a structure of tactics that defined the game. Small but crucial questions fascinated McCudden; for example, how would the wariness of two-seater gunners alter as a mission droned on? When were they truly on guard, constituting a menace? At what airspeed were they so blown about by the wind as to be unable to shoot accurately? Exactly how did two-seater climb and descent rates change as time passed over the course of a mission? When was the best time to attack?

His answers were assembled into a practical how-to article on stalking techniques. For example, to eliminate return fire,[34] the best move was to open fire with a short burst, without concern for accuracy. The object was simply to frighten the enemy into diving. Once committed, the resulting airspeed of over 130 mph produced enormous wind pressure on the standing gunner, making it impossible for him to shoot accurately. So long as the dive continued, the attacker had a free hand.

Captain J.B. McCudden

Concentrating on the downing of two-seaters, McCudden either originated or tested many tactics, helping move an uncertain art into solid practice. Source: F.A. Mumby, *The Great World War* Volume 7 (London: Gresham, 1918) p.139.

His advice was correct and well tested – unlike the sweeping maxims of Mannock. Instead, McCudden wrote narrowly, sticking to the facts, with drawbacks listed. Here was a careful man, and a most successful one. Effective both as a loner and Squadron Leader, he served as a hard-working ace. On two occasions[35] he destroyed a total of four two-seaters, all on the same day. Of these, the last group of four was downed within a total elapsed time of 1½ hours. McCudden not only developed fresh tactics, but served as his own testing means, then spreading the word by lecturing widely within the RFC.

With fame came envy and all the problems of real life. His lower class "ranker" background wasn't helpful, for he lived in an officer's society ruled by class concepts. Unappreciated was his occasional condemnation of RFC mechanics for shoddy workmanship, the result of his own bitter experience as both a pilot and mechanic. In the end, even his detailed compilations of successful tactics were put down as too specialized.[36]

McCudden died (July 1918) in a takeoff accident of the stall and spin type, a pointless death usually limited to beginners. That so careful and expert a flier could die in so ignorant a fashion seems hard to believe. However, an eyewitness report[37] permits no other conclusion. After takeoff, he " … suddenly put on speed again and rose upward to avoid collision with the tall trees … the machine now appeared to be out of control … " Once again, too high a rate of climb led to stall, and stall to spin. The final lack of control made a crash inevitable, with the pilot's death as the most likely result.

Major W.A. Bishop

A high scoring ace and winner of the Victoria Cross, he served in both World Wars, despite doubts concerning certain of his victory claims. Source: National Film Board of Canada.

In a manner suggesting Boelcke, McCudden undertook the roles of tactics researcher, ace, Squadron Leader and teacher. As did Boelcke, he achieved much, only to die in an accident. The similarity itself suggests that the same roles and types of men existed in each Air Service. However, some men were truly unique. One was "Billy" Bishop.

Major William Avery Bishop (72 victories)[38] was the son of a county official living within a small town in Ontario, Canada. As a mediocre student, but good horseman and rifle shot, he accepted conventional wisdom suggesting a military career as his best chance. However, the Royal Military College found him disappointing on moral grounds, accusing cadet Bishop of lying to authority and cheating on a critical exam[39] (crib sheets). He escaped ejection only by enlisting at the war's start.

Short, slight and accident prone, Bishop moved from an assignment as cavalryman to observer and finally to pilot training. Ham-fisted, his twenty hours of air time were unequal to the demands of a Nieuport 17. As though to make his lack of readiness clear, he crashed in a landing soon after arriving at his frontline unit. Witnessing the crash, an angry General J. Higgens slated Bishop for a return to flight school. Fate intervened, and a fresh start was managed when Bishop won his most important victory of them all – his first.

Holding the unenviable position of tail-end Charlie, Bishop responded to the jumping of his Squadron Leader Major Jack Scott by clobbering the aggressor Albatros. Raw beginner Bishop's victory undoubtedly had much to do with luck, but his bravery and shooting ability were real and evident to all.

Scott was grateful. Scratching Bishop's reassignment to flight school, he became a great supporter, serving as witness for many of his victory claims and vouching for the reality of numerous combat incidents. Unhappily, study of German sources during and after the war has been unable to authenticate many of the claimed victories.

Of all ace claims, none has been subject to more intense examination than those of Bishop, with the searchers seeking corroboration of victories more convincing than mere statements made by his friends. The resulting Bishop dossier contains much controversial material, including at least one damning work[40] and one of spirited defense.[41]

Lacking a clear resolution, we note the view of American cowboy Captain Fred Libby (14 victories) who was also there, serving in the same 60th Squadron. His report: "We have one pilot [Bishop] who writes a wicked [claims] report. God Almighty! Excuse me while I vomit … "42

One suspects that Bishop was prone to exaggerate his claims. That said, there is no doubt about his bravery, skill and influence upon tactics. For starters, there was the issue of time aloft. At the time, two missions per day, each of 1½ hours duration were considered plenty. Yet he would frequently fly a total of 7½ hours,[43] seeking not only combat, but extra practice. Never a "natural" pilot, he found endless practice a good substitute for having been shortchanged in skill. His implication: the major factor in joining "the right kind" was simple determination, rather than natural ability.

His very lack of aerobatic ability led to increased stress upon gunnery as the path to victory. Wanted in combat was a fast pass and out, as compared to an aerobatic duel – one he might well lose. However, a fast pass meant that few bullets could be fired, and much practice was spent in improving accuracy. Even given the extra drill, his slow but maneuverable Nieuport, usually armed with only a single Lewis gun in a pull-down arrangement, was far from ideal. To Bishop, the follow-on SE5a seemed an important improvement; his explanation: "It's 40 mph faster and has two guns."[44] Though the SE5a paid a price, giving up a considerable amount of maneuverability, Bishop didn't care: "This is positively the best machine in the world."[45] His determined support, coupled to a striking combat record, made a sturdy case for non-aerobatic tactics. In 1918's world of British combat tactics, consisting of the aerobatic as offered by the Camel, versus the non-aerobatic championed by the SE5a, Bishop's position was clear and persuasive. Fast pass tactics owed much to Bishop.

That Ball and Bishop should have disagreed strongly on the issue of the best machine (Nieuport 17 versus SE5a) is not surprising. Their choices reflected personal combat styles that were far different. Yet, on one secondary issue there was agreement: goggles were not to be worn. They reasoned that whatever was gained in protection from rain and flying oil droplets was lost to the usual smeared vision offered by goggles. A tendency to exaggerate the sense of murky fog experienced inside clouds was another goggle drawback. Bishop especially, convinced that shooting ability was the single most important skill any pilot brought to combat,[46] would tolerate no general reduction of vision. As for the flying debris encountered when lacking goggles, one might hope for a momentary blindness of only a second or two before full restoration of sight.

With peace, Bishop became a Canadian businessman, pioneering in air transport efforts. He rejoined the RAF in WWII to serve as a recruiting icon and glad-hander. After the war, he found it difficult to fill a satisfying role. Bishop died of illness, age 62.

The Eye-Glass Ace

(left) Blue Max winner *Fliegerleutnant* Kurt Wintgens with spectacles, worn at all times. Tony Fokker (right) congratulates Wintgens on his achievement. Source: (left) E.H. Baer, Ed. *Der Völkerkrieg* Band 14 (Stuttgart: Hoffmann, 1917) p.224. (right) *Flugsport*, October 1916, p.562.

With goggles condemned by Ball and Bishop, what hopes were there for those who required eye-glasses? Not only were eye-glasses subject to the same smeared vision problems, but their very need pointed to a serious physical defect. Breakage or loss in combat was obviously unacceptable. No Air Service welcomed men who were wearers.

Despite everything, eye-glass wearer *Leutnant* Kurt Wintgens (18 victories) of the German Air Service played an important development role as a fighter pilot, earning a Blue Max for his services. One more military brat,[47] Wintgens initially served in a communications battalion (telegraphy). As an officer, and the son of an officer, he was able to arrange an observer's slot and then pilot training. Making use of a strong gift for engineering development, he met with Tony Fokker and joined a program to test the new Fokker M5 monoplane. Possessing the key new fighter feature: a synchronized machine gun firing through the propeller disk, the package of gun plus aircraft would shortly change air combat forever. As a test pilot, he was among the first to succeed, downing a French Morane in July 1915. Fame made it unnecessary to hide his eye-glasses and many subsequent photos show him as a proud wearer.

Can one conclude that eye-glass need was not a significant drawback? Not really. They had significant disadvantages, but then all men have blind spots and disadvantages, be it slow learning, lack of strength, lack of feeling for machine logic, excess bravery or fear, lack of a sense of direction, color blindness, too young or old an age, etc. To this lengthy list, eye-glasses must be added. They were not a fatal handicap – just one more problem. In a world of mostly perfect recruits, rejection based upon eye-glass need would be logical. However, in the real world of the 1914-1918 war, the flat rejection of all eye-glass wearing pilot candidates was unwise.

Captain Edward V. Rickenbacker

When photographed he was an ambitious Lieutenant, hoping to command his unit, the 94th or 'Hat-in-the-Ring' Squadron. Source: *Air Service Journal*, July 25, 1918, p.118.

What of education? Every Air Service insisted upon a secondary school education and diploma. Were they really important? Consider the experience of a well-known American ace: Eddie Rickenbacker.

Captain Edward V. Rickenbacker (26 victories), the leading U.S. ace, became the male head of his family at age 13 upon the death of his foreman father. Those surviving included a widow and seven children. Desperate for money, Edward dropped out of school and lied about his age, working the night shift in a series of Midwest factories. Learning that he had mechanical talent: " ... engines have always talked to me",[48] he entered the world of machine tools and practical engineering.

Automobile racing had special appeal and starting as a mechanic, he became a world-class racing driver by his mid-twenties. Entry of the U.S. into the war led to the position of Engineering Officer at the American flight school in France. He would have preferred a flying job, but over-age at 27 and lacking even a high school education, there seemed no chance, until he found racing fans among the admissions officers. Excited by the presence of the truly famous Rickenbacker, his enthusiasts proved willing to ignore the rules and he was accepted for flight training. After collecting twenty five hours of solo flight in primary flight school, mostly in Nieuports, in addition to some meager gunnery training, he became a pursuit pilot assigned to the 94th Squadron, France.

Lithe, tall and athletic (6 feet 2 inches; 165 pounds) Rickenbacker was at his best in a SPAD 13. Tall, strong men had a natural preference for the roomier SPAD, choosing it over the more maneuverable Nieuports. However, more than room and personal strength was involved. A full comparison must credit the greater strength of the SPAD or SE5a, as measured against the weak-winged Nieuports. Preference alone was a good guide to user tactics; with those who opted for delicate maneuvering pressing for a Nieuport, while those who wanted a slashing dive and climb type of attack pushed for the more powerful, stronger SPAD 13.

Of the two, SE5a and SPAD 13, the latter was the stronger. Upon pulling an SE5a out of a dive with excessive "vim",[49] McCudden observed wing tip failure just outside the strut supports. The SPAD had no dive pull-out limitation. Furthermore, in the right hands, the SPAD was the more maneuverable, as demonstrated in a classic mock duel between Lewis and Guynemer.[50] High speed was another of the SPAD's features. As Rickenbacker noted, "No Fokker [D.VII] can overtake a good SPAD unless ... by diving."[51] As for the quality of his SPAD, Rickenbacker's expert knowledge of engines assured superior maintenance or better, on an every day basis.

With man, machine and tactics all in line, Rickenbacker was headed for success, requiring only judgement and luck. However, his judgement was not that of a steady guide: in part it did consist of cool evaluation, but furious emotion also had a role. An underlying drive to achieve peak combat performance and prestige may well have powered many of his decisions, made in the hope of finding a public regard equivalent to his pre-war auto racing position. Inevitably, some of his views seem odd.

On attacking observation balloons, he was a conservative. Daylight attack was too dangerous.[52] The necessary low altitude, only a few hundred feet, led to easy hits by defending anti-aircraft guns, with the result that too many attackers were lost in the process. Only attack under conditions of poor visibility – at dawn or dusk – was warranted. This very reasonable decision was countered by his own actions. Pestered by a machine gun nest while crossing over the frontlines, when at a low altitude under good visibility, he immediately swung into the attack mode, strafing the gunners.[53] His attack succeeded, but one must question tactics that frown upon the strafing of observation balloons at times of good visibility, for fear of losses, while permitting the strafing of bothersome machine gun nests. Surely destroying an observation balloon was the more important objective, for it might lead to many saved infantry lives, while destroying a machine gun nest would change nothing. On the face of it, his priorities sometimes reflected anger, instead of logic.

Similarly, there was the matter of capturing a crippled Fokker D.VII biplane.[54] Caught up in a routine two aircraft dogfight, Rickenbacker managed to hit his opponent's engine. The D.VII's propeller windmilled, reflecting the loss of all engine power. Grasping the situation, Rickenbacker decided to take his opponent prisoner, rather than shoot him down. For one thing, the German aircraft bore the red paint insignia of the Richthofen Squadron. Perhaps the pilot was a famous ace, whose capture would add prestige to that of Rickenbacker and that of his Squadron 94. While guiding the acquiescent, gliding Fokker D.VII to his side of the lines and home airfield, Rickenbacker was infuriated to see another SPAD suddenly emerge from nowhere and open fire on the Fokker – "his" Fokker. Rickenbacker's reaction consisted of firing a short burst at the "malignant SPAD" to warn him away. Despite Rickenbacker's angry response, the intruder had given the Fokker a final blow: it crashed. The pilot survived, to become a prisoner.

Again, Rickenbacker's priorities seem oddly mixed. What really mattered was ending the threat offered by the German machine and pilot. With this done, Rickenbacker's ability to turn the war into a contest for prestige was striking; his anger and action against the competing SPAD were curious indeed.

There was the matter of spare time and victories. Confirmation required trips to the front, seeking witnesses. Ideal eyewitnesses consisted of officers, equipped with binoculars and serving as anti-aircraft observers. The task of locating the proper witness and collecting signatures was one he pursued energetically, for he didn't wish to have his victories questioned, either then or later. In this he was successful: his victories stand.

However, there was an issue of available time, for each such trip might easily consume most of a day. When taken together with his insistence upon spending more time in the air than any pilot serving under him, there was difficulty in finding that time necessary for handling executive business. His solution was to appoint others as substitute managers. As a result, he claimed[55] never to have "spent more than 30 minutes a day" on administrative matters. The curtailment of administrative hours, as compared to time spent seeking victory confirmation, spelled out Rickenbacker's priorities: first came his victory count, with administrative needs dead last.

Rickenbacker did test and then push for many positive tactical procedures. He stressed the importance of small formations, especially as a means of introducing beginners to combat, and frequently led such formations. His belief in maximum frontline flying hours for himself as Squadron Commander, rather than few, set a demanding standard at a time when few existed. Having decided that only dawn attacks on balloons were worthwhile, he proved his point by organizing and leading such an attack, officially destroying 10 balloons. A strong believer in lone hand fighting, much of his success reflected the wiliness of a solo hunter enjoying the superior machine. Despite his need for prestige, he never put down the crucial importance of the machine.

Not only were positive tactics pursued, but he was willing to label and abandon broken or nonsensical techniques, even those he originated. For example, there was his early (March 1918) ethical resolve: "I will never shoot at a Hun who is at a disadvantage."[56] In reality, his very task as a fighter pilot was to place enemies at a disadvantage and then shoot them down. With the rare exception of the gliding Fokker noted above, he did so without regret.

Rickenbacker's major contribution to tactics was not that of some single, novel ploy. Instead, it consisted of evaluation of well-known tactics encountered over the Western Front in 1918. His determination to personally test, and rule on all possibilities, made Rickenbacker a powerful judge. Though certain biases were evident, so was a generally high level of personal experience and common sense.

He was that rarest of military leaders, one gifted with an instinctive feeling for the new engine-driven technology. That, and a certain sly shrewdness, yielded tactical judgements of a high order.

With tactics and air victory itself dependent upon the skills and personalities of the right kind – i.e., those with a gift for air combat – spotting talent early in the process became important. Surely efficiency would improve if only prospective aces were given flight training. Could these be recognized? Were there early signs?

The French tested for coolness in danger.[57] Wired as in a lie detector test with devices measuring blood flow and nervous activity, the subject was surprised with a pistol shot (blank) fired at close range, behind his back. The extent of startled response and time required for recovery were monitored. Considered ideal was a phlegmatic response. Those displaying an intense physical reaction were considered unsuitable candidates for flight training.

Testing for Nerves

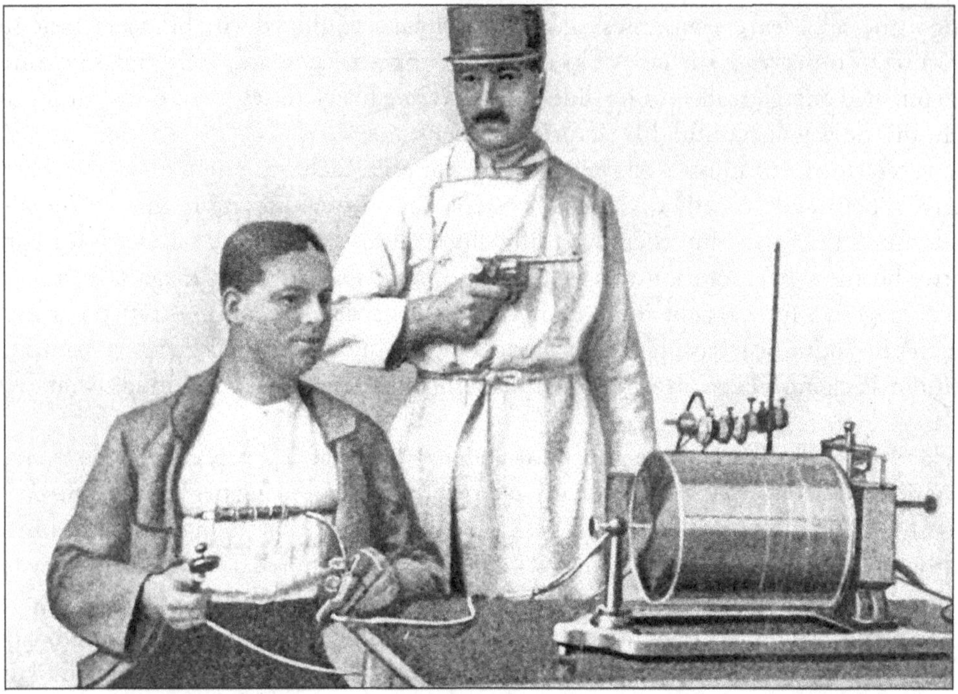

Cool types, with little reaction to shock, were believed to make good fighter pilots by the French. To find men with a phlegmatic response, reaction to the firing of a pistol was recorded on the cylinder at right. Source: *Luftfahrt*, December 1917, p.23.

The concept appears based on fictional heroes of the strong, silent type. Seeking men of this sort, respect and points were offered for a sluggish response to menace. In reality, top aces performed well despite nervousness, as demonstrated by Guynemer and Mannock. To the unimpressed British, "the French test was on the wrong tack." As pointed out by RFC Lieutenant-General David Henderson: "They might get someone constituted like an ox, but this was the very last type to produce a good pilot."[58] Yes, temperament was important, but much more than nervous response was involved. The difficulty was one of nailing down the important aspects, while ignoring the trivia.

A sense of the difficulty is supplied by Mannock's personal history. Always eccentric, he entered a period in 1918 suggesting a nervous breakdown. His sympathetic biographer[59] describes him as "a quivering wreck … saliva and tears were running down his face; he couldn't stop … " Yet he fought on, and effectively at that. Separating out those truly impaired by emotional problems was not simple.

Testing some 250 mixed subjects – some successful as fighting pilots, some failures – the RAF drew a composite picture of the candidate most likely to succeed.[60]

He was an "enthusiastic youngster … knowing little or nothing of the details of his machine … the less the fighting scout pilot knows about his machine from the mechanical point of view, the better … "

In reality, Udet frequently performed his own engine maintenance and would become a prestigious aircraft designer and manufacturer after the war. Rickenbacker and McCudden were engine experts, more knowledgeable than most RFC mechanics, with each capable of performing a full overhaul at any time. Fonck and Guynemer worked with SPAD engineers to fit a cannon into a SPAD 12, helping solve a development problem requiring much technical input from the aces. A fighter aircraft design by Ball seemed sufficiently promising to result in production by Austin. Finally, despite rejection of the triplane concept by German aerodynamicists, Richthofen succeeded in pushing for a three-winged fighter – a most successful machine – one that was ultimately made by Fokker's factory.[61]

In short, the British study resulted in conclusions that failed to meet the test of reality. Our conjecture is that the truth concerning pilot mechanical interests and skills was exactly opposite to the 1918 British conclusion. As for other practical results; for example, the value of hunting or athletics, conclusions stemming from the study are similarly unconvincing.

The temperament of men successful in the air fighting area, one of violent hunting combined with aerobatics and advanced technology, was unknown. Exactly what made for judgement of the correct lead used in shooting? The right answer might be three aircraft lengths or none, with all to be decided in a split second, with possible fatal consequences if mistaken. Adverse conditions – lack of oxygen, gun jams, an oil splattered windscreen – were all part of the picture. Not surprisingly, few were competent. Those truly gifted – the right kind – possessed an ability amounting to genius, and as with music, art or baseball, players possessing genius defy analysis.

Choosing the proper tactics required more than solid thinking. Only afterwards, when laid out for all to see, could one appreciate a daring, brilliant move. For lone hand Ball to break into a large formation, turning its key advantage of many guns into a disadvantage owing to enemy gunners fearful of hitting their own machines, required a certain brilliance. Many of the right kind exhibited this brilliance.

This chapter is concerned with the relationship between tactics and the right kind of men – those successful as fighter pilots. Ploys, schemes and personality traits have been considered. For the most part, tactics came to reflect the special abilities of available fighting machines, after a certain sifting to assure a good fit with pilot outlook and personality. Thus, a fast diving machine would lend itself to a diving attack as a key tactic, and a tight circling machine would most likely be pushed into a dogfighting role.

In the special world of air combat, machine design and logic mattered greatly but men and their special natures mattered as much, and perhaps more.

Tactics stood on three legs: those of design, military logic and temperament.

Summary and Conclusions

Richthofen versus the Rifleman

The precise cause of Richthofen's death remains unknown. Though killed in a fight seen by many, examination of the evidence submitted by contending machine gun firing claimants Sergeant C.B. Popkin, Sergeant R. Buie, and Captain R. Brown reveals serious exaggerations or flaws in reasoning. In similar fashion, eyewitness accounts (Lieutenant F.J.W. Mellersh, Lieutenant W. May, Lieutenant G.M. Travers and Sergeant H. Hart) are shown to be contradictory and to contain obvious errors, preventing acceptance.

Applying bullet scatter data, it is shown that the physical cause of death – one and only one rifle caliber bullet struck Richthofen's torso – is an unlikely result of well-aimed, ground-based machine gun fire. However, the striking of only one bullet does fit the scatter to be expected of Brown's airborne machine gun on a turbulent day.

An alternate possibility of a single unknown infantry rifleman as killer is examined in terms of altitudes flown, numbers of available marksmen and the probability of success. The likelihood of a rifleman's triumph over Richthofen is found to be significant, and at least equal to that of the other claimants.

Air Combat: Real or Nonsense?

Uncertainty concerning the reality of air combat prevented serious preparation for its occurrence. Doubts arose partly as a result of the striking aerobatics displayed by exhibition pilots, circa 1912. Many officers believed that interception of such machines, given wary pilots, was impossible. Others believed that in a coming war of millions the fate of a relatively few pilots and machines was unimportant. Sensed as a far more important task was the gathering of observation data pin-pointing the location of enemy troops. These beliefs encouraged the development of sound, stable aircraft able to observe and land anywhere. Conversely, fighting machines, but slightly developed, took the form of slow, poorly maneuverable two-seaters.

Fokker Fodder

Air war itself resulted from infantry demands. Harassed by enemy artillery, frontline troops saw observation aircraft, directing shellfire, as an immediate menace. To destroy unwanted eyes, gun-bearing aircraft were sent aloft. It was learned that the uncertain velocity and attitude of the target aircraft made accurate shooting difficult, with proper gun sight usage something of an art. It was also learned was that employment of standard fighting machines as interceptors was ineffective, for they were slow to maneuver, and carried only flexible guns. Directing such guns at the enemy required much in the way of lead correction for accuracy – a complex and uncertain process.

Anthony Fokker answered the need for an efficient fighter. His E-III was equipped with a novel interrupter device, permitting shooting through the propeller disk in the direction of flight. Emerging along the aircraft axis, bullets were aimed by pointing the entire machine, greatly simplifying gunnery. Furthermore, performance was increased by means of his single wing, single-seater, lightweight design. The resulting machine became the first effective fighter plane. Pushed by enthusiastic supporter German airman Captain Oswald Boelcke, the E-III was employed in special squadrons committed to destroying enemy aircraft.

Recognizing E-III superiority, British pilots of widely used BE2 observation aircraft ruefully referred to themselves as "Fokker fodder." Tight formations of several BE2's were a useful response, but British hopes were centered on new aircraft, still in the pipeline. In the meantime, tyro pilot Manfred Richthofen joined combat operations despite a mediocre flying school record.

After the Fokker

British plans to oppose the E-III included the FE and DH series of pushers. With its engine and propeller located in back, pushers offered superb frontal vision and clear shooting opportunities. However, shooting to the side was made tricky by lead corrections. Fixing the gun to shoot forward only (the DH2) produced a useful fighter, good at climb and velocity, but lacking in speed of maneuver and diving ability – a victim of its excess stability.

Experiments to improve the BE2 by locating extra guns, though found helpful, were ultimately denigrated as a "Christmas tree" approach. Yet, despite heavy losses the BE2 soldiered on.

Early British single-seater tractor hopes, centered on the BE12, came to nought. In combat, its extreme stability robbed it of necessary maneuverability.

French fighter design offered the successful tractor Nieuport 11 Bébé. Extremely low in weight – only 80% that of the lightweight E-III – it offered fine maneuverability, though its shooting arrangements were mediocre. Its single remote Lewis gun was difficult to reload and almost impossible to correct, should it jam.

As the E-III aged, Captain Boelcke pushed for replacement and the resulting Albatros D-I and D-II fighters were heavy, high powered, fine diving machines: features gained at some sacrifice of maneuverability. In his role as teacher, he introduced the "Dicta" or winning rules for air combat. If mostly a list of truisms and hopes, they remained a useful guide.

Meeting Boelcke by chance in 1915, Richthofen opted to become a pursuit pilot. His background is sketched, that of a cavalry officer. Pilot training proved difficult, for he had little natural feeling for flight. Sheer persistence saw him through.

Richthofen versus Two-Seaters

Tyro pilot Richthofen began fighting in the shadow of the Somme battle. Thrown against pusher British machines (FE2b), he first used Boelcke's tactic of occupying the enemy's blind spot, located behind its bottom rear. Once there, he couldn't be reached by his victim's return fire and was able to shoot straight ahead without the usual aiming concerns over the relative velocity of the target airplane as compared to his own, for they were identical. At first this tactic appeared best, and it did lead to many victories, but drawbacks arose. First, the FE2b was equipped with three guns and was quite maneuverable; as a result, attaining its blind spot was not easy. Next, shooting from a short distance immediately behind the enemy opened the possibility of collision, should a violent deceleration of the FE2 follow upon the striking of Richthofen's bullets.

Other tactics were as productive, and safer. One was to make use of every threatened FE2's natural desire to flee to safety. By opening fire prematurely it was possible to induce the FE2 to head for the frontlines and home. Diving to further increase its escape speed meant that the FE2 gunner was unable to bear the resultant wind stream, ending accurate shooting. Richthofen was then able to follow at a distance and shoot in safety. Though remote firing required many hundreds of bullets per victory, the tactic eliminated the fear of both collision and return fire.

Collision was of special concern, for Richthofen was a witness to the death of Boelcke (October 1916), caused by a light contact with his own wingman in the midst of combat. Much better, and safer, were combat tactics permitting remote positioning.

Richthofen found the BE2 an easier target than the FE2. One winning procedure was to dive on the BE2 at a great distance; one too far for accurate defensive shooting. Using the extra speed acquired by diving, he then moved quickly to a position under the BE2 tail, where the opposing gunner's vision and accuracy were poor, while his was good. In 1916-17, he downed 17 BE2's, as compared to 12 FE2's.

In general, he was betting on the superiority of twin bolted down guns equipped with a large ammunition supply, as against the uncertainty of his opponent's Lewis gun defense, worsened by a painfully limited number of rounds. The resulting odds, and score, were both heavily in his favor.

Richthofen versus Scouts, 1916

Fighting against scouts was sensed as different. With a crew of only one, scout aircraft were lightly built and lent themselves to aerobatics. Combat featuring maneuvers became widespread, leading to much tactical success. German ace *Oberleutnant* Immelmann not only employed aerobatic stunting as an important part of his combat technique, but had even incorporated a special up-going turn, accepted by every pilot as most useful. To Richthofen, who lacked a feeling for aerobatics, the resulting scene was difficult.

Engaged in denial, he put down aerobatics as so much trickery, and criticized the loop specifically as worthless, benefitting only one's enemy. As evidence, he quoted the 1915 combat death of famed French pre-war aerobatic exhibition pilot A. Pegoud. Unmentioned was the cause of his death: rather than employ aerobatics, Pegoud had entered and lost a straightforward gun versus gun duel. As for the loop, there were indeed many things that could go wrong, but in the right hands it was a useful tool.

As an alternative to aerobatics, Richthofen pushed Boelcke's philosophy of straightforward attack. Against deficient fighters, such as the too stable BE12, his procedures worked well. Similarly, the DH2 was outclassed by Albatros power and diving ability. His victory over famed opponent, British ace Captain L.G. Hawker, equipped with a DH2, further reinforced Richthofen's views. Hawker, known for Immelmann-style aerobatics, happened to be flying a machine with a defective engine. Though Hawker's skill served to hold off Richthofen for many minutes, it could not prevent his final victory.

To Richthofen, what counted was the right aircraft and the right no-nonsense tactics. Those achieving success by other means: for example, his brother's use of fake spins to trap opponents, led to Manfred's open scorn. Wanted was directness, not trickery. It would take British use of a new and extremely maneuverable fighter – the Sopwith Pup – to change his views.

Maneuverability Triumphs, 1917

Fighter aircraft design tended to achieve one or two desirable characteristics; for example, speed and climb, by trading off yet others such as maneuverability or diving ability. The Pup was that rare machine that did well in every performance category. Not only was it far superior to the BE2, FE2 and DH2, but more important, the Pup offered serious competition to the Albatros series. (Charts within this book supply detailed performance figures.)

Maneuverability when coupled with speed and climb meant success with tactics designed for a 'second act'; i.e., another attack to follow immediately upon the completion of the first. To bring this off, it was necessary to out-perform the target aircraft, as it desperately employed every possible means of evasion. Escape through superior speed or climb or maneuverability was routine. However, in the Pup, one had a machine excelling in all three traits, and escape was difficult indeed.

Another trait offered by the Pup was a longer shooting time when approaching the target; those seconds available before the need to prevent collision forced the pilot to turn away. The extra time granted by superior acceleration into the pull-away maneuver resulted in more rounds fired per attack, and led to the use of previously unpopular tactics, such as head-on attack. One indirect result was to overturn a key Boelcke dicta (# 5), putting down head-on attacks as hopeless.

Other novel Pup tactics were introduced, utilizing its fine performance. One was a slow diving attack using a deliberately stalled descent to increase firing time. A special virtue was the stalled attitude itself: just right for entering an evasive spin should the attack fail. Even attack from underneath succeeded when used by the Pup. In this case, the targeted plane had no means of shooting back, for its guns were pointed elsewhere. Secondly, the enemy pilot lost his own personal protection, that of the engine bulk. Bullets fired upward bypassed the engine, and it became possible to hit the enemy aircrew directly.

Pup design concepts were further improved upon by SPAD's designers, who managed a major power increase as well. Suddenly, new machines and tactics confronted and dominated the old.

Richthofen sensed that Boelcke's time was over. Like it or not, tricks and maneuverability mattered – and greatly at that. Sighting and impressed by a Sopwith Triplane, he struggled to obtain a German equivalent, pushing Fokker's version into mass production despite its disappointing top speed. The Fokker Triplane was to become his own special steed, driving up his victory total to 80. It was the Triplane that carried Richthofen in his last fight.

Formations and Combat

Though combat experience showed that setting one friendly aircraft against one enemy aircraft was effective, endless efforts were made to enable a number of squadron members to participate simultaneously. The hope was for greater firing power, with a larger number of fired bullets leading to a quick victory. Twin machine guns increased the stream and it was thought that several attacking aircraft would help even more. If large enough, it was thought that the mere sight of a number of attacking aircraft would frighten away smaller enemy groups.

However, in reality joint attacks tended to fail. Problems of communication between aircraft proved overwhelming, the result of a limited signaling ability permitting only crude messages of the "go" or "don't go" type. Once engaged, formation combat tended to degenerate into a 'milling about' event with much snap-shooting but no concerted fire. Casualties owed to collision were high, but those resulting from bullets were few. Large formation ineffectiveness continued through the war.

It was the small formation that achieved success, especially that of two planes working together, providing mutual defense as well as offense. Of the various possible arrangements, a side-by-side arrangement was found best. So superior was the fighting pair that larger formations were frequently directed to break up into fighting pairs upon enemy contact.

The limited scale of the two-plane formation pushed development of the triangular three-aircraft or V-type formation. Here the leader was located in front with a supporting machine above and behind, one on each side. Defended by the rear machines, the leader concentrated on offense. Successful in both defense and offense, difficulties came when maneuvering. A simple right angle turn could well result in the slowing and stalling of that machine nearest the turn center. The usual solution – an exchange of paths by the two trailing aircraft – could lead to collision as each crossed over the leader.

In the effort to attain still more firepower, V formations were sometimes stacked one above the other. The upper was charged with basic defense, the lower with offense. When employed in complex missions – those other than strafing – stacked V's lacked the necessary ease of handling. Once again, communication problems prevented success.

Yet, a few sizable formations did succeed. One was the rotating, endless circle formed by FE2's in defense. Containing roughly six machines, it was formed from a stacked V when facing attack. Each machine fired freely from its circular orbit when facing the attackers, and all combined their fire to shoot enemies trapped within the circle. Success proved that more than two or three aircraft could be profitably employed.

Richthofen settled on roughly six as the optimum number of fighters for most missions. At times he would accept the necessity for more, but his preference was for half of a full squadron register of twelve pilots. Americans drew the same conclusion, opting for fighting units containing three to seven airplanes as best. The universal preference for approximately six represented the maximum number of machines controllable by one leader. Such was the basic limitation.

Given a free choice, Richthofen would have preferred fewer machines. Single-handed combat was his free and final choice. Despite the limited firepower, it had the virtue of simplicity. To fly and fight alone eliminated all the headaches of authority and reduced combat to its essence – a duel. Others agreed. A number of lone hand aces became the highest scoring aces.

Tactics and the Right Kind

Pilot temperament exerted a great influence upon tactics. As examples: those uneasy at finding themselves alone in combat pushed for a wingman partner, while those who were loners at heart sought single hand combat. What defined a winner's outlook?

Uncertain concerning the right kind of men, recruiters employed standards favoring an upper class background. Wanted were those with a secondary or high school diploma, much organized athletics, perfect eyesight, an age of less than 25, and a height greater than 5 feet 3 inches. Richthofen himself, a military school graduate and officer, more than met the requirements. Did all?

Examining the background of top aces, we note many exceptions. Germany's second ranking ace (62 victories) *Oberleutnant* Ernst Udet was a too short, would-be artist, with no athletic experience. Attempting to enlist, he was rejected. However, his plumber father was willing to pay for Ernst's private flying lessons. His resulting pilot licence became the back door through which Udet finally gained acceptance. In action he stressed flexibility, aerobatics, a frontline air time of more than normal hours, and utilization of the latest machines. Off duty, he was a life-of-the-party sort. His success was a vote for pragmatism in pilot choice, as against official standards.

Another plumber's son was the short (5 feet 6 inches) British ace Captain Albert Ball (44 victories). Unlike Udet, Ball was a loner, withdrawn and interested in little but playing his violin. In combat, he welcomed large enemy formations by diving into and then fighting from within their interior. Protected by widespread fear of collision and German concern over hitting their own men, he was able to wrest victories where most feared to enter.

Matching temperament with exploits for other leading aces (Major Mick Mannock, Captain Ira Jones, Lieutenant Cecil Lewis, Captain Georges Guynemer, Captain René Fonck, Captain James B. McCudden, Captain William A. Bishop, Captain Edward V. Rickenbacker, *Leutnant* Kurt Wintgens) yields yet other oddities and ploys associated with their special outlook. Noted as well were the frequent exceptions to recruiting requirements: lack of formal education (Rickenbacker); defective eyesight (Wintgens); serious illness (Guynemer); too tall (Lewis).

Characteristics shared by these men include an unusually strong mechanical interest and aptitude (Udet, Rickenbacker, Fonck, McCudden, Lewis). Above all, they were marked by a fierce dedication to achievement; a desire so strong as to see them through, even when facing the trauma of a nervous breakdown (Mick Mannock, Roy Brown).

In the special world of air combat tactics, aircraft design mattered greatly, as did military logic, but men and their special natures were as important, if not more so.

Glossary

Albatros — name of German aircraft manufacturer; used to designate its products.

altitude — height above ground.

attitude — angular position held by aircraft with respect to viewer.

azimuth — left-right orientation.

bank — angular tilt of airplane; extent one wingtip is higher than the other.

Bébé — alternate, popular name for the Nieuport 11 fighter.

BE2 — British observation aircraft; good at reconnaissance but ineffective in combat; Royal Aircraft Factory product.

BE12 — British fighter; totally unsuccessful; Royal Aircraft Factory product.

Bristol fighter — Bristol F.2; high powered, highly successful; circa 1917; British & Colonial Aeroplane Co. product.

Camel — late war British fighter; arguably their best; Sopwith product.

C.G. — center of gravity; weight balance point.

cockpit — aircraft "office" enclosing aircrew member.

cyclic rate — maximum rate of machine gun bullets fired per minute without concern for safety, accuracy or endurance.

deflection — offset of aim to correct for speed and trajectory of target.

DH2 — De Havilland-designed British pusher fighter; good at tight circling, bad at diving; Airco product.

DH4 — heavy bomber, observation; Airco product.

Dicta — rules for successful air combat formulated by German ace Oswald Boelcke.

Dr. I — official designation for Fokker Triplane; much used and liked by Richthofen; Fokker Flugzeug-werke product.

D.VII — official designation for late war German biplane fighter; likely their best; Fokker Flugzeug-werke product.

E-III — the war's first effective fighter; Fokker Flugzeug-werke product.

FE2 — British pusher; used for both observation and fighting; better than BE2; Royal Aircraft Factory product.

Fliegerleutnant — German Air Service Lieutenant.

gyroscopic — that force developed at right angles to direction of motion.

handy — maneuverable.

h.p. — horsepower.

incidence — up or down angle between wing and oncoming air.

interrupter	mechanism to prevent gun from firing when propeller blade passes in front of gun.
Jagdstaffel	Pursuit squadron, often abbreviated to *Jasta*.
Jasta	Abbreviated designation for a German pursuit (i.e. fighter) squadron unit.
lead	synonym for deflection.
Lewis gun	light machine gun, drum fed; used by British, French, U.S.A.
Lieutenant, *Leutnant*	rank of Lieutenant, respectively British, U.S.A. and German.
LVG	German aircraft manufacturer; mostly bomber and observation machine types; Luft-Verkehrs-Gesellschaft.
Morane-Saulnier	French aircraft manufacturer of fighter and observation machines.
Nieuport 11, 17	successful French fighters featuring high performance and a remote Lewis gun; Société Anonyme des Establissements product.
Oberleutnant	German rank of First Lieutenant.
Oberursel	manufacturer of German air engines; poorly regarded.
pitch	nose up or down change of attitude.
Pup	highly effective British fighter airplane; Sopwith product.
pusher	aircraft with engine and propeller in back, serving to "push" aircraft.
RAF	Royal Air Force; British air service; also Royal Aircraft Factory; manufacturer.
Red Baron	ace Manfred von Richthofen, whose fighter plane was painted red as a form of "come and get me" challenge.
RFC	Royal Flying Corps; renamed Royal Air Force in 1918.
Rittm.	German rank of *Rittmeister*, or Captain of cavalry.
roll	speedy banking; with aircraft rotating about its center line.
SE5/SE5a	late war British fighter featuring two guns, high power and much stability; well-liked; Royal Aircraft Factory design.
single-seater	cockpit suited for pilot only; no passengers.
Sopwith	Sopwith Aviation Co.; British manufacturer of warplanes.
SPAD	French aircraft manufacturer; known for fighters; Société Pour l'Aviation et ses Derives.
scatter	the spread or divergence of fired bullets while in flight caused by manufacturing imperfections and barrel whip.
Staffel	German air unit designation; short for *Jagdstaffel*.
stagger	a fore and aft displacement of wings performed to shift center of lift relative to C.G., or to improve vision.
stall	separation of air flow relative to wing, resulting in low lift, high drag; may lead to spin.
swarm	a loose formation of roughly 6 aircraft; word of German origin.
tractor	aircraft with engine and propeller located at front of fuselage.
two-seater	individual cockpits for pilot and observer/gunner.

V formation	group of three aircraft, its leader flanked by two trailing machines.
Vickers gun	belt-fed machine gun, generally used as a fixed gun in British aircraft, or as a flexible gun by ground-based anti-aircraft gunners.
Vickers aircraft	the FB5 gunbus; a poorly regarded two-seater fighter; Vickers Ltd. product.
warp	a means of changing lift along the wingspan by twisting the wing; an early alternate to ailerons.
wedge	a steel shield, attached to propellers to prevent bullet damage from impinging rounds.
yaw	left-right angle between direction of flight and aircraft center line.

Notes

Abbreviations:

IWM Imperial War Museum
TNA The National Archives (formerly Public Record Office)

Prologue

1. Major Bishop, *Winged Warfare* (London: Hodder & Stoughton, 1918) p.170.
2. Ibid.
3. Frank C. Platt, Ed., *Great Battles of WWI: In the Air*, (NYC: Weathervane, 1966) p.10.

Chapter 1 – Richthofen versus the Rifleman

1. Edward V. Rickenbacker, *Fighting the Flying Circus* (NYC: Stokes, 1919) pp.334-335.
2. *Flight*, November 14, 1918, p.1273.
3. Ira Jones, *An Air Fighter's Scrapbook* (London: Greenhill, 1990) p.54.
4. James J. Hudson, *Hostile Skies* (Syracuse, N.Y.: Syracuse University Press, 1968) p.165.
5. James J. Hudson, *Hostile Skies*, p.160.
6. John R. Cuneo, *The Air Weapon 1914-1916* (Harrisburg, PA: Military Service, 1947) p.251.
7. Ernest von Hoeppner, *Deutschlands Krieg in der Luft* (Leipzig: Koehler, 1921); translated as *Germany's War in the Air* (Nashville: Battery Press, 1994) p.69.
8. Harold E. Hartney, *Up and At 'Em* (NYC: Doubleday, 1971) p.259.
9. Harold E. Hartney, *Up and At 'Em*, p.270.
10. Sholto Douglas, *Combat and Command* (NYC: Simon and Schuster, 1966) p.79.
11. Elliot Springs, *War Birds* (NYC: Grosset & Dunlop, 1926) p.203.
12. William C. Lambert, *Combat Report* (London: Kimber, 1973) p.53.
13. TNA file # AIR 2/4/87/504. For a detailed summary see Leon Bennett, *Gunning for the Red Baron* (College Station, TX: Texas A & M University Press, 2006) Chapter 1.
14. A. Mallock, *Most Dangerous Height for Aircraft Attacked from the Ground. Great Britain, Aeronautical Advisory Committee Reports & Memoranda # 621* (London: HMSO, July 1918).
15. Ibid.
16. For a popular explanation, see Amir D. Aczel, *Chance* (NYC: Thunder's Mouth, 2004) pp.30-33.
17. TNA file # AIR 1/2141/209/1/51. Appendix 3.
18. TNA file # AIR 1/2141/209/1/51. Appendix 4.
19. Ibid.
20. Ian V. Hogg, *Anti-Aircraft: A History of Air Defense* (London: Macdonald and James, 1978) p.67.
21. TNA file # AIR 1/ 2388/11/83.
22. Sources used for background include Dale Titler, *The Day the Red Baron Died* (NYC: Ballantine, 1970) plus Floyd Gibbons, *The Red Knight of Germany* (NYC: Doubleday, 1927), William E. Burrows, *Richthofen* (NYC: Harcourt, Brace and World, 1969), C.E.W. Bean, *Official History of Australia in the War of 1914-1918*, Volume 5, Appendix 4 (Sydney: Angus & Robertson, 1935) and Norman Franks & Alan Bennett, *The Red Baron's Last Flight* (Ontario: Vanwell, 1997).
23. TNA file # AIR 1/2397/262/2.
24. Ibid.
25. Ibid.
26. Popkin letter to Bean, October 16, 1935. Bean papers, Australian War Memorial Archives; or Geoffrey Miller, *Journal and Proceedings of the Military Historical Society of Australia*, Volume 39, June 1998.
27. Dale Titler, *The Day the Red Baron Died*, p.128.

28. Dolf L. Goldsmith, *The Grand Old Lady of No Man's Land* (Cobourg, Ontario: Collector Grade Publications, 1994) p.459.
29. Dale Titler, *The Day the Red Baron Died*, p.230.
30. TNA file # AIR 1/4/26/23. The guns employed direct flexible drive interrupter gears.
31. George M. Chinn, *The Machine Gun*, Volume 1, Appendix B (Washington DC: US GPO, 1951) p.661.
32. A ten round burst was given as standard by TNA file # AIR 1/699/27/3/448; p.52. However, F.W. Lanchester, *Aircraft in Warfare* (London: Constable, 1916) p.46, offered "6 or 8."
33. TNA file # AIR 1/675/21/13/1508; p.18.
34. TNA file # AIR 1/675/21/13/1508; p.17.
35. TNA file # AIR 1/675/21/13/1508; p.19.
36. TNA file # AIR 1/675/21/13/1508; pp.16, 27, 31, 32, 33, 97.
37. TNA file # AIR 1/675/21/13/1508; p.33.
38. TNA file # AIR 1/675/21/13/1508; p.20.
39. Dale Titler, *The Day the Red Baron Died*, pp.245, 246.
40. TNA file # AIR 2/51/AB275/2355.
41. TNA file # AIR 1/2427/305/19/942.
42. Norman Franks & Alan Bennett, *The Red Baron's Last Flight* (Ontario: Vanwell, 1977) pp.22, 24.
43. Australian War Memorial; numbers given in caption of negative #E02381.

Chapter 2 – Air Combat: Real or Nonsense?

1. Ernest von Hoeppner, *Deutchland's Krieg in der Luft* (Leipzig: Koehler, 1921). Translated as *Germany's War in the Air* (Nashville: Battery Press, 1994) p.19.
2. Royal Engineers; served in various balloon companies 1905-1909.
3. *Aeronautics*, January 1912, pp.18,19.
4. *Flying* (UK) October 1912, p.39.
5. *Aeronautics*, January 1912, p.20.
6. Ernest von Hoeppner, *Germany's War in the Air*, p.17.
7. Ibid, p.23.
8. Claude Graham-White, *Aviation* (London: Collins, 1912) p.193.
9. *Aeronautics*, January 1912, p.19.
10. Mervyn O'Gorman, *Technical Reports of the Advisory Committee for Aeronautics, Reports & Memoranda # 86* (London: HMSO, 1913) p.246.
11. Captain A. Bott, *An Airman's Outings* (London: Blackwood, 1917) p.170.
12. Mervyn O'Gorman, *Technical Reports of the Advisory Committee for Aeronautics, Reports & Memoranda # 86* (London: HMSO, 1913) p.259.
13. Mervyn O'Gorman, *Technical Reports of the Advisory Committee for Aeronautics, Reports & Memoranda # 86* (London: HMSO, 1913) pp.260, 261.
14. Mervyn O'Gorman, *Technical Reports of the Advisory Committee for Aeronautics, Reports & Memoranda # 127* (London: HMSO, 1914) p.312.
15. Geoffrey de Havilland, *Sky Fever* (London: Hamish Hamilton, 1961) p.72.
16. De Havilland, *Sky Fever*, p.147.
17. General S. Brancker's testimony, minutes of the Committee on the Administration of the RFC, IWM file # 73/183/1, p.14.
18. Computed for Standard Atmosphere, velocity = 100 ft/sec, drag coefficient = 0.9.
19. *The Aeroplane*, March 12, 1914, p.274. Passenger killed was E.T. Haynes, Factory civilian scientist.
20. *The Aeroplane*, March 5, 1914, pp.219, 220.
21. Ibid.
22. *Flight*, June 12, 1914, p.633.
23. Ibid.
24. *Flight*, March 8, 1913, p.278.
25. David Henderson, *The Art of Reconnaissance* (London: John Murray, 1915) pp.171, 172.
26. Mervyn O'Gorman, *Technical Reports of the Advisory Committee for Aeronautics, Reports & Memoranda # 86* (London: HMSO, 1912) p.198.
27. Ibid.
28. Paul R. Hare, *The Royal Aircraft Factory* (London: Putnam, 1990) p.278.

29. de Havilland, *Sky Fever*, pp.80-81.
30. Norman Macmillan, *Sefton Brancker* (London: Heinemann, 1935) p.51.
31. Herman Glauert, *The Longitudinal Control of an Aeroplane. Technical Reports of the Advisory Committee for Aeronautics, Reports & Memoranda # 592* (London: HMSO, 1918) p.5.
32. *Flight*, June 26, 1919, p.853.
33. *The Times* (London) November 6, 1914, p.10.
34. de Havilland, *Sky Fever*, p.81.
35. Constance Babington-Smith, *Testing Time* (NYC: Harper, 1961) pp.38, 39; Lord Mottistone, *Fear and Be Slain* (London: Hodder & Stoughton, 1931) pp.133, 135.
36. Babington-Smith, *Testing Time*, p.41.
37. Mary A. Busk, *E.T. and H.A. Busk* (London: John Murray, 1925) p.69.
38. H.A. Jones, *The War in the Air* Volume 7 (Appendices) (Oxford: Oxford University Press, 1937) Appendix XXVII chart.
39. Ibid.
40. H.A. Jones, *The War in the Air* Volume 7 (Appendices), Appendix XXXII chart. For a rough conversion into today's $, multiply wartime pound values by 155.
41. F.H. Sykes, *Aviation in Peace and War* (London: Arnold, 1922) p.67.
42. Ibid.

Chapter 3 – Fokker Fodder

1. He favored the Morane-Saulnier Parasol and the Nieuport machines.
2. A variation of the Hotchkiss gun, the St. Étienne was generally disliked. French thirst for the British Lewis gun started with this lemon. See George M. Chinn, *The Machine Gun*, Volume 1 (Washington D.C.: USGPO, 1951) p.185.
3. Claude W. Sykes, *French War Birds* (London: Greenhill, 1987) p.185.
4. A.R. Weyl, *Fokker: The Creative Years* (London: Putnam, 1965) Chapter 4.
5. *Flugsport*, September 1914, p.805; also *Zeitschrift fur Flugtechnik und Motorluftschiffahrt*, November 1915, p.170. Patent # 276, 396.
6. Anthony Fokker and Bruce Gould, *Flying Dutchman* (London: Routledge, 1939), p.117.
7. Interview took place in early 1919. TNA file # AIR 1/2429/305/30/3.
8. Fokker and Gould, *Flying Dutchman*, p.144.
9. Director US Air Service, *Rotary Engines* (Washington, D.C.:USGPO, 1919) p.15.
10. Darrol Stinton, *The Design of the Aeroplane* (London: Blackwell, 1983) p.129.
11. In addition to horizontal tail area, stability is determined by factors including C.G. location, distribution of mass, airfoil type, etc. A complete analysis is beyond the scope of this work.
12. Grover C. Loening, *Military Aeroplanes* (Boston: Best, 1917) p.157.
13. J.M. Bruce, *British Aeroplanes 1914-1918* (London: Putnam, 1969, 2nd ed.) p.369.
14. J.M. Bruce, *British Aeroplanes 1914 – 1918*, p.399.
15. Calculated from official 3-views given by *L'Aérophile*, August 1917, p.276.
16. *The Aeroplane*, January 25, 1912, p.83.
17. *Aerial Age Weekly*, January 17, 1916, p.428.
18. View of French engineer M.J. Lagorgette as given by *Aerial Age Weekly*, September 11, 1916, p.786.
19. Johannes Werner, *Knight of Germany* (London: Greenhill, 1985) p.134.
20. *Flight*, April 27, 1916, p357.
21. Christopher Cole, ed., *Royal Flying Corps Communiqués 1915-1916* (London: Kimber, 1969) p.134.
22. Leon Bennett, *Gunning for the Red Baron* (College Station, Texas: Texas A & M University Press, 2006) pp.36-40.
23. Franz Immelmann, *The Eagle of Lille* (London: Greenhill, 1990) p.106.
24. Werner, *Knight of Germany*, p.159.
25. von Hoeppner, *Germany's War in the Air*, p.38.
26. von Hoeppner, *Germany's War in the Air*, p.41.
27. Oswald Boelcke, *An Aviator's Field Book* (NYC: National Military Publishing, 1917) p.76.
28. Boelcke, *An Aviator's Field Book*, p.82.
29. L.Bairstow et al, *Notes on the Performance of Aeroplanes. Technical Reports of the Advisory Committee for Aeronautics, Reports & Memoranda # 268* (London: HMSO, 1917); Jones, *The War in the Air* Volume 7 (Appendices), chart XXVII; TNA file # AIR 1/1192/205/5/2599.

30. Vivian Voss, *Flying Minnows* (London: Arms & Armour, 1977) p.161.
31. Andrew Boyle, *Trenchard* (London: Collins, 1962) p.155.
32. Christopher Cole, ed., *Royal Flying Corps Communiqués 1915-1916*, p.108.
33. Werner, *Knight of Germany*, p.131.
34. John E. Johnson, *Full Circle* (NYC: Ballantine, 1964) p.18.
35. Boyle, *Trenchard*, p.162.
36. Speech in the House of Commons, January 20, 1916. *The Aeroplane*, January 26, 1916, p.172.
37. Ibid.

Chapter 4 – After the Fokker

1. New York Times, *The European War* April-June 1916 Volume VII (NYC: NY Times, 1917) pp.131-132.
2. New York Times, *The European War* April-June 1917 Volume XI (NYC: NY Times,1917), p.329.
3. E. Angelucci and P. Matricardi, *Les Avions*, Volume I (Brussels: Elsevier, 1978) pp.141, 257.
4. Edward P. Warner, *Aerodynamics* (NYC: McGraw-Hill, 1927) pp.509-511.
5. For bank and other influences upon circling diameter, see Leon Bennett, *Gunning for the Red Baron* (College Station, Texas: Texas A&M University Press, 2006) Chapter 8. As compared to the Bébé, the E-III's larger wing area didn't compensate for its greater weight.
6. For a good English translation, see Walter A. Musciano, *Eagles of the Black Cross* (NYC: Obolensky, 1965) pp.60, 61.
7. Ibid.
8. As described in *L'Aérophile*, February 1917, pp.49-53.
9. *Aircraft*, June 1917, p.106.
10. Manfred von Richthofen, *The Red Air Fighter* (London: *The Aeroplane* & General Publishing Company, 1918) chapters 1 and 2. This is the only authentic WWI translation.
11. Richthofen, *The Red Air Fighter*, p.24.
12. Richthofen, *The Red Air Fighter*, p.88.
13. de Havilland, *Sky Fever*, p.97.
14. Herman Glauert, *The Longitudinal Control of an Aeroplane. Technical Reports of the Advisory Committee for Aeronautics, Reports & Memoranda # 470* (London: HMSO, May 1918) p.5.
15. Anon., *Final Report of the Committee on the Administration and Command of the RFC, etc.* (London: HMSO, 1916) p.13.
16. Sholto Douglas, *Combat and Command* (NYC: Simon and Schuster, 1963) p.80.
17. Boyle, *Trenchard* , p.162.
18. *Luftfahrt*, October 1918, p.16.
19. Jones, *The War in the Air* Volume 7 (Appendices) (Oxford: Oxford University Press, 1937) Appendix XXVII.
20. Ibid.
21. General Brancker's letters, Imperial War Museum file # IWM 73/183/1. Unpaginated, "presumably written by Lieutenant Colonel Brooke-Popham."
22. Friedrich von Bernhardi, *Germany and the Next War* (NYC: Longmans, Green, 1914) p.200.

Chapter 5 – Richthofen versus Two-Seaters

1. Ira Jones, *Tiger Squadron* (London: W.H. Allen, 1954) p.44.
2. TNA file # AIR 1/1625/204/89/8; Harold E. Hartney, *Up and At 'Em* (NYC: Doubleday, 1971) p.45.
3. Arch Whitehouse, *The Fledgling* (NYC: Duell, Sloan and Pierce, 1964) p.99.
4. Richthofen, *The Red Air Fighter*, p.76.
5. Richthofen combat reports: TNA file # AIR 1/2397/262/1, AIR 1/686/21/13/2250.
6. Richthofen, *The Red Air Fighter*, p.77.
7. Douglas, *Combat and Command*, p.100.
8. TNA files # AIR 1/1625/204/89/8, AIR 1/ 2087/207/7/38.
9. For biographies of downed RFC fliers, see Norman Franks, H. Giblin and N. McCrery, *Under the Guns of the Red Baron*, (London: Grub St., 1998); for the first victory see p.15.
10. Douglas, *Combat and Command*, p.97.
11. TNA file # AIR 1/2087/207/7/38.
12. Oliver Stewart, *Words and Music for a Mechanical Man* (London: Faber and Faber, 1967) p.148.
13. TNA file # AIR 1/ 1625/204/89/8, p.16.
14. TNA file # AIR 1/ 1625/204/89/8, p.19.

15. TNA file # AIR 1/ 1625/204/89/8, p.21.
16. Whitehouse, *The Fledgling*, p.131.
17. Richthofen, *The Red Air Fighter*, p.56.
18. TNA file # AIR 1/1625/209/89/8/ p.20.
19. Ibid.
20. Alan Bott, *Cavalry of the Clouds* (NYC: Doubleday, Page Co., 1918) p.303.
21. TNA file # AIR 1/2386/228/11/16.
22. TNA file # AIR 1/1625/204/89/8/ p.21.
23. Interview with Boelcke, *Aeronautics*, October 18, 1916, p.249.
24. TNA file # AIR 1/2398/267/16.
25. Richthofen, *The Red Air Fighter*, p.77.
26. Richthofen, *The Red Air Fighter*, p.18. While this 1918 translation of Richthofen's book is the most authentic of the many available, its use of "yards" is likely incorrect. Richthofen thought in terms of meters, rather than yards, and the two differ by about 10%. Thus what is given as "50 yards" should be read as 50 meters or 55 yards.
27. TNA file # AIR 1/1625/209/89/8, p.47.
28. Bennett, *Gunning for the Red Baron*, p.52-57.
29. Maurice Baring, *Flying Corps Headquarters 1914-1918* (London: Bell, 1920) p.127.
30. Richthofen frequently assigned mistaken ID's to his victims. As a result, standard references continue to disagree. Our basic source is Walter Musciano, *Eagles of the BlackCross* (NYC: Obolensky, 1965).
31. TNA file # AIR 1/1625/204/89/8.
32. Ibid.
33. Richthofen combat reports: TNA file # AIR 1/2397/262/1, AIR 1/686/21/13/2250.
34. Richthofen combat report of March 4, 1917. Ibid.
35. Laddie Lucas, *Out of the Blue* (London: Hutchinson, 1985) p.24.
36. *The Aeroplane*, November 27, 1918, p.1970.
37. Richthofen combat report March 12, 1918. TNA file # AIR 1/686/21/13/2250.

Chapter 6 – Richthofen versus Scouts, 1916

1. *Die Luftflotte*, September 1918, pp.194-195. *Aircraft*, February 1917, p.54 for details concerning a July 1916 fight. The looper was a Nieuport Scout. For the importance of E-III aerobatics, see *The Sphere*, January 29, 1916, p.108.
3. Richthofen, *The Red Air Fighter*, p.88, 130.
4. Floyd Gibbons, *The Red Knight of Germany* (NYC: Doubleday, 1927) p.126.
5. Gibbons, *The Red Knight of Germany*, p.127.
6. *L'Aérophile*, September 1915, pp.195-196.
7. As quoted by *L'Aérophile*, Ibid.
8. Richthofen combat reports October 7, 16, 25, 1916; TNA file # AIR 1/2397/262/1, AIR 1/686/21/13/2250.
9. *Test Reports RFC Machines*; TNA file #AIR 2/165/MR/10723.
10. Data from J.F. Wise, *Canadian Airmen and the First World War* (Canada: University of Toronto Press, 1980) p.384.
11. See detailed analysis of tight circling: Bennett, *Gunning for the Red Baron*, Chapter 8.
12. Richthofen combat reports November 23, 1916; TNA file # AIR 1/2397/262/1, AIR 1/686/21/13/2250.
13. Richthofen's estimated 3 to 5 minutes of descent seems too little, leading to an unlikely descent rate.
14. Richthofen combat reports December 11, 1916; TNA file # AIR 1/2397/262/1, AIR 1/686/21/13/2250.
15. Ibid.
16. *Aerial Age Weekly*, February 5, 1917, p.535.
17. Richthofen, *The Red Air Fighter*, p.127.
18. Richthofen, *The Red Air Fighter*, p.132.
19. Paul R. Hare, *The Royal Aircraft Factory* (London: Putnam, 1990) p.231.
20. Peter Gray & Owen Thetford, *German Aircraft of the First World War* (NYC: Doubleday, 1970) p.44.
21. Ibid., p.48. Climb rate from ground level to 1000 meters.
22. Richthofen, *The Red Air Fighter*, p.130.
23. Richthofen combat reports January 4, 1917. Op. cit.

Chapter 7 – Maneuverability Triumphs, 1917

1. Richthofen, *The Red Air Fighter*, p.86.
2. Richthofen, *The Red Air Fighter*, p.87.

3. Richthofen, *The Red Air Fighter*, p100.
4. Data from Jones, *The War in the Air* Volume 7 (Appendices), Appendix XXVII.
5. Karl Bodenschatz, *Hunting with Richthofen* (London: Grub Street, translated from the 1936 German ed., 1998) p.46.
6. Major W.A. Bishop, *Winged Warfare* (London: Hodder and Stoughton, 1918) p.231.
7. Converting 100 mph into Ft/Sec, we have (5280 Feet/Mile x 100 Mile/Hour) / (60 Minutes/Hour x 60 Seconds/Minute) equals 147 Feet/Second. Two airplanes would converge at twice this speed, or roughly 300 Feet/Second, or 100 yards per second.
8. *Fighting Instruction Data*, TNA file # AIR 1/1625/204/89/8.
9. *Notes on Air Fighting*, TNA file # AIR 1/2087/207/7/38.
10. *Fighting Instruction Data*, TNA file # AIR 1/1625/204/89/8.
11. *Notes on Air Fighting*, TNA file # AIR 1/2087/207/7/38.
12. *Notes on Air Fighting*, TNA file # AIR 1/ 2087/207/7/38.
13. *Aerial Fighting*, TNA file # AIR 1/920/204/5/885.
14. Ibid.
15. *Notes on Air Fighting*, TNA file # AIR 1/2087/207/7/38.
16. *Fighting Instruction Data*, TNA file # AIR 1/ 1625/204/89/8.
17. Eddie V. Rickenbacker, *Fighting the Flying Circus* (NYC: Stokes, 1919) p.337.
18. Martin C. Windrow, Ed. *Aircraft in Profile* Volume 3 (NYC: Doubleday, 1966) p.76.
19. For a full treatment of Sopwith Triplane aerodynamics see Leon Bennett, *Three Wings for the Red Baron* (Shippensburg, PA: White Mane, 2000) Chapter 6.
20. E.A. Griffiths and C.H. Powell, *Forces and Moments on Triplanes. Technical Reportsof the Advisory Committee for Aeronautics, Reports & Memoranda # 250* (London: HMSO, July 1916) p.158.
21. At 6500 feet altitude. Jones, *The War in the Air* Volume 7 (Appendices), Appendix XXVII.
22. Gray and Thetford, *German Aircraft of the First World War*, p.48.
23. Fokker and Gould, *Flying Dutchman*, p.158.
24. Hans Herlin, *Udet: A Man's Life* (London: Macdonald, 1960) p.158.
25. Fokker and Gould, *Flying Dutchman*, p.199.
26. Franks, Giblin and McCrery, *Under the Guns of the Red Baron*, pp.134-136.
27. Walter A. Musciano, *Eagles of the Black Cross* (NYC: Obolensky, 1965) p.276. Also see Gibbons, *The Red Knight of Germany*, p.381.
28. H.F. King, *Sopwith Aircraft 1912-1920* (London: Putnam, 1980) pp.135, 137.
29. *Luftfahrt*, July 1918, p.28.
30. Fokker and Gould, *Flying Dutchman*, p.147.
31. A.J. Fairbanks, *Distribution of Pressure over Model of the Upper Wing and Aileron, NACA (National Advisory Committee for Aeronautics) Report # 254*, (Washington D.C.: USGPO, 1925) pp.541-600.
32. Ibid, p.552.
33. Accounts of Richthofen's losing battle differ in important details. For example, the range was reported as unusually long by Gibbons, pp.296-299 and Bodenschatz, pp.17-20, suggesting a hit by pure chance. In contrast, Franks et al, pp.148-151, suggested a short range, implying misjudgement of the risk on Richthofen's part.
34. A.R. Weyl, *Fokker: The Creative Years* (London: Putnam, 1965) p.229-231. The measured safety factor for a well-built wing was roughly 8.0.
35. William E. Burrows, *Richthofen* (NYC: Harcourt, Brace & World, 1969) pp.173-174.
36. Thomas Nevin, *Ernst Junger and Germany* (Durham, NC: Duke University Press, 1996) p.48.
37. Richthofen, *The Red Air Fighter*, p.88.
38. von Hoeppner, *Germany's War in the Air*, p.109.

Chapter 8 – Formations and Combat

1. TNA file # AIR 1/1625/204/89/8.
2. Richthofen, *The Red Air Fighter*, p.80.
3. TNA file # AIR 1/1625/204/89/8.
4. TNA file # AIR 1/2150/209/3/212.
5. TNA file # AIR 1/1625/204/89/8.
6. TNA file # AIR 1/ 2150/209/3/212.
7. TNA file # AIR 1/1625/204/89/8.
8. John Tanner, Ed. *Fighting in the Air*, Volume 7 (London: Arms & Armour Press, 1978) p.99.

9. Tanner, Ed. *Fighting in the Air*, Volume 7, p.91.
10. TNA file # AIR 1/1625/204/89/8.
11. Tanner, Ed. *Fighting in the Air*, Volume 7, p.10.
12. Tanner, Ed. *Fighting in the Air*, Volume 7, p.91.
13. Bishop, *Winged Warfare*, pp.143-144.
14. Hartney, *Up and At 'Em*, pp.42, 59.
15. Stewart, *Words and Music for a Mechanical Man*, p.125.
16. James McCudden, *Flying Fury* (London: Aviation Book Club, 1930. Reprint: London: Greenhill, 1987) p.155.
17. Hartney, *Up and At 'Em*, p.59.
18. Whitehouse, *The Fledgling*, p.163.
19. Ibid.
20. Bishop, *Winged Warfare*, p.231.
21. Stewart, *Words and Music for a Mechanical Man*, p.148.
22. Stewart, *Words and Music for a Mechanical Man*, p.124.
23. TNA file # AIR 1/1625/204/89/8.
24. Tanner, Ed., *Fighting in the Air*, Volume 7, p.93.
25. Hartney, *Up and At 'Em*, p.75.
26. Bishop, *Winged Warfare*, p.236.
27. Ibid.
28. Bennett, *Gunning for the Red Baron*, pp.142-147.
29. *Air Service Journal*, November 8, 1917, pp.565, 566.
30. Hartney, *Up and At 'Em*, pp.77-80.
31. Gibbons, *The Red Knight of Germany*, p.125.
32. Karl Bodenschatz, *Hunting With Richthofen*, (London: Grub Street, 1996) pp.54, 55.
33. Air Service Technical School, *Pursuit*, (Washington, D.C.: USGPO, 1926) p.7.
34. Hartney, *Up and At 'Em*, p.78.
35. Gibbons, *The Red Knight of Germany*, p.126.
36. Richthofen, *The Red Air Fighter*, p.116.
37. Richthofen, *The Red Air Fighter*, p.130.
38. Bodenschatz, *Hunting With Richthofen*, pp.54, 55.
39. Bodenschatz, *Hunting With Richthofen*, p.46.
40. TNA file # AIR 1/2427/305/29/AP942.
41. Richthofen, *The Red Air Fighter*, p.100.
42. Richthofen, *The Red Air Fighter*, p.112.
43. Richthofen, *The Red Air Fighter*, p.132.
44. Bodenschatz, *Hunting With Richthofen*, p.47.
45. Richthofen, *The Red Air Fighter*, p.127.
46. Bodenschatz, *Hunting With Richthofen*, p. 46.
47. Richthofen, *The Red Air Fighter*, p.130.
48. Stewart, *Words and Music for a Mechanical Man*, p.131.
49. TNA file # AIR 1/ 2386/228/11/2.
50. Ibid.
51. Gibbons, *The Red Knight of Germany*, pp.327, 328.
52. Bodenschatz, *Hunting With Richthofen*, p.61.
53. Bodenschatz, *Hunting With Richthofen*, p.170. The precise number of losses remain uncertain. A more recent study offers 11 to 4. See Brereton Greenhaus, *The Making of Billy Bishop*, (Toronto: Dundurn Press, 2002) p.176.
54. Contact (pseud.) *An Airman's Outings*, (London: Blackwood, 1917) pp.299, 300. The author's real name was Captain Alan Bott.
55. Jones, *Tiger Squadron*, p.84.
56. Rickenbacker, *Fighting the Flying Circus*, p.154.
57. Hartney, *Up and At 'Em*, p.195.
58. Duncan Grinnell-Milne, *Wind in the Wires*, (NYC: Ace, 1968) p.180.
59. Victor W. Page, *Modern Aircraft Engines* Volume .1 (NYC: Henley, 1929) p.332.
60. TNA file # AIR 1/1625/204/89/8.
61. *Air Service Journal*, July 12, 1917, p.93.

62. Bodenschatz, *Hunting With Richthofen*, p.179.

Chapter 9 – Tactics and The Right Kind

1. H.A. Jones, *The War in the Air* Volume 5 (Oxford: Oxford University Press, 1935), p.469.
2. Frederick Sykes, *From Many Angles* (London: Harrap, 1942) p.220.
3. Ernst von Hoeppner, *Germany's War in the Air*, p.137.
4. Ernst von Hoeppner, *Germany's War in the Air*, p.109.
5. Udet background obtained from Armand Van Ishoven, *The Fall of an Eagle* (London: Kimber, 1979), Armand Van Ishoven, *Ernst Udet* (Herrsching, West Germany: Pawlak, 1977), Hans Herlin, *Udet: A Man's Life* (London: Macdonald, 1960).
6. Average height was lower in those low protein times. Pre-war USA Army required 5 feet 4 inches. With war, the standard was lowered to 5 feet 0 inches. See Provost Marshal General Report, *On the Operations of Selective Service* (Washington DC: USGPO, 1919) p.156.
7. For details, see Armand van Ishoven, *The Fall of an Eagle*, pp.200-208.
8. Detailed by Stanley M. Ulanoff, Ed., *Ace of the Iron Cross* (NYC: ARCO, 1981) pp.42-44. A slightly different version given in French by Bernard Marck, *Le Dernier Vol de Guynemer* (Paris: Acropole, 1991) pp.94, 95.
9. Chaz Bowyer, *Albert Ball, V.C.* (London: Kimber, 1977), p.25.
10. Chaz Bowyer, *Albert Ball, V.C.* p.85.
11. Chaz Bowyer, *Albert Ball, V.C.* p.24.
12. In a lengthy fight, even strong pilots found it difficult or impossible to develop the force necessary to maneuver machines that were either too stable or unstable. See H.Glauert, *The Longitudinal Control of an Aeroplane. Great Britain, Aeronautical Advisory Committee Reports & Memoranda # 470* (May 1918).
13. A.J. Insall, *Observer* (London: Kimber, 1970) p.118.
14. *Air Service Journal*, August 8, 1918, p.190.
15. Mannock sources include J.M. Dudgeon, *Mick* (London: Robert Hale, 1981), Fred Oughton and Vernon Smyth, *Ace With One Eye* (London: Muller, 1963) and Ira Jones, *King of the Air Fighters* (London: Nicholson & Watson, 1934).
16. J.M. Dudgeon, *Mick*, p.134.
17. J.M. Dudgeon, *Mick*, pp.123, 125.
18. Ira Jones, *Tiger Squadron* (London: W.H. Allen, 1954; reprint, London: Award, 1966) pp.102, 124.
19. J.M. Dudgeon, *Mick*, p.121.
20. Cecil Lewis, *All My Yesterdays* (Dorset, UK: Element, 1993.) p.12; Cecil Lewis, *Sagittarius Rising* (London: Davies, 1936; reprint, Warner, 1994) p.10.
21. Cecil Lewis, *Sagittarius Rising* p.170.
22. Guynemer sources include Claude W. Sykes, *French War Birds* (London: Hamilton, 1937), Bernard Marck, *Le Dernier Vol de Guynemer* (Paris: Acropolis 1991), Jacques Mortane, *Guynemer, The Ace of Aces* (NYC: Moffat, Yard, 1918).
23. William Arthur Bishop, *The Courage of the Early Morning* (Toronto: McClelland & Stewart, 1965) p. 52.
24. Jacques Montane, *The Ace of Aces*, p. XXVII.
25. Ibid.
26. Ibid.
27. Bernard Marck, *La Dernier Vol de Guynemer*, Chapter 16.
28. René Fonck, *Ace of Aces* (NYC: Doubleday, 1967) p.124.
29. Charles Christienne and Pierre Lissarrague, *French Military Aviation* (Washington, DC: Smithsonian, 1986) p.163, assigned 127 probables to Fonck
30. Ibid.
31. René Fonck, *Ace of Aces*, pp.124-125.
32. Claude W. Sykes, *French War Birds*, p.148.
33. Christopher Cole, *McCudden, V.C.* (London: Kimber, 1967), p.17.
34. James McCudden, *Flying Fury – Five Years in the RFC* (London: Aviation Book Club, 1930; reprint London: Greenhill, 1987) p.129.
35. *Flight*, April 4, 1918, p.359.
36. Christopher Cole, *McCudden*, p.204.
37. *Aeronautics*, July 17, 1918, p.359.

38. Bishop sources included: William Arthur Bishop, *The Courage of the Early Morning* (Toronto: McClelland & Stewart, 1965), William Avery Bishop, *Winged Warfare* (London: Houghton & Stoughton, 1918), William Avery Bishop, *Winged Peace* (NYC: Viking, 1944), Robert Jackson, *Fighter Pilots OF WWI* (NYC: St. Martin's Press, 1977).
39. William Arthur Bishop, *The Courage of the Early Morning*, p.18.
40. Brereton Greenhous, *The Making of Billy Bishop* (Toronto: Dundurn Press, 2002).
41. H. Clifford Chadderton, *Hanging a Legend* (Ottowa: War Amputations of Canada, 1986).
42. Frederick Libby, *Horses Don't Fly* (NYC: Arcade, 2000) p.227.
43. William Avery Bishop, *Winged Warfare*, p.227.
44. William Arthur Bishop, *The Courage of the Early Morning*, p.112.
45. William Arthur Bishop, *The Courage of the Early Morning*, p.116.
46. William Avery Bishop, *Winged Warfare*, p.170.
47. Wintgens background source: *Flugsport*, October 1916, p.562.
48. Edward V. Rickenbacker, *Rickenbacker* (NJ: Prentice-Hall, 1967) p.43. Much background material obtained from this source.
49. James McCudden, *Flying Fury–Five Years in the RFC*, p.220.
50. Cecil Lewis, *Sagittarius Rising*, p.196.
51. Edward V. Rickenbacker, *Fighting the Flying Circus* (NYC: Stokes, 1919) p.310.
52. Edward V. Rickenbacker, *Fighting the Flying Circus*, p.320.
53. Edward V. Rickenbacker, *Fighting the Flying Circus*, p.236.
54. Edward V. Rickenbacker, *Fighting the Flying Circus*, p.341.
55. Edward V. Rickenbacker, *Fighting the Flying Circus*, p.261.
56. Edward V. Rickenbacker, *Fighting the Flying Circus*, p.338.
57. *Luftfahrt*, December 1917, p.23; *Flugsport*, July 1916, p.14.
58. *Flight*, June 14, 1917.
59. Adrian Smith, *Mick Mannock, Fighter Pilot* (London: Palgrave, 2001) p.119.
60. *Aeronautics*, October 9, 1918, pp.344-347.
61. Leon Bennett, *Three Wings for the Red Baron*, Chapter 7.

Bibliography

Archives

For specific references see Notes.
Australian War Memorial Photo Database (Canberra, Australia)
IWM (Imperial War Museum, London, UK)
TNA (The National Archives, London, UK)

Official Government Publications

Air Service Technical School (Washington D.C., USA)
Great Britain – Technical Reports of the Advisory Committee for Aeronautics (London, UK)
NACA (National Advisory Committee for Aeronautics) Reports (National Advisory Committee for Aeronautics, Washington D.C.)

Books

Aczel, Amir D. *Chance*. NYC: Thunder's Mouth, 2004.
Anon., *The Times History of the War*, Volumes 9, 14. London: *The Times*, 1916.
Angelucci, E. and P. Matricardi. *Les Avions*, Volume 1. Brussels: Elsevier, 1978.
Babington-Smith, Constance. *Testing Time*. NYC: Harper, 1961.
Baer, E.H. Ed. *Der Völkerkrieg* Band 14. Stuttgart: Hoffmann, 1917.
Baring, Maurice. *Flying Corps Headquarters 1914-1918*. London: Bell, 1920.
Bean, C.E.W. *Official History of Australia in the War of 1914-1918*. Volume 5. Sydney: Angus & Robertson, 1935.
Bennett, Leon. *Three Wings for the Red Baron*. Shippensburg, PA: White Mane, 2000.
Bennett, Leon. *Gunning for the Red Baron*. College Station, Texas: Texas A&M University Press, 2006.
Bernhardi, Friedrich von. *Germany and the Next War*. NYC: Longmans, Green, 1914.
Bishop, William Arthur. *The Courage of the Early Morning*. Toronto: McClelland & Stewart, 1965.
Bishop, Major W. Avery. *Winged Warfare*. London: Hodder and Stoughton, 1918.
Bishop, Major W. Avery. *Winged Peace*. NYC: Viking, 1944.
Bodenschatz, Karl. *Hunting With Richthofen*. London: Grub Street, 1998. (translated from 1936 German ed.)
Boelcke, Oswald. *An Aviator's Field Book*. NYC: National Military Publishing, 1917.
Boelcke, Oswald. *Hauptmann Boelcke's Feldberichte*. Gotha: Perthes, 1917.
Bott, Captain A. *An Airman's Outings*. London: Blackwood, 1917.
Bott, Captain A. *Cavalry of the Clouds*. NYC: Doubleday, Page, 1918.
Bowen, Ezra. *Knights of the Air*. Alexandria, VA: Time-Life 1980.
Bowyer, Chaz. *Albert Ball, V.C.* London: Kimber, 1977.
Boyle, Andrew. *Trenchard*. London: Collins, 1962.
Bruce, J.M. *British Aeroplanes 1914-1918*. London: Putnam, 1969.
Burrows, William E. *Richthofen*. NYC: Harcourt, Brace & World, 1969.
Busk, Mary A. *E.T. and H.A. Busk*. London: John Murray, 1925.
Chadderton, H. Clifford. *Hanging a Legend*. Ottowa: War Amputations of Canada, 1986.
Chinn, George M. *The Machine Gun*, Volume 1. Washington D.C.: USGPO, 1951.
Christienne, Charles and Pierre Lissarrague. *French Military Aviation*. Washington, DC: Smithsonian, 1986.
Cole, Christopher. *McCudden, V.C.* London: Kimber, 1967.
Cole, Christopher. *Royal Flying Corps Communiqués 1915-1916*. London: Kimber, 1969.
Cuneo, John R. *The Air Weapon 1914-1916*. Harrisburg PA: Military Service Pub., 1947.
Contact (pseud.) *An Airman's Outings*. See Bott, Captain A.
Director US Air Service. *Rotary Engines*. Washington D.C.: USGPO, 1919.
Douglas, Sholto. *Combat and Command*. NYC: Simon & Schuster, 1963.
Dudgeon, J.M. *Mick*. London: Robert Hale, 1981.

Floerke, Hans. *Deutschland in der Luft Voran.* Munich: Muller, 1915.
Fokker, Anthony H.G. and Bruce Gould. *Flying Dutchman.* London: Routledge, 1939.
Fonck, René. *Ace of Aces.* NYC: Doubleday, 1967.
Franks, Norman; H. Giblin and N. McCrery. *Under the Guns of the Red Baron.* London: Grub Street, 1998.
Franks, Norman & Alan Bennett. *The Red Baron's Last Flight.* Ontario: Vanwell, 1997.
Gibbons, Floyd. *The Red Knight of Germany.* NYC: Doubleday, 1927.
Goldsmith, Dolf L. *The Grand Old Lady of No Man's Land.* Cobourg, Ontario: Collector Grade Publications, 1994.
Graham-White, Claude. *Aviation.* London: Collins, 1912.
Graham-White, Claude and Harry Harper. *Air Power.* NYC: Stokes, 1917.
Gray, Peter and Owen Thetford. *German Aircraft of the First World War.* NYC: Doubleday, 1970.
Greenhous, Brereton. *The Making of Billy Bishop.* Toronto: Dundurn, 2002.
Grinnell-Milne, Duncan. *Wind in the Wires.* NYC: Ace, 1968.
Hare, Paul R. *The Royal Aircraft Factory.* London: Putnam, 1990.
Hartney, Harold E. *Up and At 'Em.* NYC: Doubleday, 1971.
Havilland, Geoffrey de. *Sky Fever.* London: Hamish Hamilton, 1961.
Henderson, David. *The Art of Reconnaissance.* London: John Murray, 1915.
Hoeppner, Ernest von. *Germany's War in the Air.* Nashville: Battery Press, 1994. (translated from *Deutschlands Krieg in der Luft.* Leipzig: Koehler, 1924).
Hogg, Ian V. *Anti-Aircraft: A History of Air Defense.* London: Macdonald and Jane's, 1978.
Hudson, James J. *Hostile Skies.* Syracuse NY: Syracuse University Press,1968.
Herlin, Hans. *Udet: A Man's Life.* London: Macdonald, 1960.
Immelmann, Franz. *The Eagle of Lille.* London: Greenhill, 1990.
Insall, A.J. *Observer.* London: Kimber, 1970.
Ishoven, Armand van. *Ernst Udet.* Herrsching, West Germany: Pawlak, 1977.
Ishoven, Armand van. *The Fall of an Eagle.* London: Kimber, 1979.
Jackson, Robert. *Fighter Pilots of WWI.* NYC: St. Martins, 1977.
Johnson, John E.. *Full Circle.* NYC: Ballantine, 1964.
Jones, H.A. *The War in the Air* 7 Volumes. Oxford: Oxford University Press, 1937.
Jones, Ira. *King of the Air Fighters.* London: Nicholson & Watson, 1934.
Jones, Ira. *Tiger Squadron.* London: W.H. Allen, 1954; reprint, London: Award, 1966.
Jones, Ira. *An Air Fighter's Scrapbook.* London: Greenhill, 1990.
King, H. F. *Sopwith Aircraft 1912-1920.* London: Putnam, 1980.
Lambert, William C. *Combat Report.* London: Kimber, 1973.
Lanchester, F.W. *Aircraft in Warfare.* London: Constable, 1916.
Lewis, Cecil. *All My Yesterdays.* Dorset, UK: Element, 1993.
Lewis, Cecil. *Sagittarius Rising.* London: Davies, 1936; reprint, London: Warner, 1994.
Libby, Frederick. *Horses Don't Fly.* NYC: Arcade, 2000.
Loening, Grover C. *Military Aeroplanes.* Boston: Best, 1917.
Lucas, Laddie. *Out of the Blue.* London: Hutchinson, 1985.
Macmillan, Norman. *Sefton Brancker.* London: Heinemann, 1935.
Marck, Bernard. *Le Dernier Vol de Guynemer.* Paris: Acropole, 1991.
Masmejean, A. *Les Avions Allemands.* Paris: Librarie Aeronautique, 1917.
McCudden, James. *Flying Fury–Five Years in the RFC.* London: Aviation Book Club, 1930. Reprint London: Greenhill, 1987.
Mortane, Jacques. *Guynemer, The Ace of Aces.* NYC: Moffat, Yard, 1918.
Mottistone, Lord. *Fear and Be Slain.* London: Hodder & Stoughton, 1931.
Mumby, Frank A. *The Great World War* Volume 7. London: Gresham, 1918.
Musciano, Walter. *Eagles of the Black Cross.* NYC: Obolensky, 1965.
Nevin, Thomas. *Ernst Junger and Germany.* Durham, NC: Duke University Press, 1996.
New York Times. The European War, Volumes 7 and 11. NYC: *New York Times,* 1917.
Oughton, Fred and Vernon Smyth. *Ace With One Eye.* London: Muller, 1963.
Page, Victor W. *Modern Aircraft Engines.* Volume 1. NYC: Henley, 1929.
Platt, Frank C., Ed. *Great Battles of WWI: In the Air.* NYC: Weathervane, 1966.
Provost Marshal General Report. Report. *On the Operations of Selective Service.* Washington, DC: USGPO, 1919.
Richthofen, Manfred von. *The Red Air Fighter.* London: *The Aeroplane* & General Publishing Company, 1918.

Rickenbacker, Edward V. *Fighting the Flying Circus*. NYC: Stokes, 1919.
Rickenbacker, Edward V. *Rickenbacker*. NJ: Prentice-Hall, 1967.
Scott, A.J.L. *Sixty Squadron, RAF*. London: Heinemann, 1920.
Smith, Adrian. *Mick Mannock, Fighter Pilot*. London: Palgrave, 2001.
Springs, Elliot. *War Birds*. NYC: Grosset & Dunlop, 1926.
Stewart, Oliver. *Words and Music for a Mechanical Man*. London: Faber and Faber. 1967.
Stinton, Darrol. *The Design of the Aeroplane*. London: Blackwell, 1983.
Sykes, Claude W. *French War Birds*. London: Hamilton, 1937; reprint, London: Greenhill, 1987.
Sykes, F.H. *Aviation in Peace and War*. London: Arnold, 1922.
Sykes, Frederick *From Many Angles*. London: Harrap, 1942.
Tanner, John, Ed. *Fighting in the Air*. London: Arms & Armour, 1978.
Titler, Dale. *The Day the Red Baron Died*. NYC: Ballantine, 1970.
Udet, Ernst. *Hals und Beinbruch*. Berlin: Wilhelm Kolf, 1928.
Ulanoff, Stanley M., Ed. *Ace of the Iron Cross*. NYC: ARCO, 1981.
Voss, Vivian. *Flying Minnows*. London: Arms & Armour, 1977.
Warner, Edward P. *Aerodynamics*. NYC: McGraw-Hill, 1927.
Werner, Johannes. *Knight of Germany*. London: Greenhill, 1985.
Werner, Johannes. *Boelcke der Mensch, der Flieger, etc.* Leipzig: Koehler, 1932.
Weyl, A.R. Fokker: *The Creative Years*. London: Putnam, 1965.
Whitehouse, Arch. *The Fledgling*. NYC: Duell, Sloan and Pierce, 1964.
Windrow, Martin C., Ed. *Aircraft in Profile*, Volume 3. NYC: Doubleday: 1965.
Wise, J.F. *Canadian Airmen and the First World War*. Toronto: Toronto Press, 1980.

Journals

Aerial Age Weekly, USA. Also sometimes given as *Air Age Weekly*, USA
Aerial Service Journal, USA.
Aeronautics, UK.
L'Aérophile, France.
The Aeroplane, UK.
Aircraft, UK.
AVIA, Netherlands.
Deutsche Luftfahrter Zeitung, Germany (also given as *DLZ*).
Die Luftflotte, Germany.
Flight, UK.
Flying, UK.
Flugsport, Germany.
Illustrierte Flugwoche, Germany.
La Guerre Aerienne, France.
Luftfahrt, Germany.
Journal and Proceedings of the Military Historical Society of Australia, Australia
The New York Times, USA.
Scientific American, USA.
The Times, UK.
Zeitschrift fur Flugtechnik und Motorluftschiffahrt, Germany (also given as ZFM).

Index